Celebrating the Lives
of Jewish Women
Patterns in a Feminist Sampler

HAWORTH Innovations in Feminist Studies
Esther Rothblum, PhD and Ellen Cole, PhD
Senior Co-Editors

New, Recent, and Forthcoming Titles:

When Husbands Come Out of the Closet by Jean Schaar Gochros

Prisoners of Ritual: An Odyssey into Female Genital Circumcision in Africa by Hanny Lightfoot-Klein

Foundations for a Feminist Restructuring of the Academic Disciplines edited by Michele Paludi and Gertrude A. Steuernagel

Hippocrates' Handmaidens: Women Married to Physicians by Esther Nitzberg

Waiting: A Diary of Loss and Hope in Pregnancy by Ellen Judith Reich

God's Country: A Case Against Theocracy by Sandy Rapp

Women and Aging: Celebrating Ourselves by Ruth Raymond Thone

Women's Conflicts About Eating and Sexuality: The Relationship Between Food and Sex by Rosalyn M. Meadow and Lillie Weiss

A Woman's Odyssey into Africa: Tracks Across a Life by Hanny Lightfoot-Klein

Anorexia Nervosa and Recovery: A Hunger for Meaning by Karen Way

Women Murdered by the Men They Loved by Constance A. Bean

Reproductive Hazards in the Workplace: Mending Jobs, Managing Pregnancies by Regina Kenen

Our Choices: Women's Personal Decisions About Abortion by Sumi Hoshiko

Tending Inner Gardens: The Healing Art of Feminist Psychotherapy by Lesley Irene Shore

The Way of the Woman Writer by Janet Lynn Roseman

Racism in the Lives of Women: Testimony, Theory, and Guides to Anti-Racist Practice by Jeanne Adleman and Gloria Enguidanos

Advocating for Self: Women's Decisions Concerning Contraception by Peggy Matteson

Feminist Visions of Gender Similarities and Differences by Meredith M. Kimball

Experiencing Abortion: A Weaving of Women's Words by Eve Kushner

Menopause, Me and You: The Sound of Women Pausing by Ann M. Voda

Fat—A Fate Worse Than Death?: Women, Weight, and Appearance by Ruth Raymond Thone

Feminist Theories and Feminist Psychotherapies: Origins, Themes, and Variations by Carolyn Zerbe Enns

Celebrating the Lives of Jewish Women: Patterns in a Feminist Sampler edited by Rachel Josefowitz Siegel and Ellen Cole

Celebrating the Lives of Jewish Women

Patterns in a Feminist Sampler

Rachel Josefowitz Siegel, MSW
Ellen Cole, PhD
Editors

The Harrington Park Press
An Imprint of The Haworth Press, Inc.
New York • London

Published by

The Harrington Park Press, an imprint of The Haworth Press, Inc., 10 Alice Street, Binghamton, NY
13904-1580

The editors wish to thank Emma Root and Mae Rockland Tupa for permission to adapt Emma's
Genealogy Sampler for our cover design. Emma Root's sampler was published in *The new work
of our hands: Contemporary Jewish needlework and quilts* (Mae Rockland Tupa, 1994, Radnor,
PA: Chilton Book Company).

Cover design by Monica L. Seifert.

Library of Congress Cataloging-in-Publication Data

Celebrating the lives of Jewish women : patterns in a feminist sampler / Rachel Josefowitz Siegel,
Ellen Cole, editors.
    p.   cm.
Includes bibliographical references and index.
ISBN 1-56023-913-1 (alk. paper).
    1. Jewish women–United States–Biography. 2. Jewish women–Canada–Biography. 3. Femi-
nism–Religious aspects–Judaism. I. Siegel, Rachel Josefowitz. II. Cole, Ellen.
DS115.2.P58 1997
305.48'6'96–dc21   97-5263
                                                                       CIP
                                                                        r97

Because of our unshakeable commitment to family connectedness, learned above all from growing up Jewish, we lovingly dedicate this book to our daughters and sons.

To:

Charles Ellis Siegel
Hyman Barry Siegel
Ruth Vivian Siegel

Anton Goldman Cole
Gabriel Lucas Cole
Jeffrey Seaton North
Elisabeth Sewell North

CONTENTS

Editors   xi

About the Authors   xiii

Foreword   xxi
     Marcia Cohn Spiegel

Preface   xxvii
     Rachel Josefowitz Siegel
     Ellen Cole

SECTION I: FROM GENERATION TO GENERATION: THE MEANINGS OF MISHPACHA

Chapter 1. Living in a Glass Bowl: Tales of a Rabbi's Daughter   3
     Elisheva Glass

Chapter 2. Bris, Britah: Parents' First Lessons in Balancing Gender, Culture, Tradition, and Religion   9
     Susan Steinberg-Oren

Chapter 3. Married – Without a Chupa   19
     Roslyn Mendelson

Chapter 4. Queer Jewish Women Creating Families: New Perspectives on Jewish Family Values   29
     Susie Kisber

Chapter 5. Mothers, Judaism, and True Honor   39
     Paula J. Caplan

Chapter 6. Backwards and Forwards in America   45
     Sandra Butler

Chapter 7. Personal Reflections on Being a Grandmother:
L'Chol Dor Va Dor   57
    Rachel Aber Schlesinger

SECTION II: WANDERING JEWS: LIVES FRACTURED BY GEOGRAPHY

Chapter 8. Jewish Identity Lost . . . and Found   69
    Trudi Alexy

Chapter 9. Trials and Tribulations in the First Year
of a "Mixed Sephardi/Ashkenazi Marriage"   81
    Sarah Taieb Carlen

Chapter 10. The Joys of Mitsvoth   95
    Rebecca L. Bradley

Chapter 11. In Search of Eden   111
    Pnina Granirer

Chapter 12. Family Memories and Grave Anxieties   119
    Susan Weidman Schneider

SECTION III: THE JOURNEY HOME

Chapter 13. Really Jewish   125
    Jane Marie Law

Chapter 14. You Don't Know Me Because You Can
Label Me: Self-Identity of an Orthodox Feminist   139
    Norma Baumel Joseph

Chapter 15. The Journey Home: Becoming
a Reconstructionist Rabbi   147
    Elisa Goldberg

Chapter 16. Becoming Jewish   159
    Brenda Lynn Siegel

Chapter 17. How Jewish Am I?   167
     Hannah Lerman

Chapter 18. The Politics of Coming Home:
     Gender and Jewish Identities in the 1990s   177
     Rachel N. Weber

Chapter 19. "Why Kafka?" A Jewish Lesbian Feminist
     Asks Herself   187
     Evelyn Torton Beck

**SECTION IV: EVE AND THE TREE OF KNOWLEDGE:
WOMAN'S PLACE AMONG THE PEOPLE OF THE
BOOK**

Chapter 20. "I Don't Know Enough": Jewish Women's
     Learned Ignorance   201
     Rachel Josefowitz Siegel

Chapter 21. Learning to Leyn   211
     Michele Clark

Chapter 22. Better Late Than Early: A Forty-Eight-Year-
     Old's Bat Mitzvah Saga   219
     Nina Perlmutter

Chapter 23. Exploring Adolescent Jewish Female Identity:
     Reflections About Voice and Relation   231
     Carol Philips

Chapter 24. First There Are the Questions   247
     Ellyn Kaschak

**SECTION V: PAIN AND HEALING,
SORROW AND HOPE**

Chapter 25. Jewish Battered Women: Shalom Bayit
     or a Shonde?   261
     Lenore E. A. Walker

Chapter 26. Canadian Jewish Women and Their Experiences
    of Antisemitism and Sexism   279
        Nora Gold

Chapter 27. We Are Not As We Were: Jewish Women
    After the Holocaust   291
        Joan Fisch

Chapter 28. Violent Legacies–Dialogues and Possibilities   301
        Judith Chalmer

Glossary   313

Index   321

Editors

Rachel Josefowitz Siegel, MSW, is a Jewish mother, grand-mother, and great-grandmother. Recently retired from her feminist therapy private practice, she now has more time to write, travel, and visit with friends and family. She has co-edited *Seen but Not Heard: Jewish Women in Therapy* with Ellen Cole, *Women Changing Therapy* with Joan Hamerman Robbins, and has written numerous articles on women over sixty and on Jewish women. She continues to lecture and lead workshops on women's issues.

A wandering Jew of Ashkenazi background, she is an active and activist member of her synagogue, and feels most at home in an egalitarian or feminist conservative environment.

Ellen Cole, PhD, is Professor of Psychology at Alaska Pacific University in Anchorage. She co-edits the Haworth Press book program, "Innovations in Feminist Studies," conducts a small private practice in sex therapy, and co-hosts a radio call-in show for Alaska Public Radio.

"I grew up in Queens, New York in a nonobservant, anti-religious household, but I attended Hebrew School at a Reform temple for about a year, my brother had a Bar Mitzvah, and I barely even knew anyone who wasn't Jewish until I went to college in Boston at the age of seventeen. I considered myself an atheist for many years, but recently that label has seemed too harsh. The more time I'm away from Jewish centers (having spent my adult years in Vermont, Arizona, and now Alaska), the more Jewish I feel."

About the Authors

Trudi Alexy, MA, was born in 1927 in Rumania and emigrated to the United States with her thoroughly assimilated family during World War II. At the age of sixty she embarked on a search for the Jewish roots of which she was deprived as a child in Hitler's Europe. This spiritual journey is chronicled in her book, *The Mezuzah in the Madonna's Foot: Marranos and Other Secret Jews, A Woman Discovers Her Spiritual Heritage* (Harper/San Francisco, soft cover; award, Jewish Book Council, Autobiography/Memoir, 1994). Trudi Alexy lives in Tarzana, California. She is a licensed marriage and family counselor and art therapist and divides her time between her private practice, writing, and lecturing on "Jewish Identity in a Hostile Climate" as a member of the National Speakers' Bureau of the United Jewish Appeal.

Evelyn Torton Beck, PhD, is Professor of Women's Studies, Jewish Studies and Comparative Literature at the University of Maryland—College Park. Among her books are *Nice Jewish Girls: A Lesbian Anthology; The Prism of Sex: Essays in the Sociology of Knowledge;* and *Kafka and the Yiddish Theater: Its Impact on His Work.* Born in Vienna, Austria the year that Hitler came to power in Germany, to a Polish-born father and a Viennese-born mother, she came to understand early on that multiculturalism begins at home. She rebelled against her parents' way of legislating Jewish observance by joining a Marxist-Zionist youth group whose philosophy eventually led her to feminism. Although she is a member of *Bet Mishpacha,* Washington, DC's lesbian/gay synagogue, she identifies as a cultural Jew whose forms of observance are highly personal and somewhat unpredictable.

Rebecca L. Bradley, JD, has been a trial lawyer for over twenty-five years, practicing in Denver, Colorado, USA. Her main interests include travel, the study of world cultures (she speaks, reads, and writes in Russian, Hebrew, and Spanish), art, music . . . and new experiences. Born to a humanist mother and an atheist father, with ancestors from Scotland, Ireland, England, and Native America (Cherokee), she has been a "Jew by assimilation'" since age seventeen and underwent formal Halakhic conversion in 1982 in time for the Bat Mitzvah of her daughter, Morgan. Ms. Bradley studies Talmud with a weekly group and has made seven trips to Israel in the past thirteen years.

"I am more of an 'activist Jew' than a religious Jew, but am becoming more religious in the traditional sense."

Sandra Butler is the author of *Conspiracy of Silence: The Trauma of Incest* and *Cancer in Two Voices*. Currently she is the co-director of the Institute for Feminist Training and is preparing a handbook for feminist activists on the political and psychological intersections of social change.

"I am a white Eastern European Ashkenazi Jew on both sides of my family. The Judaism of my childhood and early adolescence was the Reform Judaism of the liberal patriarchs, filled with fewer rules about Judaism but just as many about gender. The Judaism of my mid-life, after decades of secular activism is a tentative, but deeply felt, commitment to the daily practice of feminism informed by the Jewish ethic of Tikkun Olam."

Paula J. Caplan, PhD, CPsych, is a clinical and research psychologist, actor, playwright, and author of *The Myth of Women's Masochism; Don't Blame Mother: Mending the Mother-Daughter Relationship; Lifting a Ton of Feathers: A Woman's Guide to Surviving in the Academic World; Thinking Critically About Research on Sex and Gender* (co-authored by her son, Jeremy B. Caplan), and *They Say You're Crazy: How the World's Most Powerful Psychiatrists Decide Who's Normal.*

Sara Taieb Carlen, PhD, "I was born in Tunisia, studied at the Sorbonne, the London School of Economics, the Hebrew University of Jerusalem, and got my PhD in Sociology from York University where I teach a course in the Division of Social Science—Interethnic Relations: The Sephardi Communities of Europe, Asia, and Africa. I have given several conferences, written articles or book chapters, and attended conferences on the following topics: Race and Ethnic Relations, Sephardi Jews, Islam and the Jews, Migration, Jewish identity, assimilation, identity maintenance, identity and colonization, identity and education, racism, discrimination, etc. I am now working on a book (in French) about the Jewish communities of North Africa that the Editions Maisonneuve of Paris, France, are interested in.

"I am a traditional Sephardi Jew for whom Shabbat, cashrout, all religious holidays, and not just the so-called High Holidays are important, worthy of being celebrated with as much pomp and beauty as possible. My approach to Judaism reflects my upbringing as well as the traditional Sephardi philosophy which emphasizes joy, flexibility, tolerance, and respect for other people's creeds and ways of practicing."

Judith Chalmer, MFA, is part of an unaffiliated, eclectic, loud-mouthed and fiercely loyal Jewish community in central Vermont. She is the daughter of a German-Jewish, Holocaust-survivor father and a Russian-Jewish, American-born mother. She was raised Reform, by her mother. She currently teaches literature and creative writing at Norwich University. Her first book of poems, *Out of History's Junk Jar,* was published in 1995 by Time Being Books of St. Louis.

Michele Clark, MEd, "My professional life is divided between counseling at a nonprofit agency and teaching psychology at Vermont College in an undergraduate program for adults. I have written on Jewish identity issues for *Bridges, The Reconstructionist,* and in an edited volume, *Jewish Women Speak Out* (Canopy Press, 1995). I grew up in a moderately observant Conservative household. As my essay indicates, I attend services regularly and move slowly toward more Jewish observance."

Joan Fisch, MSW, BCD, is a licensed clinical social worker in practice in Menlo Park, CA, and a member of the clinical faculty in the Department of Psychiatry and Behavioral Sciences at the Stanford University Medical School. She is an active member of the Jewish Women's Caucus of the Association of Women in Psychology and has served as its coordinator. Joan Fisch grew up with a strong identity as a secular Jew. Her parents were politically progressive and nonreligious. Her mother's parents were Syrian Sephardic Jews, her father's parents Lithuanian Catholics. She has become interested in religious practice and now thinks of herself as a Liberal Jew.

Elisheva Glass, "I am fifteen years old, live in Ithaca, New York, and am a sophomore at Ithaca High School. I have attended the Rabbi Felix Aber Religious School of Temple Beth-El for eleven years, and I have also been educated at Camp Yavneh in Northwood, New Hampshire. I am part of an observant, conservative family whose lives are centered around Judaism." (Photo by Amanda Brady)

Nora Gold, PhD, is Associate Professor at the School of Social Work, McMaster University. She is an active Jewish feminist in Toronto; she has been involved in the creation of Sukkah-by-the-Water, a feminist Sukkah ceremony that draws 450 women each year, and has raised over $100,000 for feminist projects in Israel. She, along with others, leads the services at her egalitarian rabbi-less shul, and she is a member of a dialogue group for Jewish and Palestinian women. Her ethnic background is Ashkenazi.

Elisa Goldberg is a third-generation Ashkenazi Jew who grew up in the Northeast. She has variously expressed her Judaism in paper mache, collage, household and community, hospital chaplaincy and rabbinical school. She lives in Philadelphia with her family-by-choice: her partner and two teenage stepdaughters.

Pnina Granirer was born in 1935, in Braila, Romania, in a secular, Jewish family. She immigrated to Israel in 1950, and graduated from the Bezalel Art Academy in Jerusalem. She went to the United States in 1962 and to Canada in 1965, where she became a citizen. Married with two sons, she is an atheist, but feels strongly Jewish. She lives and paints in Vancouver, BC, Canada.

Dr. Norma Baumel Joseph, PhD, is Assistant Professor in the Department of Religion at Concordia University, Montreal, and is also an associate of the Chair in Quebec and Canadian Jewish Studies. For the past 18 years she has been teaching, lecturing, and publishing on women and Judaism, Jewish law and ethics, and women and religion. She has lobbied for Jewish women's rights, forming local and international groups to further those goals. President of the International Coalition for Agunah Rights (ICAR) and consultant to the Canadian Coalition of Jewish Women for the Get, she founded the Montreal Women's Prayer group. Norma appeared in and was consultant to the film *Half the Kingdom*. Her doctoral dissertation focused on the legal decisions of Rabbi Moses Feinstein as they describe and delineate separate spheres for women in the Jewish community. She lives in Montreal where she raised four children with her husband, Rabbi Howard Joseph.

Ellyn Kaschak, PhD, is Professor of Psychology at San Jose State University and the author of *Engendered Lives: A New Psychology of Women's Experience.* She has been involved in the the the development of the theory and practice of feminist psychology since its inception and was one of the founders, in 1972, of the Women's Counseling Service of San Francisco. She is currently co-director of the Institute for Feminist Training and is active in international teaching and training. "My family background is Ashkenazi from the Eastern European exile. My grandparents were all immigrants to the United States in the early part of the twentieth century, and continued, throughout their lives, to practice Orthodox Judaism. The Judaism of my parents' generation became Conservative and Americanized. My own current practice is feminist and questioning, secular and celebratory."

Susie Kisber is a PhD Candidate in Clinical Psychology, completing a dissertation entitled "Queer Jewish Women Becoming Parents Within the Jewish Community: Issues of Invisibility, Social Support, and Affiliation." She identifies as a Reconstructionist Jew, drawing on the creative force of a nonhierarchical divinity, the Canaanite pagan roots of Judaism, and the Ashkenazi, Sephardic, Mizrachi, and Jewish Renewal traditions. She is a co-founder of *Pardes Rimonim,* a Jewish feminist, earth-centered, inclusive, ritual community, and is actively involved in Queer Minyan, a *chavurah* which meets monthly to celebrate *Kabbalat Shabbat.*

Jane Marie Law, PhD, was born and raised in Kalispell, Montana. Deeply interested in comparative religions from an early age, she received her undergraduate degree in Religious Studies and Japanese from the University of Colorado at Boulder and her PhD in History of Religions from the University of Chicago in 1990, with a focus on Japanese ritual performance. She is currently Assistant Professor of Japanese Religions at Cornell University. She converted to Judaism in 1991, has a Jewish household, and is active in her local Conservative congregation. She lives in Ithaca, New York with her husband, Adam, her two children Samuel and Tamar, and their very ordinary cat Kado.

Hannah Lerman, PhD, "I am a feminist psychologist in practice in Las Vegas and the author of *A Mote in Freud's Eye,* published in 1986, and *Pigeonholing Women's Misery,* published by Basic Books in 1996. My chapter contains a description of my present nonpracticing Jewish identity."

Roslyn Mendelson, PhD, is a psychologist in independent practice in Calgary, Alberta, Canada, specializing in work with children and families. She and her Protestant husband have two young daughters. Roslyn has conducted workshops on interfaith marriages.

Of Ashkenazi origin, brought up in a traditional Jewish home, she is currently affiliated with a Reform Temple and is active in her community: She serves as chairperson for the Daycare in the Jewish Community Centre and has recently co-chaperoned the Calgary delegation for the *March of the Living, 1996,* a trip in which 6,000 international Jewish youth tour concentration camps, ghettos, and old Jewish cities and towns in Poland. Judaism continues to be an important part of her life.

Nina Perlmutter, MA, teaches Western and Eastern Philosophy and Religion at Yavapai Community College in Prescott, Arizona. She holds BA and MA degrees in Philosophy with emphases in Cross-Cultural Studies and Environmental Ethics. She is currently working on a Masters degree in Jewish Studies. Of Polish-Russian descent, Nina attended religious school through sixth grade, but was raised mostly as a secular Jew. Her late-blooming passion for Judaism surprised her even more than it did her friends. She calls herself a "postdenominational" Jew, and is becoming more observant, especially of Shabbat. She and husband Tom keep a Jewish-Buddhist home.

Carol Philips is a doctoral student in Human Development and Psychology at the Harvard Graduate School of Education. She has taught art, writing, social sciences, and interdisciplinary studies at the college level for over twenty years. She is proud of her progressive, secular Jewish heritage and, as she has done throughout her life, continues to uphold that tradition.

Rachel Aber Schlesinger, EdD, is Associate Professor at York University. She teaches courses dealing with education and social change, women and aging. She also serves on the Executive Board of the Centre for Jewish Studies at York University, conducts research in the Jewish community, and gives workshops and seminars on Jewish topics. Her current research deals with Jewish women as gatekeepers of family and community memories.

Rachel's mother came from a long line of Ashkenazi rabbis; her father was a rabbi and scholar. Born in Germany, she came to the United States with her family and moved to Canada with her husband Ben. They have lived in Israel, India, Jamaica, Australia, and New Zealand thanks to academic sabbaticals. They are blessed with four wonderful children and numerous equally wonderful grandchildren.

Susan Weidman Schneider is Editor-in-Chief and founding editor of *LILITH, the Independent Jewish Women's Magazine,* published since 1976. She is the author of the highly acclaimed *Jewish and Female: Choices and Changes in Our Lives Today,* among other books. She is an Ashkenazi Jew, belongs to a Conservative synagogue (where she is often bored and occasionally stimulated), and grew up in a strongly Jewish-identified household in Winnipeg, where Yiddish and Hebrew were equally appreciated, and where, because Yiddish was the language of concealment, she learned quite a bit of it. (Photo by Joan Roth.)

Brenda Lynn Siegel is a nineteen-year-old sophomore in college. She is studying dance and law. When her grandmother, the co-editor of this book, asked her to write this chapter she was thrilled! She has always been interested in the cultural aspects of her religion and will continue to learn more about them as her life goes on.

Marcia Cohn Spiegel, MA, earned her degree in Jewish Communal Service from Hebrew Union College-Jewish Institute of Religion. She is working to create change in the attitudes of the Jewish community toward addiction, violence, and sexual abuse. Author of *The Heritage of Noah: Alcoholism in the Jewish Community Today,* and co-author of *The Jewish Women's Awareness Guide,* and *Women Speak to God: The Poems and Prayers of Jewish Women,* she recently wrote the introduction to *The Jewish Woman: A Bibliography* by Ann S. Masnik.

"My grandparents were Orthodox; my parents raised me to be Conservative; I participated in building a Reform synagogue, belong to a Conservative synagogue, and feel most at home in Jewish Renewal or Reconstructionist settings. I am a member of the creative feminist spiritual communities *B'not Esh,* the *Mikveh* Ladies, and *Shabbat Shenit.*"

Susan Steinberg-Oren, PhD, is a clinical psychologist living in Los Angeles. She is the mother of two young children whom she just enrolled in the local synogogue pre-school. She enjoys Jewish culture and religion and loosely defines her denomination as "liberal-conservative."

Lenore E. A. Walker, EdD, ABPP-CL, FAClinP, is a licensed psychologist in independent practice with Walker & Associates in Denver, Colorado, and Miami Beach, Florida, and Executive Director of the Domestic Violence Institute. An international lecturer who trains at the invitation of governments, private groups and world health organizations, she has done research, clinical intervention, training, and expert witness testimony on the psychology of battered women and dynamics of the battering relationship. She is author of ten books and over fifty journal articles and book chapters including *The Battered Woman; Terrifying Love: Why Battered Women Kill*; and *How Society Responds,* as well as *Abused Women and Survivor Therapy: A Practical Guide for the Psychotherapist.*

She was raised in the Bronx, New York with Jews of all backgrounds. As an adult she rejected her Conservative background where she had training in culture, holidays, and Jewish cooking, for the social consciousness of the Reform movement. She has been a member of Congregation Emanuel since arriving in Denver twenty years ago and both her son and daughter attended religious and Sunday school there.

Rachel N. Weber, MRP, is a doctoral candidate in the Department of City and Regional Planning at Cornell University. She has worked as an economic development consultant to local governments, and holds a Masters in Regional Planning from Cornell and a BA from Brown University. Ms. Weber was a Fulbright Scholar in Calcutta, India.

"I was brought up attending a suburban Conservative synagogue, and went through a period of devout, almost fanatical observance between the ages of ten and thirteen. I kept kosher, attended Services, and spent summers at Camp Ramah, experiences which affirmed my devotion to Jewish rituals, songs, and faith. After my Bat Mitzvah, I was more attracted to punk rock than praying, and have only recently come back to reclaiming a Jewish identity. I am trying to find meaningful, feminist ways of celebrating Jewish holidays and rituals."

Foreword

For almost 2,000 years Jewish women were silenced, excluded from full participation in Jewish life by a series of laws that prohibited them from study, public prayer, and positions of religious leadership. The sound of a woman's voice was said to create the danger of sexual provocation, *kal be-ishah ervah*. Rabbi Eliezer ben Hyrrcanus taught that it is better to burn the Torah than to teach it to your daughter. Our prayers remained private and personal, and we were taught only enough of the laws to maintain a proper Jewish home and raise our children. Our stories were told in private; our wisdom shared through *bobbe meises*, grandmother stories.

Silence was expected. We were raised to listen and be obedient, not make waves. Our needs were subservient to those of the family. I never questioned the status quo when I was growing up; I didn't share my feelings with my mother, nor did she share hers with me. Today, Jewish women are telling their stories across the generations, as in the pages of this book.

My own search for my mother's story was triggered by a statement she made as we returned from my grandmother's funeral. "Now," she said, "I'll never know if she loved me." I embraced her as she wept, but I was filled with confusion. My grandmother was a gentle, kind woman, generous with hugs and physical affection. How could my mother question her love? In that instant I understood that the very people we think we know best, we may not know at all. I vowed to uncover the source of my mother's pained statement, and in the process discovered some of the causes of the friction between my mother and me.

I knew my grandmother well from the weekends I spent with her during my childhood in Chicago, and as an adult when we both lived in Los Angeles. She loved nothing better than teach me to cook brisket and *tsimmis* and *tagelach*, or to have me assist in Shabbat dinner preparations. We kneaded *challah* together as she talked about growing up in *Kovnogebernya*. She was expected to marry a learned man as befitted the daughter of a learned man. But she fell in love with and married a handsome redheaded soldier. She described his hasty flight to Chicago to flee the tsar's army and the terrible uncertainty of the long silence following his departure; then the tickets arrived that brought her to Maxwell Street, a big family, the chicken store, the boarders, and finally the life on Turner Avenue that I knew and participated in. My memories of these conversions are vivid, permeated with the aroma of baking bread and of her soft touch on my arm.

My mother's memories were of growing up too poor to buy the daily paper that the teacher asked them to bring to school. She and her sister, Lottie, mothered their five little brothers, made beds, prepared dinner, set the table, and saved pennies to buy treats for the boys. They both finished two years at Marshall High and went to work as secretaries. Without their salaries it would have been impossible for the boys to go to college. My mother was a good girl who anticipated her parents' wishes and tried to do what was expected before it was asked. And so her deeds and sacrifices were barely noticed. Lottie and the boys were showered with love and physical affection, yet my mother hungered for thanks and praise.

My early life was different from either of theirs, growing up in Columbus Park, middle-class and assimilating. Ours was a neighborhood of Greeks, Italians, Irish, and Jews mixed together. It was a time of deep economic depression but I was not aware of any deprivation. I always knew that I would go to college, and then get married. While I worked to earn money for shoes or clothes, the family didn't depend on my earnings to put food on the table.

My mother once said, "You were lucky to have parents who loved you and could make anything possible for you. But you were never grateful for that. You never appreciated what we did for you." I couldn't imagine what she was talking about. Later, after I had pulled together the threads of her story I did understand. Of course she was angry; I was given the opportunity for piano lessons, Hebrew school, concerts, museums, and even college, things she had coveted but never had, and which I, having them without asking, didn't appreciate. She was showing me love by giving me what she had always wanted, and I, acting as if it was nothing out of the ordinary, did not value her gift.

Through three generations of women who loved and thought we knew each other ran the different colored threads of our separate lives: where we came from, our cultural and class backgrounds, the limitations and expectations defined by our mothers of who we should be and how we should live. These threads created different designs for each of us. The colors were similar but the patterns varied, and would never be an exact match. During my mother's final illness I tried to show her the appreciation she craved, but I couldn't do it. The reward she wanted was from her mother, and her mother was gone. Nothing her sister or brothers or children could do would ever fill that empty place.

As I traced my own story, I paid closer attention to the stories of other women, their mothers and grandmothers. I once made assumptions about all Jewish women, but now I was forced to recognize that each of us is a unique combination of those who preceded us, the circumstances of their births and lives as well as of our own. Other second and third generation Ashkenazi Jews often make these same assumptions: that all Jewish immigrants to these shores came from Eastern Europe, were poor, Orthodox, Yiddish speaking, moved to a big city, became middle-class, worshipped in a Conservative synagogue, and voted Democratic. Sometimes this is true; often it is another story. When I stopped making assumptions about my own family, I was able to recognize the wide variety of our experiences and realize the myriad strands that come together to create each individual life story.

In *Celebrating the Lives of Jewish Women* we read about Sephardi women whose food, celebrations, and customs differ dramatically from the Ashkenazi; we hear the stories of women who rejected their parents' Jewish practice to seek new practices and rituals, and others who returned to traditional Judaism; we learn about marriages between Jews and non-Jews, the deep satisfaction as well as the difficulties facing converts to Judaism and of lesbian and bisexual women who are establishing Jewish families. We read about the impact of the Holocaust on all of us. The myth of *shalom bayit*, peace in the house, is shattered in a description of family violence. We read about women who have transcended tradition to become rabbis, to chant from the Torah, to assume nontraditional roles. These stories reveal both the joys and pleasures, and the ambivalence and marginality that Jewish women feel. Through their voices and tales, we are forced to reconstruct our image of a Jewish woman.

As the authors search for a clearer understanding of their Jewish identity, they may uncover family secrets that they no longer wish to conceal. We each have family secrets: secrets as benign as a change of name, or a "nose job," or as devastating as incest or early child-hood sexual abuse, alcoholism, drug addiction, or gambling. Some-times our family history is so carefully concealed that there is no way to uncover the mysterious forces that shaped our attitudes and expectations.

When I asked my mother-in-law to tell me something about her early life and where she came from, she replied, "I don't know why you are so nosy. It's none of your business. You wouldn't know about it. It's a small place." For years I tried to get her to open up, but she never revealed anything about her life in the old country. Comparing stories with cousins who survived Auschwitz, I found them equally mystified about the family history. Since the death of their parents and grandparents, and the total destruction of their homes and family records, there was no one left to tell the story. To this day we all wonder what was being hidden. Did someone leave a wife and marry another without a divorce? Was there a cruel parent or step-parent? Was there violence or incest? Was someone a crimi-nal? Or was it a story of pogroms, terrible poverty, and unhappiness that caused my mother-in-law to want to forget that life—not uncover her pain for a "nosy" daughter-in-law? In the face of this silence there aren't even any *bobbe meises* to shed light on the past.

The silence has been broken. We trace our own strength and courage to our mothers and grandmothers and celebrate our new awareness of their vitality. We no longer have to hide our contribu-tions to Jewish life and survival, nor the darker aspects of our histories. We are exploring where we came from and the influences that shaped our lives, so that we can understand who we are and where we are going. We will keep silent no more. We are speaking out in clear voices, not concealing the truth from one another. We are learning to support each other as we move forward. And we are treasuring our differences as we treasure our similarities.

We are stepping forward as equals, to share in the full responsibilities of Jewish life, to be counted, and above all to be heard. We are changing Jewish life forever. Not only are women serving as religious leaders and scholars, but we are compelling community organizations to address problems of family dysfunction that were once concealed in our silence about addiction, family violence, and sexual abuse. We are listening to the pain of those who have been isolated and marginalized, and will no longer accept this as the norm. As we find our voices, we are changing Judaism forever. In *Celebrating the Lives of Jewish Women: Patterns in a Feminist Sampler*, Rachel Josefowitz Siegel and Ellen Cole have provided a vehicle to tell some of these stories, to share the experiences of others, so that we can illuminate our own lives.

Marcia Cohn Spiegel

Preface

This book is a Jewish women's sampler, and within its pages Jewish American and Canadian women have contributed pieces of writing that, like pieces of embroidery, illustrate their lives. A sampler is a carefully and lovingly crafted collection of varied stitches and patterns that represent a culture's and family's heritage as well as the innovations of the individual woman who created it. The stitches and patterns are arranged to convey a message that may contain the maker's values, spirituality, intellectual curiosity, aesthetic sensibilities, and sense of humor. Together, the stitches and patterns form an expression of personal and communal identity.

The sampler is part of our North American women's heritage; it is part of our Jewish women's heritage. Within Judaism, women traditionally presented their samplers to the synagogue as Torah binders or Torah covers.

> From the seventeenth century onwards it was received on the Sabbath with the following blessing: ". . . the One who blessed our mothers, Sarah, Rebecca, Rachel, and Leah, may He give His blessings to every daughter of Israel who makes a mantle or cloth for the honor of the Torah, may the Lord reward and remunerate her and let us say amen." (Parker, 1989, p. 164)

Embroidery in general and sampler making in particular have provided a source of both pleasure and power for Jewish women. While employed to inculcate traditional sex roles and values, sampler making also enabled women to "negotiate the constraints of femininity" (Parker, 1989, p. 11). Jewish embroiderers from the seventeenth century, for example, celebrated courageous women whose acts of courage saved their people. Samplers, too, particularly in the verses that were embroidered into the fabric, reflected the religious changes of the times. And so we use as our defining metaphor an activity that has historically been important to women, that has represented both the traditional and the courageous, and that has reflected changing times.

In drawing together this collection, our basic principle was one of inclusivity in order to convey the multiplicity of patterns in Jewish women's lives, the multiplicity of issues that Jewish women grapple with in a changing world. Within each section we have identified a major pattern, although, true to the concept of a sampler, the same pattern reappears as subtext in other chapters and other sections. Thoughts and feelings, impressions and reflections, Jewish and feminist concepts and values, are echoed from author to author, or appear in sharp and startling contrast. Might it be that their coexistence within the frame of our sampler could serve as a model for Jewish women learning to listen and to respect each other across our similarities and through our differences?

Section I, *From Generation to Generation: The Meanings of Mishpacha,* focuses on Jewish family patterns, new and old, from bris to mother-honoring and grandmothering, from intermarriage to lesbian and queer families. Section II, *Wandering Jews: Lives Fractured by Geography,* reflects the personal and often heartrending displacements, migrations, and adaptations that Jewish women and their families have made throughout Jewish history, enriching our sampler with the vibrant colors that accompany the bridging of varied Jewish cultures. Section III, *The Journey Home,* explores the many personal journeys that women make in search of an individual Jewish identity, journeys that include introspection, connection to Jewish mothers and foremothers, commitment to Jewish values, intellectual pursuits, informed spirituality, and interaction with Jewish communities. Section IV, *Eve and the Tree of Knowledge: Woman's Place Among the People of the Book,* addresses the relationship for Jewish women between Jewish learning and Jewish ritual, grappling with the historical taboos against women's participation, asking our own questions, speaking our own voice, claiming our place. Finally, Section V, *Pain and Healing, Sorrow and Hope,* examines the painful topics of family violence, socially sanctioned antisemitism and sexism, and the lasting impact of the Holocaust on us all.

Jewish women are seen in this sampler as survivors, as witnesses, as defenders, innovators, and healers. We hope to impart an overall impression of positive female energy and wisdom. In each section the patterns are presented from different perspectives, all questioning, searching, adapting, celebrating, transmitting, and living Jewish values. All our authors and editors are Jewish women. We range from adolescent to great-grandmother, atheist to orthodox, convert to areligious, heterosexual to queer, immigrant to fifth generation. We are Sephardi and Ashkenazi, Canadian and American, secular and observant. Our Jewish education ranges from none at all to preparation for the rabbinate.

What we have in common is an individual consciousness of our Jewishness, and that is the thread that binds together the stitches of our sampler. *Tikkun Olam*, the concept of healing the world, is a common denominator of this Jewish consciousness, appearing over and over again in the pages of this book. "Eve tries again," (Granirer, 1989) this time to heal the world; this time the forbidden tree bears fruits of Jewish knowledge, healing, and inclusivity. Eve dares again, with the support of her sisters, biting into the apple herself, then offering it to all.

Many hands have produced the stitches and patterns of this book. We would like to acknowledge and thank all of our authors for their generosity in sharing so much of themselves in these pages; Nicky Morris and Barbara Johnson for consultations and cheerleading; Marion Poliakoff for wisdom and support in the early stages; Rabbi Morris Goldfarb for glossary expertise; Bess Schomacker and Jude Keith Rose for secretarial assistance; Charles Siegel for computer coaching; Bill Palmer at The Haworth Press for initial encouragement and continuing support; Bettina Kipp for painstaking reference checking; and Doug North, for everything.

This has been a deeply fulfilling project for us as co-editors. At times it has felt like a sacred ritual of connection with each other, akin to the joys and excitement of preparing a holiday banquet together, our favorite ingredients and recipes shared across the miles between Ithaca, New York, and Anchorage, Alaska. It has also felt like a sacred bond with Jewish women everywhere, many hands bringing precious offerings to the altar of Jewish consciousness and Jewish continuity. Shalom.

Rachel Josefowitz Siegel
Ellen Cole

REFERENCES

Granirer, Prina (1989). *The trials of Eve/Les Epreuves d'Eve.* Vancouver, BC: Gaea Press.

Parker, Rozsika (1989). *The subversive stitch: Embroidery and the making of the feminine.* New York: Routledge.

SECTION I:
FROM GENERATION
TO GENERATION:
THE MEANINGS OF MISHPACHA

Chapter 1

Life in a Glass Bowl:
Tales of a Rabbi's Daughter

Elisheva Glass

I am a fifteen-year-old young woman growing up in Ithaca, New York. For those of you unfamiliar with Ithaca, it is a very diverse community full of liberals and leftover hippies, professors, and aspiring actors. I live downtown in this multicultural city — the part of town with a few more extremists and a little less safety. I go to the public high school — there is only one — and can't wait to graduate in two years.

It was difficult for my parents to have me and my siblings attend public school and receive so little Jewish education. They provided us with a excellent religious school education, but it can't compare in the long run to *yeshivas* or day schools. I wasn't, and still am not, fazed by this in the least. People have tried to start a day school here, and although we have a good Jewish community, the idea never got more than two feet off the ground.

Our Jewish community is terrific. We have active, young members running a Conservative synagogue that is thriving as never before. All feel welcome within a few moments of entering the synagogue; people are overwhelmed by a sense of warmth and caring that our community holds and extends to others . . . or so I've heard. You see, I'm not your normal congregant; I'm the rabbi's daughter. Not many people can say they have 275 parents, but I can. Everything I do or say is watched and reported to fellow congregants or to my father. Even non-Jews recognize me because they know my father and his role. They watch me to discover mine, I suppose. It's awful at times; I almost feel like a constant hostess, smiling and putting on an act at all times. It's hard, and I don't think anyone should have the pressure of growing up under constant, watching eyes. It is enough to drive a person insane. At other times it is nice because there is a support system and an extended family that is always there for me.

Fortunately for me, I have two siblings who share the burdens. My older sister, Ann, has probably had more to deal with than my younger brother Calman and I put together, but we love her anyway. In all seriousness, the three of us get along remarkably well. We all hold the stereotypical roles in our family: Ann is a natural born leader who thrives on control and responsibility; Calman is the one who gets off a little easier and doesn't have to fight with my parents over such silly things as bedtime, and is frequently found to be in his own world making plans for the future while we do chores; and then there is me, suffering from Middle Child Syndrome, occasionally forgotten, mistaken for my older sister, and always caught in the middle. My sister and I have a relationship that is peerless, full of love and trust. She truly is my best friend and has been there for me through everything, helping my parents raise me. My brother and I have an incredible closeness which is sometimes hard to find, but it is always there. We grew up playmates and friends, sometimes living in a castle made of cardboard bricks, sometimes working in imaginary grocery stores. I have to believe that the three of us get along so well because of my father's position and the fact that no one else can really understand what we go through as his children.

All the insanity leads many RKs, as we call ourselves, to rebellion — which I completely understand. But it has helped me to become a good socializer and people person. I have had to grow up a lot faster and have developed a much better public persona than I imagine I otherwise would have. But, I am also extremely self-conscious and a perfectionist of sorts. I have become so afraid of what others will think of me, and I always aim to please others, but rarely myself.

My actions and behavior are greatly affected by all of this as I constantly mask my true feelings and desires. I must be prim and proper in all aspects of my life because my private life *is* my public life. There is no separation between the two and, as one can imagine, this is extremely difficult to handle at times.

Because everyone knows my position in the community, they know I'm Jewish, and this makes it both easier and harder to express my

Judaism. I dress the same as every teen except for the occasional Hebrew lettering on a shirt or *Magen David*, *Hamsa*, or *Hai* jewelry. No one can be certain of my religion until I wear these things, but I choose to do so with pride. On the other hand, this also means teachers turn to me during class discussions with questions about our religious views and practices. This is usually very uncomfortable because although I am perfectly tolerant and accepting of my religion, I know many others are not. I want to present Judaism in the best possible light while accurately describing our lives. Only when I need to go on the defensive do things get really bad. When I am set against the whole class or I am trying to educate others and show them our side of the issue — this is when I am pained the most by the ignorance and arrogance of others.

The teen years are generally known as the years when a young woman discovers her identity, finds herself. This is difficult for anyone to go through, and while Judaism makes many aspects of life a little easier, it only complicates this particular process for me. I am so uncertain about everything, and every decision seems to carry the weight of the world. There are more choices to be made than ever. Lots of people say that it is wonderful for our religion to provide adolescents with a *Bar/Bat Mitzvah* to help them and make them proud of themselves — but I'm not so sure we need it at that age. When I was twelve, I had an amazing year. Some of this did have to do with my Bat Mitzvah and the *B'nai Mitzvah* of my peers, but it was also just the flow of my life at the time. In actuality, I could use a ceremony like that now as I am full of self-doubt and awkward feelings. As my brother prepares for his, I can't help but feel jealous and wish I had another chance now, with my present-day friends and family, so I could at least feel special for one weekend. I've come to accept the fact that being a teenager is difficult. But, I do feel that things are harder for me as a Jew. I have two identity crises to go through—secular and religious.

Unlike many others, I don't challenge my religion. Perhaps my parents have sufficiently taught me about all the open ends of our religion and the fact that it is a religion full of choices for the individual, but whatever it is, I understand the origins of our customs and beliefs. This is not to say I am absolutely certain there is a God, because in that department I am clueless. I think even the most religious of us doubt God's presence at times. It is hard not to; there is no proof or anything tangible for us to know God is there, but my parents say it is a faith we must have. If God was God, wouldn't He make all humans good and make it a perfect world? Why would evil things happen? The fact that I question God's presence, I think, only shows that part of me believes or wants to believe that there is a God, and for now that is enough to hold my faith.

Women have an extremely complicated position in our community when it comes to affiliation. The religion itself doesn't change from Reconstructionist to Reform to Conservative to Orthodox, but women's places, practices, and obligations change drastically. By being Orthodox you give up your right to have an *Aliyah* or pray aloud or practice some *mitzvoth*. You must be more modest in your clothing and relationships with men. There's a huge difference between a Reform *shul* where both men and women wear *kippot* and *tallitot*, or neither are wearing them, and singing together to musical instruments, and an Orthodox shul where the women can't see the men or the leader.

The choice of where to align yourself in this wide spectrum is truly first addressed upon entering college, but that doesn't mean I haven't started to think about it already. I am not comfortable in a Reform service, perhaps because I am not used to it. I've never been to a Reconstructionist service. I like the ideas behind a Conservative service, but I almost feel more comfortable in an Orthodox setting because more people know what they are doing and want to be there (or they at least act like they do). But how could I turn on all I've grown up with, especially since my father is a rabbi? I feel that I can't.

On the up side, our religion does provide us with many morals. Where other teens struggle with decisions about whether or not to drink or take other drugs, the answer is clear to me. Part of this, of course, has to do with the fact that if I were to experiment with drugs, word of this would get home to my parents before I did. My parents have never out and out named consequences for these acts, but I am sure I would not be allowed out of their sight for a long time. What would the community think if I were caught doing something like this? I would be shunned, and while my parents would be pitied, they would also lose face in the community. Who would trust a rabbi who can't keep his own child from trying drugs? They would keep their children out of shul so I wouldn't be a bad influence, and then they would be the ones hurt from the loss of Judaism.

Interdating is taboo in Judaism. I understand that intermarriage is a problem, but interdating seems so harmless. My parents explain that "not every date leads to marriage, but every marriage starts with a date." Fine, but how do you know the boyfriend won't convert later? It's a hard enough issue to handle on its own, but even harder in Ithaca where in my grade there are a total of eight Jewish guys. That definitely is a limited selection, and I could never date most of them because I've grown up closely with them; it would be like incest. So, basically, having a social life full of various boyfriends and exciting dates isn't part of my future. I could always choose to rebel against this, but that would cause the scandal of the century in the Jewish community of Ithaca. We must act the part of the model family full of happiness and respect and wonderful children. But, more important, my parents would be deeply upset, and that would simply make life more difficult for me.

The people who help me through all the insanity of my life are my friends. And while one should never fish for compliments, *complements* are always good to find. As you can imagine, growing up in a community as small as Ithaca, I have had relatively few friends who were Jewish. In some ways having Jewish friends makes life easier in terms of explaining when I cannot do things on *Shabbat*, or being absent for holidays, or even just life cycle events. But it also makes things a lot more uncomfortable when Jews, who should know about all these things, don't know about them, and I have to explain.

The social aspect itself is no different except that I go a lot farther back with my Jewish friends from religious school and play groups, and having a history and memories with people is nice. My female Jewish friends are no different from my gentile female friends, except that I might see them in services and have the extra social time with them. The males are no different either, except that my parents like them a whole lot more than the non-Jewish guys. I understand that they want me to date Jewish guys, but they're all just friendships, and none are developing into anything more, so there really should be no partiality. I've always gotten along better with guys than girls, and my whole life I've always had more male friends than female. This wasn't an issue until adolescence when it became a problem for my parents. I can't spend time with my non-Jewish male friends in case someone sees us and thinks I have a gentile boyfriend. I don't, and I resent the fact that I miss out on friendships because of what congregants might think. I don't see why I can't do things with friends; I'm not interdating. The bottom line is, even if I were with a Jewish male friend half the congregation wouldn't know if he was Jewish, so what is the difference? My parents would know. Well if my parents know I'm with a *friend*, what is the problem? I don't see why they aren't happy about the fact that I am truthful with them. The good thing about having female friends would be not having to deal with this problem, but for some reason I just don't get along well with girls. It is not as if I don't try.

I'm also restricted in terms of friendships because of Shabbat. I can't do anything with my friends on Friday night or Saturday. I can only do things on Sunday, but I need to do homework then, so I virtually have no time to socialize. This also means I miss virtually all parties. Missing parties is the worst because everyone has a great time without me and plenty of memories, which also helps to exclude me during the week. Then there are the times I'm just not invited because I can't come anyway, but that hurts, too; they could at least let me know I'm wanted there. So, as you can see from all these limitations, having friends at the time in my life when I need them most is extremely difficult.

All aspects of my life are affected by the occupation my father chose. Everyone in my community knows me and watches over me; I must be a representative for the Jewish people and the state of Israel in class discussions; and my social friendships are limited because of interdating or the implication thereof. While I feel strongly about our heritage and its benefits along with the moral values it instills, there is also a side of me that blames Judaism for these problems in my life. In spite of it all, Judaism has molded my character and helped me become who I am today. For that alone I must cherish and pass on our traditions. I am sure that our religion will help guide me through the many roads of my life, for like Carl Sandburg, "I am an idealist. I don't know where I'm going, but I'm on my way."

Chapter 2

Bris, Britah: Parents' First Lessons in Balancing Gender, Culture, Tradition, and Religion

Susan Steinberg-Oren

Like good Jewish parents, my husband and I, shortly after our marriage, obeyed the first commandment in the Bible — be fruitful and multiply. As we began our partnership in life, we also embarked upon our new duty of co-parenting the innocent little love of our life. Although we were both raised as Jews, and wish to pass on that identity in a meaningful way to our children, we had no idea how much conflict would be raised between us over this matter. After all, this wasn't a mixed marriage. The extent to which we differed in our thoughts, expression, and experience of Judaism rapidly became evident in those exciting, exhausting, and emotionally draining days just following our son's birth. Although our first parental thoughts were the same, "What a miracle!" followed by, "Oh, no, we have to have a *bris*," the similarity in our positions ended there. As we faced the decision regarding whether or not to have a bris, it was as if we were speaking different languages—Hebrew and English, to be exact.

No, ours is not a mixed marriage, but a bicultural one. I was raised in the United States. My husband was raised in Israel. While our ancestors three generations back were probably neighbors in eastern Europe, their journeys led them to different destinations. I would argue that it was these destinations that strongly shaped each of our own unique experiences of Judaism.

Well, back to the bris. To circumcise or not to circumcise, that was the first question. While today the majority of males from

Western countries, Jewish and non-Jewish alike, are circumcised, controversy has been raised in the past and once again today regarding the medical/sanitary benefits of circumcision. Aware of this debate, but ignorant of the exact details, we both knew without question that we would circumcise our son. As I probed myself further, I thought of the covenant of Abraham. Far be it from me to break a 3,500-year chain of commitment to Judaism. My husband's response was simply: "All Jewish people circumcise their sons." Since we quickly decided we were going to circumcise, we moved to the second question: How should it be done? This decision was much more difficult and we debated it for a while. The question of doctor vs. *mohel* raised considerable anxiety in us. Which is safer? Who has more experience? Which way is less traumatic physically, emotionally? Do we need this procedure to be meaningful, and to whom? Does, or will, our son need it to be meaningful?

My husband, who takes his Jewish identity as a given, felt that there were many options. We could go to a doctor's office, or we could have a small bris at home. If we were more concerned about medical safety but wanted to include meaning, we could make a circumcision in a doctor's office more religious by inviting a mohel or a rabbi or by saying our own prayers. If tradition was more important but we were concerned about medical safety, we could make a circumcision in our home more medical by inviting a surgeon to do the job. My husband's view was that we didn't have to be so concerned about structuring Judaism into our son's life. By being the son of an Israeli he would have an inherent and important connection with Israel which would be sufficient to impart a strong Jewish identity.

I, on the other hand, do not take my Jewish identity for granted. I believe I have to work to keep it alive. I also believe I have to work hard to impart a Jewish identity to my children. Such work involves careful decisions. Not surprisingly, I had concerns about every option. The decision seemed to be complicated by the fact that I had no guarantees concerning safety, and preventing trauma. Consequently, I felt impelled to focus on the meaning of the act. Since circumcision according to Jewish law is a mark of peoplehood, I wanted the act to happen in a manner symbolic of its meaning. Thus,

I wanted to have the bris in our home, surrounded by family and friends, our community.

At this time in our development, our life was fairly devoid of community. We had just started working after many years in school. We moved to a new and very large city. Our families lived far away and many of our close friends lived out of state. We commuted far to our jobs. We did not belong to a synagogue. I felt that it was time to start building a sense of community for ourselves as well as for our child and children to come. My husband disagreed: "The community thing will happen; you don't have to impose it."

Here is our second difference of opinion: community needs to be created versus community will develop. In looking back, a common thread in our differences appeared: Judaism needs to be imparted versus Judaism will occur naturally. I believe this difference is strongly related to our countries of origin. Let's take a simple look at how Judaism functions in Israel. A Jewish child raised in Israel automatically follows the traditions of Judaism. For one thing, s/he learns Jewish history in school, regardless of the family's commitment to provide a Jewish education. Also, the child absorbs Jewish customs and traditions even if the family does not follow the rules of religious observance. For example, most shops are closed from late Friday afternoon to Sunday morning. There is not much to do, so everyone rests or visits with families or friends, essentially practicing the Shabbat. People are given vacations for all Jewish holidays so that they can appropriately celebrate them. There are abundant *Brit Milahs, B'nai Mitzvahs*, weddings, and funerals, and most members of the community attend these affairs. Most everyone speaks Hebrew, and those who don't may learn by taking courses that are subsidized by the government. Judaism happens naturally in this country.

Let's contrast this view with Judaism in America. The Jewish child raised in America is faced continuously with obstacles to traditional practices. In order to learn Jewish history, one must go to a private Jewish or religious school. The financial investment to do so requires a strong commitment toward Judaism from the parents. While Saturday is the weekend, many business establishments are open. The child is faced with many choices for activities such as movies, sports events, music lessons, errands, etc. Children are not given time off for religious holidays unless they go to a Jewish school. There are not so many Brit Milahs, B'nai Mitzvahs, weddings, and funerals. And usually the child, school-age and above, does not attend because of play dates, Little League games, piano lessons, and homework. If one is not careful, the Jewish child will not be exposed to many traditions of Judaism. Judaism does not just exist in the United States; it has to be worked at.

So, how does one work at being Jewish? What do parents do to help their children to internalize a Jewish identity? Here we come to the third and most pronounced difference in my husband's and my approaches to Judaism: the synagogue. This sacred building represents the most controversial aspect of our Jewish union. The root of this conflict more accurately is the religious component of Judaism, not the synagogue, per se. But in America, and probably in all other countries where Jews live outside of Israel, it is the synagogue which houses the difficult task of connecting the religious and cultural experiences. For me, involvement in the synagogue is part and parcel of the Jewish experience. For my husband, it is an obligatory exercise that is tolerated reluctantly.

My husband lives by the Yiddish proverb, "The best synagogue is the heart." For him, the private and familial aspects of Jewish life, Shabbat dinners with our children, Passover Seders, trips to Israel, are the most meaningful and all that are necessary. The fulfillment one receives from these events is immediate and powerful. Who needs anything else? Especially when visits to the synogogue result in confusion, frustration, and profound ambivalence. My position is that our private Jewish experiences require social/public support to stay alive, particularly in the absence of extended families. Jews in America are dependent upon the organized Jewish community, most notably the synagogue, to support them in their decision to live as Jews. This is something my husband has reluctantly come to understand through years of living in this country.

At the time of our son's bris, the synagogue was not a huge issue. It looms much larger now as he and his younger sister are becoming increasingly conscious of the world around them and how they fit into it. While finding a synagogue was not immediately in our thoughts, finding a rabbi/mohel to perform the circumcision was. We did not belong to a temple and we did not know many rabbis. One couldn't just look in the phone book or call 1-800-dial a mohel. Instead, I talked to friends and got some leads. In addition, we were recommended a wonderful sourcebook to help Jewish parents to make decisions, *The Jewish Baby Book,* by Anita Diamant (1988).

The first mohel we located was a rabbi who specialized in circumcisions. "He does eight a day," boasted a friend who used him for his son's bris. "He's extremely reliable and accessible. He even carries a beeper. Here's his pager number." This rabbi's efficiency and mass production concerned me. "How meaningful could the ceremony be, if he is rushing off to the next one?" I asked my husband. Even he agreed we should cross this one off the list. The image of a man performing one circumcision after another all day long, all year long, seemed to haunt my husband.

The second mohel was referred by a friend who was in rabbinical school. The friend recommended first that we check with a recent customer. Upon calling the mother of the 18-month-old child who had been circumcised by this mohel, I was horrified to find out that he had botched the job. "My son may need an operation to correct for the original circumcision. It is too early to tell." Four to six days away from the act, I was aghast at hearing my worst nightmare and beginning to run out of options. I called my friend back in tears: "I need another referral." Taking pity on me, he called numerous colleagues and got me the name and number of someone who came with excellent reviews. Phew! "Let's just use him!" I pleaded with my husband. Exhausted by these difficult decisions, he succumbed.

Those two or three or four days prior to the bris were nervous ones. My husband returned to work, while I began to learn how to mother an infant. Every experience was new, and somewhat overwhelming, as I was performing at about a 50 percent level because of the postpartum healing process. And the countdown to the bris was in the back of my mind.

Are you or aren't you going to have a bris? This seemed to be the question of the week as I phoned friends and relatives to notify them of the birth. "It's so barbaric," some quipped, while others swore that mohels outperformed MDs. There were questions about whether we would give him a local anaesthetic, as well as quasi-professional opinions that wine is sufficient to numb the pain. The more I spoke about it, the more my head began to spin.

When the big day arrived, my husband and I were quite anxious. We had invited about 30 people to the event. Our anxieties were distinct and, surprisingly, gender-related. My husband, I believe, was suffering from castration anxiety. His identification with our son brought him in touch with the imminent physical pain of the circumcision act. I could have sworn that I saw him touching his penis repeatedly that day. He denies it. My worries involved care-giving in a fishbowl. In other words, how would I be able to care for my postsurgical son while hosting so many people in my home for this "happy" event? While traditional Judaism does acknowledge the bittersweet aspect of this rite, there is not enough written to prepare parents for the myriad of feelings evoked by it.

My husband and I were not the only ones to experience marked ambivalence during the ceremony. So were many of our guests. A passionate debate emerged among several men as the ceremony began. It concerned the extent of pain experienced by the child. "A baby cries no more than when you take his blanket away," one friend commented. "How would you like to undergo surgery without anaesthesia?" another retorted. Several women in the room glanced empathically in my direction, as if to say this must be hard for you. I felt myself withdrawing further and further and when our baby started crying, I was so preoccupied and upset I had to leave the room.

Once the circumcision was complete I took our son into his room and stayed there during most of the reception. My husband visited us often, he too wanted to take a break from the guests. He wore the baby monitor like a beeper, ducking into the "recovery room" at the slightest peep or sigh. Female friends came to see me and ask how we were doing. "Okay," I replied. But, for all of us, it was not fun. It was not joyful. We did not have that warm fuzzy feeling of belonging. We just wanted to get through it. Any meaning we wished to glean from this rite of passage was overshadowed by anxiety and discomfort. The whole affair felt imposed and impersonal. I even felt some embarrassment about being the one to encourage my family to go through this stressful exercise. My husband felt angry and voiced our sentiment best: "If we have another son, I will not go through that again!"

Two years later, a baby girl was born to us. We were overjoyed to have a daughter, just as we had been to have a son. We felt particularly blessed with the miracle of having one child of each sex. And in those first few minutes after discovering it's a girl and fantasizing wildly about all that would entail for us as parents, there was tremendous relief in knowing we wouldn't have to have a bris.

During those first few days and weeks with our daughter, we basked in the wonder of parenting an infant. With maternity leave and few social obligations, total merger ensued, except for that frequent arm pulling of her two-year-old brother who repeatedly whined: "Come on, let's go play." "This time I don't want to make the same mistakes," I reminded myself frequently. I strove toward conscious consistent parenting as much as possible. Rocking till he dropped was replaced with baby self-calming techniques. Overfeeding was solved by more awareness of the various forms of discomfort symbolized by her cries. And, I pondered long and hard about how we could make a welcoming ceremony more fulfilling and meaningful.

Brit habat, the most common name for the ceremony to celebrate the birth of a Jewish daughter, is a recent addition to the list of communal Jewish customs. Some propose that it is a revival of an ancient ritual in which new mothers brought thanksgiving offerings to the Temple for the birth of their daughters sixty-six days after the birth. Others believe it is a novelty created in the 1970s by progressive Jewish parents to correct for the lack of community acknowledgment of the birth of girls. Because there is no record of the ancient ceremony, there is also no associated normative liturgy. Jewish parents have considerable freedom to decide how and when. This freedom to create our own ceremony was a blessing for us, having been traumatized by the strict rules for the brit milah.

I knew from the time of her birth that I wanted to have a naming ceremony for our daughter. It was equally as important for me to welcome her into the community as it had been to welcome her brother. And, from the position I described earlier, this ceremony is just one in a long list of events that imparts a sense of Jewish identity. My husband, consistent with his position, was less sure. In our discussions, however, it became apparent we both wanted a chance to redeem ourselves, and thought the *britah* could allow us this opportunity. We realized that we had significantly more knowledge having gone through the bris and having located literature about bris and britah celebrations. We thought that we really could do it differently this time.

Family was coming from out of state to see the baby, and we decided to make that an occasion for the celebration. We located the rabbi who married us, who was very happy to perform the ceremony. We wanted him to contribute the religious and traditional components of the service which we wanted to augment with our own meaning and rituals. Thankfully, this time, we also had the breathing room to do this. By breathing room, I mean the actual time and the peace of mind which comes with freedom from concerns about safety and physical pain. We spent weeks acquiring information about our cultural and family heritage, finding blessings, and writing poems. This time the focus was not on a body part, but on the wholeness of a person, her family and community.

The ceremony surrounded our daughter's ties to her female ancestors. We read narratives created by us and our parents describing the lives of the three women after whom she had been named. By recalling the strengths and virtues of her namesake relatives, we reminded ourselves of the value of these women within our own lives and within the communities in which they lived. As the female is symbolized by cycles and seasons, our daughter's ceremony helped us to connect the generations, essentially continuing the familial cycle. It also provided us with an opportunity to recognize and praise the accomplishments of our foremothers, a practice long neglected by traditional Judaism.

My husband, a reluctant participant in the bris, seemed to embrace our daughter's naming ceremony. He focused on the personal and familial aspects of the ceremony. Because his parents would not be there in person, he asked them ahead of time to compile descriptive histories of his relatives. At first they joked about the relevance of this ceremony as it is not accepted by traditional Judaism. Brit habat ceremonies have been fairly uncommon in Israel because of the predominance of Orthodox Judaism relative to other forms of Jewish thought and practice. However, *Saba* and *Safta* met the task 150 percent by faxing us informative and humorous biographies of the treasured women. My husband was delighted to share these stories with other family members and our closest friends. This was truly meaningful for him.

I focused on the spiritual and feminist aspects of this celebration by emphasizing the intimate connection with God and womankind. We created a ritual in the service by which all female relatives gathered to light the candles and quote traditional blessings for our daughter. My mother and I then acknowledged the miracle of being female, the wisdom of our own foremothers, and our intimate connection to each other as we celebrated our female Godsend.

My husband and I, our differences notwithstanding, joined in our Judaism that day. Together, we made "Jewish choices," a term coined by Anita Diamant and Howard Cooper in their book, *Living a Jewish Life* (1991). By "Jewish choices," we sought to express our Judaism through rituals or actions based not only upon the knowledge of traditions but also upon personal reflection and insights from psychology and feminism. Collaboratively creating our own ceremony allowed us to communicate our differences and similarities in the open, deciding each of our limits and where we could compromise. We were able to define the important pieces of our identities, family values, and cultural and religious practices so that we could express them in ways that felt right and made sense to both of us. The end result was a Jewish ceremony which was personal, dynamic, and meaningful. There were no power struggles, sense of doubt, feelings of anxiety, alienation, or imposition. Constructing the service was a lesson in conscious Jewish co-parenting. Thus, not only did we welcome our daughter, but our own bicultural coming together in the long and lovely journey of being Jewish parents.

REFERENCES

Diamant, Anita (1988). *The Jewish baby books*. New York: Summit Books.
Diamant, Anita and Cooper, Howard (1991). *Living a Jewish life*. New York: Harper Perennial.

Chapter 3

Married – Without a Chupa

Roslyn Mendelson

This is the story of being in an interfaith marriage and the challenges it has presented to me: isolation, confrontation, and self-discovery.

I am a Jewish woman and a feminist. I grew up in the primarily *Ashkenazi* Jewish community of Montreal, Canada, a city which had a Jewish population of 125,000 at that time. My family had a very traditional Jewish outlook on life, and perpetuated traditional Jewish values. My contact with non-Jews was quite small. Ninety percent of my classmates in the public schools were Jewish, as were all of my parents' friends. Most of the smaller stores that we frequented were owned and managed by Jewish people. I went to afternoon and Sunday school for five years where I learned Hebrew and Yiddish. I belonged to and was active in the B'nai Brith Youth Organization and went to Jewish summer camps. My family belonged to an Orthodox and then a Conservative synagogue, I was brought up with Jewish people, Jewish knowledge, Jewish holidays, Jewish pride and a Jewish soul. I was married at a young age to a Jewish man under a *chupa*. That marriage ended in divorce.

Later in life, like the daughters in *Fiddler on the Roof,* I broke with tradition: I married a non-Jewish man, but we did not have a

I would like to express my gratitude to the women who have participated in my workshops. In particular, I would like to thank the following people: Willa Miller, Lynne Sloane, and Carolyn Larson for their thoughtful editorial comments, their challenging questions, and their encouragement in writing this article; Roberta Nitkin for sharing her experiences and inspiring my thinking; Melanie Loomer for her input in developing the original workshop; and my husband, David Hodgins, for his loving support in all aspects of this project.

chupa, because that was one of the compromises I made when I married a Protestant man. We now live in Calgary, a western Canadian city with a Jewish population of 7,000 people where we are bringing up our two small daughters. I work as a psychologist and have been active as a feminist since the early 1970s.

I sometimes read about people like myself in various articles where I have found statistics about the rates of interfaith marriages (Rabinowitz, 1989) and their chance of surviving (Chiswick and Lehrer, 1991). Therapists grapple with the problem of how to counsel couples in interfaith relationships and how the implications of religious differences may be addressed (Eaton, 1994). People are concerned about the effect of interfaith marriages on the children and the best way to raise the children (Clamar, 1991). And of course, I am aware that intermarriage is viewed as a crisis within the Jewish community with respect to the continuity and integrity of Jewish life.

The concerns that have been raised in the literature are interesting and important. However, they do not address what, for me, are fundamental issues in making a commitment to the man I love, a man who happens to come from outside the religion and the community that I love. Marrying outside my faith placed me in a position where I have had to examine my values closely and make careful decisions on many important aspects of my life, a process that has been interesting and challenging. I call it a journey in isolation, confrontation and self-discovery which I believe is specific to my experience of being a *Jewish* woman in an interfaith marriage.

My journey is complex and multifaceted. It involves making decisions on such fundamental issues as how to handle life transitions, how to celebrate holidays, how to raise children, where to live and the extent to which I want to be affiliated with the Jewish community. It affects my relationship with my husband and children, as well as other relationships in my life. It includes a confrontation and clarification of values regarding two other important aspects of my life, Judaism and feminism.

ISOLATION

The isolation I speak of is twofold: It predates the marriage and it comes from marrying a non-Jewish man. Isolation from Judaism occurred before my marriage and set up the conditions which in part fostered my choice to intermarry.

Before considering marrying my husband, I lived as a student in a small university town not far from Montreal. The townspeople were English speaking, and there was a very small Jewish population, even among the university community. However, living so close to my hometown, I was not concerned about the lack of Jewish affiliation in my life. As a graduate student, most of my friends were not Jewish. In fact, my Jewishness and my commitment to Judaism, although not a secret, were perhaps not as obvious to people as they were to me. As a student, I lived a very sectarian life: I went to Montreal for holidays and *simchas* where I expressed my Judaism.

Although, on the one hand, I identified and felt connected to being Jewish, I was also conflicted because I felt isolated from my religion. Spiritually, I was not provided with many opportunities or models for being involved in Judaism as a single woman, and I questioned the role of women in Judaism.

This conflict was magnified by the fact that my first husband was refusing to give me a *get*. At that time, there was little support for *agunot*, and I felt powerless. My non-Jewish friends counseled me that this system was unfair and perhaps I should question the system that put me in this position. Despite the fact that this advice did not really reflect my own feelings, I went along with the values of my peers.

Given my student lifestyle and my religious questioning, I felt very connected to my friends and turned to them for support and understanding. However, after I became involved with my future husband and began to grapple with the decision of whether or not I should marry a man who came from a different religion and a different culture, my impression was that my friends did not understand this struggle, as they in fact had not understood my struggle with the get. To them, religion was not as important as loving another person and should not be a barrier, keeping two people who loved each other apart. Their values were those of universal acceptance and compromise. These values were not useful, however, when trying to make decisions about how to bring up children or about my feelings concerning the celebration of Christmas.

Interestingly, I received most support and understanding from women who were committed to their own religious upbringing if the women understood that there were fundamental differences between Judaism and Christianity.

There are many aspects of the experience of isolation within an intermarriage: spiritual isolation, isolation from known sources of support, from families, during mourning and death, and regarding my identity. Other Jewish women who are married to non-Jews have shared their experience of spiritual isolation with me. As Jews, we celebrate our religion in the home and join synagogues and temples as families. Worship is shared. Women have described the feeling of wanting desperately for their partners to go to synagogue with them, and then feeling dreadfully uncomfortable because they are aware of their husbands' lack of connection to the service. I can relate to the feelings of longing, wishing that my partner would share in worship, and then having him in synagogue, sitting next to me without a *tallit*, not knowing the songs and prayers. Similarly, as women grow and further develop their relationship with Judaism, they express fear of alienation from their partners. I know that in my own marriage I cannot take my own exploration of Judaism for granted without monitoring the effect that this exploration has on my husband.

Like other Jewish women I sometimes feel isolated around holidays and simchas. When celebrating Jewish holidays, our husbands may not share the joy and the history. In the early stages of our life together, I spent time teaching my husband my traditions, so that they would become familiar to him. He was a willing participant. His only objection was that he was inconvenienced by not eating bread in our home on *Pesach*, or shopping on *Rosh Hashanah*. Despite his openness, however, I was teaching him rather than sharing a common history with him.

Being involved in the non-Jewish holidays can be a source of difficulty for a Jewish woman. When celebrating my husband's holidays, even when I am enjoying myself, I feel threatened, I fear assimilation and I feel that I am doing something that I have been brought up not to do. I am also faced with breaking the sex role expectation of creating the holidays as I do not bake or shop for the Christmas presents. In the dominant culture, names such as Scrooge and The Grinch are applied to those who do not feel Christmas joy and I am isolated in my discomfort with the holiday.

An aspect of isolation that I have considered, but thankfully not experienced, is the experience of death in an interfaith marriage. As a Jew, I was brought up to be comforted by Jewish ritual surrounding death. My grandparents are buried side by side and my parents visit their graves at least three times a year. I cannot tolerate the idea of cremation, not only because it is against Jewish law, but because I associate burning bodies with the Holocaust. I had always expected to be buried and to have my husband next to me. I have difficulty imagining the experience of dealing with my husband's death and my husband having a non-Jewish funeral. I cannot imagine being comforted by a Wake or gaining strength from the words of a minister. Although my husband does not share my feelings regarding cremation, he will respect my wishes. However, I am still uneasy about being buried alone as I will not be buried in a non-Jewish cemetery.

Marrying a non-Jew has challenged my personal identity and my identity as a Jew as well as my ability to let people know and understand me. I experience this differently when relating to non-Jews and to Jews. Before marrying my husband, I was aware of some people stereotyping me as a Jew. In response, I could use my Jewish involvement as a way of educating people about what is important to me as a Jew and who I am. For example, when non-Jews would ask me what I would be doing for Christmas, I could say that I do not celebrate Christmas because I am Jewish. However, once married, when my colleagues ask me what I am doing for Christmas, I sometimes feel uncomfortable, and unsure about how to communicate my thoughts and feelings or how to establish my identity.

After marrying a non-Jew, I also feel Jews see me differently than before in terms of my commitment to Judaism. When the problem of Jewish continuity is described as the "problem of intermarriage," I feel alienated among my people and defensive about my choice of marriage partner and my commitment to Judaism. I also worry that my husband will not find a place where he feels comfortable and accepted. In reality, I am very concerned about Jewish continuity and am grateful that parts of the Jewish community welcome my family, thus allowing me to fulfill my commitment to raising a Jewish family and to Jewish continuity. Thus, among Jews and non-Jews, I have to find new ways of showing myself and proclaiming my involvement as a Jew.

Being married outside of my faith leads to isolation from parents and parents-in-law. There is now a part of my experience that has no common thread with those of my parents; I know this causes them discomfort. They share my fears of the assimilation of their grandchildren, but as people who hold traditional values regarding a wife's role and who value compromise, they believe that I should support my husband in celebrating his holidays. For example, before my husband and I had children, I chose to visit my parents during the Christmas holidays while my husband went to his home Although my parents appreciated seeing me, they suggested that perhaps I should have shown my husband more support by being with him on his holiday. On the other hand, when I do celebrate my husband's holidays, my parents and I barely discuss the events of the holidays. I suspect they are as conflicted as I am. In some areas, our conflicts originate from different sources, I believe, and it is difficult to discuss our ambivalence concerning this issue.

Likewise my parents-in-law do not have the framework to understand my past, my experience, or my feelings regarding my involvement in their traditions. I suppose that the decisions my husband and I make regarding our children's lives are foreign and perhaps painful for them despite the fact that they may genuinely try to understand our choices. I cannot imagine how they feel about their grandchildren being named in synagogues rather than being baptized, attending Hebrew day school, rather than Sunday school, and eventually being *Bat Mitzvahed* rather than being confirmed in church. Yet, from their perspective, by celebrating their holidays with me, they are inviting me to be one of the family and are treating my children as they treat the rest of their grandchildren. They do not realize that at times being part of the family causes me to give up something of myself, and that having my children involved in their holidays arouses fear in me.

CONFRONTATION AND SELF-DISCOVERY

Dealing with the religious issue in my relationship with my husband has also led to confrontation and self-discovery, which are both painful and rewarding. For me, the confrontations have occurred when my beliefs about Judaism and feminism have been challenged.

In making decisions regarding how I wish to live and how to bring up my children I have had to examine my feelings about and commitment to Judaism in a way that many of my Jewish friends have not. I have also had to confront the limitations of feminist thinking in terms of handling minorities and diversity. These confrontations interface with my identity as a Jew.

Important questions arose as my worldview was challenged: Over the years, how supportive have feminist thought and values been to me as a Jew? Where did Judaism fit into my life? When I examined my decision-making process regarding my relationship with Judaism against the background of feminist values in the mid-1980s, I found that feminist principles were not helpful to me; they did not take into account the perspective of a Jewish woman.

At that time there was much feminist criticism of patriarchal religions, encouraging women to leave, explore, expand, and experiment spiritually rather than to perpetuate organized religion. I too realize the extent to which patriarchal religions have oppressed women, and I value women finding our own spiritual voices. These concerns both spoke to and perpetuated my isolation from Judaism. Consequently, I did not initially explore Judaism to see if there was a place for me. However, my emotional struggle surrounding my religion brought my personal split to my consciousness. I began to speak to other Jewish women who were more visibly Jewish and found some writings by Jewish feminists which were enlightening in that they reflected my world view (Beck, 1982).

After much soul searching I discovered that my own need is to belong to and perpetuate Judaism, despite the fact that some aspects of Judaism are contradictory to my feminist values. For example, before I married my husband, I did receive a get as I ultimately realized this patriarchal symbol held meaning for me in finally dissolving my first marriage and ensuring the religious status of my children. As well, my husband and I decided to raise our children as Jews as I could not compromise about that issue. Furthermore, I ultimately came to the realization that Judaism is a part of me that I could not divorce. Despite being married to a non-Jew, Jewish survival is important to me. I believe that as a member of a minority, I cannot take my religion or my Jewish identity for granted lest it be overshadowed by the majority culture or its religion. Throughout this process I have learned that my worldview regarding what is important is a Jewish worldview and is not generally known by non-Jews. Thankfully, since I began this journey other feminists have begun to write and speak about issues of diversity, racism, and antisemitism.

Given that both my friends and my husband were surprised at my commitment to Judaism, what did that say about my outward involvement as a Jew? I realized that a number of forces were influencing my visibility as a Jew. As I had learned that we live in an antisemitic society, it was safer to keep my Judaism to myself. Furthermore, there were aspects of the stereotype of Jewish women with which I did not want to be identified and, like many others, I internalized antisemitism and covered up these parts of myself. From this process of examining my Jewish identity, and my relationship with Judaism, I have learned that if I allow myself to be less visible as a Jew, people will not know what a Jew is, and if I do not turn to Judaism for answers I will not know what a Jew is.

Finally, and most profoundly, I have had to confront my fears on many levels. As a Jewish person, born in the shadow of the Holocaust, Jewish survival and the privilege of living a Jewish life are very important and emotional issues to me. I am afraid that by marrying a non-Jew, 5,000 years of history may end with me. My children may marry non-Jews and may not choose to live a Jewish life. This risk would exist if I were married to a Jewish man, of course, but I would not feel that I had created the conditions to make this possible. As I involve myself in my husband's life and traditions, I question whether I am threatening my children's connection to Judaism and betraying the memory of my people. For the most part I do not see this happening as my children take joy in lighting the *Shabbot* candles and comment on their love of Jewish holidays. They have been brought up to identify themselves as Jews who have a Christian father and heritage. However, when they ask when Christmas will be here and identify themselves as half-Christian, I feel concerned.

The final fear concerns the safety of the man I have married. Recently, a letter bomb detonated at the Jewish Community Centre where my children are in daycare. Before marrying my husband, I had told him that he was giving up the safety of being a member of the cultural and religious majority. Although I could not imagine another Holocaust, he might be in the position of having to choose between me and safety. I do not know if he connected his decision and my warnings to the feelings he must have had as he rushed from his workplace to the Jewish Centre to collect our three-year-old daughter minutes after the bomb exploded. The bombing scared me, but only confirmed my sense of reality that as a Jew, my family and I are not safe in this world. Although being a target of a bombing was the reality to which I was born, this was a reality that my husband chose.

The intensity of the process that I describe has ebbed and flowed over the years. My feelings of isolation regarding the decision to marry were paramount during the early years and when my children were born. As my husband and I grow together, we are becoming more comfortable with each other and for the most part simply live our lives without considering the interfaith aspect. However, Jewish and Christian holidays come about to remind us of our struggle. With each developmental phase of our children, we are faced with new challenges. As our daughters are young, we have yet to deal with the further crises that will come with life transitions in their and our own lives. Other Jewish women have described this experience as a combination of the joy of being married to someone whom they love, joined with profound grief, or a crying inside, for the losses and struggles which this love has evoked.

REFERENCES

Beck, E. T. (1982). *Nice Jewish girls*. Trumansburg, NY: The Crossing Press.

Chiswick, C. U. and Lehrer, E. L. (1991). Religious intermarriage: An economic perspective. *Contemporary Jewry, 12*, 67 – 97.

Clamar, A. (1991). Interfaith marriage: Defining the issues, treating the problems. *Psychotherapy in Private Practice, 9*, 79 – 83.

Eaton, S. C. (1994). Marriage between Jews and non-Jews: Counseling implications. *Journal of Multicultural Counseling & Development, 22*, 210 – 214.

Rabinowitz, J. (1989). The paradoxical effects of Jewish community size and Jewish communal behavior: Intermarriage, synagogue membership, and giving to local Jewish federations. *Contemporary Jewry, 10*, 9 – 15.

Chapter 4

Queer Jewish Women Creating Families: New Perspectives on Jewish Family Values

Susie Kisber

Intermarriage and assimilation are often cited as serious threats to the survival of the "Jewish People." At the same time there are Jews who want to identify with the Jewish community but feel marginalized or excluded. Queer (gay, lesbian, bisexual, and/or transgendered) Jews are not yet fully accepted in mainstream Judaism. Despite this, many are affiliating with Jewish institutions; taking active roles in shaping current Jewish theology, politics, and spiritual traditions; setting up Jewish homes; and raising Jewish children. This article explores some salient issues that queer Jewish women face, examples of how we are creating families, and some new perspectives that we offer on Jewish family values.

As I begin, I want to discuss my *kavannah*, intention, about why I have chosen to use the term "queer" in this article. Those of us who are gay, lesbian, bisexual, and/or transgendered do not agree on one word or phrase that feels comfortable to all of us. "Queer" is used here as a proactive term that encompasses the diversity of the entire sexual minority community. I believe that using language that comes

I am grateful to my *besherts:* Judith Sachs, my soulmate, and Manuel Marks, my lover, for the intimacy and love they bring to my life and the support they provided as I wrote this article. As our connections deepen, I find myself learning more and more about what it means to create family. I also want to thank Juliet Stamper for her friendship, clarity, and many hours of editorial assistance, and Andrea Beth Damsky, Diana Lion, Alina Ever, Jennie Schacht, and Hinda Seif for their feedback about this article as well as the important role each plays in my life. I would also like to acknowledge my mother, Emily Loveman Kisber, for her continued love and support.

29

from within the community and adequately reflects the complex and diverse aspects of our culture and identities is important. By naming ourselves and reclaiming this once derogatory label, we can change how we use the word and how it is viewed by society at large.

Rabbi Rebecca Alpert, when speaking in August 1995 at the Fourteenth International Conference of Gay and Lesbian Jews, made a convincing argument for the community to adopt the word "queer" to define ourselves. She pointed out that some Jews who came to the United States after World War II adamantly refused to adopt the label "Jew." Instead they used terms such as "Israelites," "Hebrews," or "Hebrew People" One rarely thinks of the word "Jew" as offensive today even though it was a charged term then. Similarly, the inverted pink and black triangles used by the Nazis in the Death Camps to mark "homosexuals" and "asocials" (a term sometimes applied to lesbians) have been successfully reclaimed by queer communities throughout the world.

Personally, I use the term "queer" with the awareness that it makes a statement emphasizing my willingness to be "different from the usual" (*Webster's New World Dictionary*, 1987, p. 489) heterosexual majority. Just as I most commonly identify myself as a Reconstructionist when speaking about my spiritual orientation as a Jew, I usually call myself a bisexual when I refer to my sexual orientation. My sexual identity, like my Jewish one, is a cultural identity that is multifaceted. Unfortunately, I often find that the political, ethical, and social aspects of my queer identity get over-shadowed because the dominant culture primarily focuses on the sexual component.

I also use the word queer to counter the invisibility experienced by subgroups within the community. For example, the majority of literature about queer parenting is written by and for lesbians; thus the experiences of bisexual and transgendered women, whatever their sexual orientation may be, becomes subsumed under "the lesbian experience." Using the term queer reflects a broader picture of the diversity of our community.

The definition of what it means to be Jewish is also controversial. Individual Jews may have varying levels of Jewish lineage; religious/spiritual observances and/or practices; Jewish cultural, political, and social involvement and backgrounds; and commitment to a

Jewish identity. Anyone who self-identifies as a Jew is, for the purposes of this article, considered to be one.

Language, as illustrated above, has tremendous sociopolitical power to construct one's experience. Words such as "family" and "marriage," as they are commonly used, have narrow definitions and do not take into account the diversity of families that actually exist. A "family" is usually understood to contain two married people of opposite gender who either have, or plan to have, children. A "marriage" is recognized by the state and is generally assumed to be a union between two heterosexual opposite-gendered people. Much of the language used in Jewish curriculum and outreach programs is designed with only traditional nuclear families in mind. This ignores the needs of many different types of queer and heterosexual families. Designing these types of programs with an understanding of queer oppression is one way the Jewish community can begin to address society's limited notions about families.

Heterosexism is the attitude and assumption that heterosexuality is presumed and considered to be the only or best, not to mention the "natural," option for individuals and families. Barbara and Nancy, a bisexual and a lesbian who are in a committed partnership, decide to enroll their child, Ted, in religious school. The enrollment form has spaces to fill in the father's and mother's names. It does not ask who is in the family. Heterosexist assumptions like this are common and often so insidious that they go unnoticed by most people.

When someone who is queer experiences the feelings that a queer lifestyle is not normal or a valid option, she is being affected by internalized heterosexism. Naomi is a lesbian who readily identifies herself as such. In other words she is "out" and proud of her sexual orientation. After rethinking a decision she recently helped make on behalf of her congregation, she became aware of some ways in which she has internalized the larger society's belief that only heterosexual rabbis reflect Jewish family values. As part of her synagogue's search committee for a new religious school principal, she agreed with the rest of the committee that Rabbi C was the most qualified candidate. In the end, the committee decided not to hire Rabbi C because they thought that, as an "out" lesbian Rabbi, she would not be an appropriate role model for the congregation.

Naomi later realized that it was her internalized heterosexism that led her to agree with the other committee members.

Homophobia, like heterosexism, when expressed in its subtle and more blatant forms actively restricts queers' civil rights. Homophobia is the fear and hatred of queers and queer culture. Leora is a lesbian living with her lover and her lover's child from a former heterosexual marriage. They live in Virginia, which is one of many states that is known for its legislation which negates queer civil rights.[1] She is aware that merely coming out could jeopardize her and her lover's safety, employment, and right to maintain child custody. She avoids questions at work about how she spends her free time and feels uncomfortable developing close friendships with her co-workers. The gay and lesbian synagogue in Washington, DC, provides a place where she and her family can develop supportive relationships without the fears and consequences of homophobia.

Queers who experience internalized homophobia feel self-hatred, fear, anger, and shame within themselves, toward other queers, or in response to queer culture. Evelyn Torton Beck is the editor of *Nice Jewish Girls: A Lesbian Anthology* (1989a) and a prominent Women's Studies scholar. She is also the mother of Nina Rachel, a lesbian who came out before her mother did. She describes the feelings of internalized homophohia she struggled with throughout her twenty-year marriage.

> My passions for women always felt like some dread disease I had contacted and could neither control or get rid of. I was terribly ashamed of these feelings and at the same time treasured them as my most valued possession, my secret source of joy, comfort, and nourishment, right through the years of my marriage. (p. 10)

Just as queer oppression can be external or internalized, so can antisemitism. Often these attitudes are so commonplace in everyday life that the damage they are causing is not obvious. When a Jew feels or expresses hatred, disrespect, disdain, or stereotypes about Jews or being Jewish, she is being affected by internalized antisemitism. Beck poignantly describes her struggle, as a Holocaust survivor, with internalized antisemitism.

> Part of my freak-out at becoming a mother, and especially birthing a girl child, had to do with my history with antisemitism and the sense of being unwanted and slated for murder. If I had no right to live, how could I have the right to reproduce another like me? (p. 23)

As minorities, both Jews and queers live with the negative stereotypes that are prevalent in Western cultures. As queer women decide to have children, they are faced with internalized conflicts and pain about their identities. Vaughn (1987) warns her readers of the insidiousness of internalized heterosexism.

> All of us have grown up as the unwilling participants in a system that has negated our very existence. Unless we shake ourselves free of dominant cultural values and assumptions about The Family, we are almost bound to recreate something which not only doesn't work, but which oppresses us. (p. 24)

Often the first step in freeing ourselves from mainstream values and assumptions is to identify them within ourselves.

Many queer Jewish women creating families find themselves confronted with their feelings about their multiple identities. They may question each facet of their identity, contemplating how the multiple layers fit together. For example, a woman may consider the implications of being a queer Jew, a Jewish parent, a Jewish family, a queer parent, a queer family, a queer Jewish parent, and a queer Jewish family. Beck (1989b), in a transcribed conversation with her daughter, describes how coming out as a lesbian freed her to begin to address the oppression she feels as both a lesbian and as a Jew. "Becoming visible as a lesbian made me less safe in the world but more secure in myself, so maybe I could face the unsafety of being Jewish" (p. 22). Understanding and sorting through the array of identity issues that arise as queer Jewish women create families is difficult because we have few role models. Most of society's models of forming relationships are based on traditional ideas about male and female roles and/or the division of labor being split only between two married adults. There are also few models of queer Jews and queer Jewish family life.

Some opposite gendered queer Jewish parents rely on feminist theory, process, and practice to create new child-rearing models. Many of these models go beyond simple egalitarianism. They often take into account the emotional, temporal, financial, psychological, and physical resources of each person who is involved in parenting. There is an emphasis placed on making conscious choices about how these resources are shared. Throughout the parenting process, talking about and being aware of issues of class, physical ability, past oppression, and culture is also important. The entire experience is looked upon as an evolving journey. The process is as important as the outcome. The current baby boom among queers is providing fertile ground for these feminist models of parenting to be tested and for us to figure out what works well and what does not.

Queer Jews have met the challenge of having few role models and prescribed methods of creating families by making conscious choices and decisions about our lives. Many heterosexuals never have this opportunity because their roles and choices are laid out by society's preconceived expectations. Gambill (1987) sees the many options available to queer parents as a gift.

> As Lesbians, who are automatically placed on the fringe of society by the choice of our lives, we can bring to parenting and to young children the positive aspects of being on that fringe—of possibility instead of control, acceptance instead of rejection, diversity instead of commercial homogeneity, and, yes, importantly, a world of many families in changing and varied forms, not limited by the term *traditional.* This, then, can be a politics of the heart, the expression of love not as a possession, handed down through the marriage ceremony, but love as a verb in motion, daring the boundaries and stretching each of us to our full possibilities. (p. 300)

Bringing a child into their relationships places queer Jewish parents in contact with the larger heterosexual and predominantly Christian world. Those who have previously found it possible to push aside their internalized oppressions find themselves confronted with thoughts about what they want to and will pass down to the next generation. Suddenly, the impact of a decision not to be "out" as queer or Jewish affects more than just oneself. This decision makes a statement to a child that the family has something to be ashamed of, to be fearful about, or to hide. By being "out" and proactive in addressing oppression and ignorance, these queer Jewish parents are working toward *tikkun olam*, repairing the world. They are helping to educate the wider Jewish community and the queer community about diversity issues.

Queers also offer society many new ideas about co-parenting.[2] Some queer parents are coming together not as lovers, but as individuals interested in child rearing. Others have several layers of parenting involvement depending on the particular circumstances and interests of those involved "Family of choice" is a term commonly used within queer culture to describe family members who may not be recognized by the state as legal relatives. These are significant and committed relationships. Often these relationships are not bound by sex-roles or heterosexist stereotypes. They do not fit into the more familiar relationship patterns or categories of the blood-related nuclear or extended family. For instance, Elaine, a nonpartnered lesbian, has decided that she does not want to be a primary parent. She does, however, want to be involved in child rearing. She has chosen to live with Ahuva, a bisexual, and Ahuva's male lover, Marty. Ahuva and Marty have a five-year-old daughter, Shoshi. Joel and Doug, who are partners, also live with Elaine, Ahuva, Marty, and Shoshi. They are all family to one another, and each adult is involved in child care. Varied types of family configurations like this one not only provide new paradigms for the larger community but also role models for future generations.

Queer Jewish women have much to offer the larger Jewish community based on the many positive aspects we can draw from our dual identities as queers and as Jews. As Jews, we have a long history of culturally defining ourselves, maintaining close-knit community and familial connections, and surviving centuries of oppression. As queers, our civil rights movement only really began to coalesce in the last twenty-five years. The creativity and flexibility with which we approach creating families comes from not having the same preconceived notions as the majority culture about how our relationships should be. Thus we challenge the status quo in many ways.

Queer Jewish families, by our very existence, redefine Jewish family values. This can offer hope to all of us who are concerned with the survival of the "Jewish People." We can provide a model that celebrates the many layers of our individual cultural identities as well as the diversity that exists within the community. We have a heightened sensitivity to external and internalized oppression that has resulted from our experiences of marginalization and exclusion. Many of us also approach creating families and understanding what it means to be a Jew with a feminist analysis. These are just some of the ways that queer Jews can offer new perspectives on Jewish family values. I believe that the larger Jewish community can learn from our experiences. I look forward to a future in which each Jew is respected and valued for the unique contributions she has to offer the family, the larger Jewish community, and humankind.

REFERENCE NOTES

1. The Sharon Bottoms' custody case in Virginia has drawn national media attention to queer civil rights issues. For more information about legal issues and queer families see Arnup, 1995; Benkov, 1994; Davies and Weinstein, 1987; Polikoff, 1987; and Ursel, 1995.

2. For some examples of queer parenting experiences see: Clunis and Green, 1995; Cooper, 1987, 1988; Henderson, Lubarr, Neumann, Royster, 1987; Lorde, 1987a,b; Martin, 1993; Polikoff, 1987; Pollack and Vaughn, 1987; Rounthwaite and Wynne, 1995; and Vaughn, 1987.

REFERENCES

Alpert, Rebecca (1995, August). *What's in a name?* Talk presented at the 14th international conference of Gay and Lesbian Jews. New York, NY.

Arnup, Katherine (1995). Living in the margins: Lesbian families and the law. In Katherine Arnup (Ed.), *Lesbian parenting: Living with pride and prejudice* (pp. 378 – 398). Charlottetown, PEI, Canada: Gynergy Books.

Beck, Evelyn Torton (1989a). Daughters and mothers: Three generations (essay). In Evelyn Torton Beck (Ed.), *Nice Jewish girls: A Lesbian anthology* (rev. ed.) (pp. 5 – 13). Boston, MA: Beacon Press.

Beck, Evelyn Torton (1989b). Mother and daughter, Jewish and Lesbian: A conversation (1989). In Evelyn Torton Beck (Ed.), *Nice Jewish girls: A Lesbian anthology* (rev. ed.) (pp. 16 – 27). Boston, MA: Beacon Press.

Benkov, Laura (1994). *Reinventing the family: The emerging story of Lesbian and Gay parents.* New York: Crown Publishers.

Clunis, D. Merilee and Green, G. Dorsey (1995). *The Lesbian parenting book.* Seattle, WA: Seal Press.

Cooper, Baba (1987). The radical potential in Lesbian mothering of daughters. In Sandra Pollack and Jeanne Vaughn (Eds.), *Politics of the heart: A Lesbian parenting anthology* (pp. 233 – 240). Ithaca, NY: Firebrand Books.

Cooper, Baba (1988). Mothers and daughters of invention. In H. Alpert (Ed.), *We are everywhere* (pp. 306 – 321). Freedom CA: The Crossing Press.

Davies, Rosalie G. and Weinstein, Minna F. (1987). Confronting the courts. In Sandra Pollack and Jeanne Vaughn (Eds.), *Politics of the heart: A Lesbian parenting anthology* (pp. 43 – 45). Ithaca, NY: Firebrand Books.

Gambill, Sue (1987). Love in motion. In Sandra Pollack and Jeanne Vaughn (Eds.), *Politics of the heart: A Lesbian parenting anthology* (pp. 296 – 300). Ithaca, NY: Firebrand Books.

Lesbian Mother's Group: Henderson, Pearl; Lubarr, Debbie; Neumann, Barbara; Royster, Shirley (1987). Our lovers will never be fathers, but our community can be our family. In Sandra Pollack and Jeanne Vaughn (Eds.), *Politics of the heart: A Lesbian parenting anthology* (pp. 289 – 295). Ithaca, NY: Firebrand Books.

Lorde, Audre (1987a). Man child: A Black Lesbian-feminist's response. In Sandra Pollack and Jeanne Vaughn (Eds.), *Politics of the heart: A Lesbian parenting anthology* (pp. 220-226). Ithaca, NY: Firebrand Books.

Lorde, Audre (1987b). Turning the beat around: Lesbian parenting 1986. In Sandra Pollack and Jeanne Vaughn (Eds.), *Politics of the heart: A Lesbian parenting anthology* (pp. 310 – 315). Ithaca, NY: Firebrand Books.

Martin, April (1993). *The Lesbian and Gay parenting handbook: Creating and raising our families.* New York: Harper Perennial.

Polikoff, Nancy D. (1987). Lesbian mothers, Lesbian families: Legal obstacles, legal challenges. In Sandra Pollack and Jeanne Vanghn (Eds.), *Politics of the heart: A Lesbian parenting anthology* (pp. 325 – 332). Ithaca, NY: Firebrand Books.

Pollack, Sandra, and Vaughn, Jeanne (1987). Introduction. In Sandra Pollack and Jeanne Vaughn (Eds.), *Politics of the heart: A Lesbian parenting anthology* (pp. 12 – 17). Ithaca, NY: Firebrand Books.

Rounthwaite, Jane and Wynne, Kathleen (1995). Legal aliens: An alternative family. In Katherine Arnup (Ed.), *Lesbian parenting: Living with pride and prejudice* (pp. 81 – 97). Charlottetown, PEI, Canada: Gynergy Books.

Ursel, Susan (1995). Bill 167 and full human rights. In Katherine Arnup (Ed.), *Lesbian parenting: Living with pride and prejudice* (pp. 341 – 351). Charlottetown, PEI, Canada: Gynergy Books.

Vaughn, Jeanne (1987). A question of survival. In Sandra Pollack and Jeanne Vaughn (Eds.), *Politics of the heart: A Lesbian parenting anthology* (pp. 20 – 28). Ithaca, NY: Firebrand Books.

Webster's New World Dictionary. (1987). New York, NY: Warner Books.

Chapter 5

Mothers, Judaism, and True Honor

Paula J. Caplan

As children, when most of us learned the Ten Commandments, we learned that, unlike "Thou shalt not commit adultery," some commandments applied immediately to our lives. Probably the most immediately relevant was "Honor your father and your mother," which continues with a phrase more meaningful as we get older, "that your days may be long upon the land which the Lord your God is giving you" Exodus 21:12 (Revised Standard Version). This commandment is said to serve as a bridge between the preceding commandments, whose prime concern is people's relationship to God, and those that follow, whose prime concern is people's relationships with people. Our parents are said to be God's human representatives.

When I first learned this commandment as a child in Springfield, Missouri, our rabbi explained that "father" was mentioned first because we are naturally inclined to honor our mothers anyway. That struck me as odd when I thought about the way that the mothers I knew, even Jewish mothers, are treated. My grandmother worked to the point of exhaustion to feed us royally on *Rosh Hashono* and *Pesach*, so that "the menfolk" could devote their time to prayer. We enjoyed her food. We loved her. We adored her wit and sparkle. We did not particularly honor her, I am deeply sad to say. It is praying and doing paid work that have tended to be honored by Jews in North America, not mothering work.

"Honor" means "to hold in respect" or "to revere." Even today, among Jews in North America, we train our girls and women to feel

---

This article is a revised version of one that appeared in *The Reconstructionist*, January/February 1989, and is reprinted by permission.

that a major part of their worth comes from their ability to mother, to provide nourishing and attractive food, and a pleasant environment, to take care of children, husbands, and others. But instead of acknowledging that what these women do makes the world go— keeps people together, functioning, and happy— people say, "Listen to those women. They're talking about recipes, and furniture, and diapers" (Caplan, 1989). Thus the incredible value of what mothers do is swiftly dismissed. North American Jews are as guilty of this as are non-Jews.

The failure to honor mothers is a part of Judaism's more general failure to honor women. In the same *Torah portion* in which the Ten Commandments appear, Moses warns his people, in preparation for their receiving the commandments, "Do not go near a woman" Exodus 19:15 (Revised Standard Version). Apparently, women were not to receive the *Torah*. And apparently, only men were being addressed at that point. As Judith Plaskow writes, "Moses does not say, 'Men and women, do not go near each other.' At the central moment of Jewish history, women are invisible" (Plaskow, 1990, p. 26). When I first read that verse in the Torah, I thought it must be *my* mistake, that I must be misreading it—which is so often women's initial response to evidence that individuals or institutions important to us do not value us.

Jewish feminist Judith Arcana points out how women in the Torah are valued only as bearers of children—a role that is not honored but simply expected:

> Four mothers, ironically called "the matriarchs," served in Genesis to beget sons "in the name of the Lord": Sarah, Rebekah, Leah, and Rachel. All but Leah, who is undesired and unloved, are described as "barren" until "the Lord" sees fit to open their wombs, to produce male children in keeping with His covenant with the husbands, the patriarchs: Abraham, Isaac, and Jacob. The bodies of these women are owned by men and their pregnancies are quickened by God. They have no fertility of their own: "And the Lord remembered Sarah as He had said, and the Lord did unto Sarah as He had spoken. And Sarah conceived, and bore Abraham a son" Genesis 21:1, 2 (Revised Standard Version). Their very femaleness is incon-

sequential, for "it had ceased to be with Sarah after the manner of women" Genesis 18:11 (Revised Standard Version). These women are vessels—like their spiritual daughter and blood-descendant, the Virgin Mary—carrying God's seed for men. Less powerful even than these were the concubines, slave women who also bore sons toward the wealth of their masters. (Arcana, 1986, pp. 187–188)

There is a complex interplay between Jews and the surrounding culture. As a Jewish psychologist, I have observed that Jews represent a large proportion of the mental health professions and have made significant and influential mother-blaming contributions to the clinical and research literature. Furthermore, Jews in all walks of life often look to mental health professionals for knowledge and truth as they used to look to Torah and the rabbis. But that secular arena is just as riddled with antiwoman—and antimother—sentiment as is traditional Judaism.

As an example of how our *Jewish* experience shapes our views of mothers, and how those views can be improved, I want to mention a terrific book titled *The Jewish Woman in America* (Baum, Hyman, and Michel, 1976). Like many Jews, I grew up feeling embarrassed about the kind of Jewish woman who bleached her hair, had her nose fixed, talked loudly, and dressed flamboyantly, with too many jewels, too much makeup, fur coats, and gold wedgie shoes. I thought that she gave Jews a bad name.

In reading *The Jewish Woman in America.* I came to understand these Jewish women in a new light, for in that book one finds a description of how generations of Jewish mothers in the Old Country were trained to be strong and energetic. Since the men had to be free to study, it was the mothers who learned the language and customs of the surrounding culture, so that they could deal with the outside world in ways that allowed their families to survive.

When Jewish mothers immigrated to North America, they discovered that a good woman was quiet and passive. She was supposed to be a showpiece for her husband's material success. Women with this history of energy and power, then, had no place to channel that power, except into buying more and more clothes, furs, and jewels. Trying to show that their husbands were successful "providers," they changed their hair and noses to look like the women of the surrounding culture.

As an example of how our secular environment regards mothers, I will describe briefly some work I did with a student assistant (Caplan and Hall-McCorquodale, 1985). We read 125 articles from a variety of mental health journals, in which the professionals offered explanations for people's emotional problems. We found that mothers were blamed for seventy-two different kinds of problems, ranging from arson to the inability to deal with color blindness, to the commission of homocide by some transsexuals, to something called "self-induced television epilepsy," in which a child seemed to bring on his seizures by watching TV. It didn't matter whether the authors were psychoanalysts, family therapists, or other types of mental health workers. They all blamed mothers, and, sadly, the mother-blaming had not lessened with time and the influence of the women's movement.

There is hope. The light begins slowly to shine in the mental health professions, led by people such as Jean Baker Miller, Rachel Josefowitz Siegel, and Janet Surrey (Miller, 1987; Siegel, 1987, 1988; Surrey, 1985), who have recognized the importance of the emotional nurturing that mothers do. They have renamed mothers' alleged emotional dependency and inability to separate from their children as what these things usually are, namely, love of, and considerable skill at, being in relationships.

I have suggested that what is often called mothers'—especially Jewish mothers'—masochism and martyrdom is not in fact their enjoyment of suffering which is, after all, the definition of masochism (Caplan, 1993). When women say, "Look what I've sacrificed for you!" it is often a justified plea for the appreciation and recognition that mothers so rarely receive, except perhaps on Mother's Day.

When appreciation comes only on sentimental occasions, it feels empty. People who do boring, even stressful jobs still feel valued when they get their weekly paycheck. But mothers are unpaid and overworked and do not receive regular appreciation. No one says, "You did a great week's worth of dusting, Mom" (Caplan, 1989).

There is hope within Judaism as well. Feminists are examining women's—and, therefore, mothers'—roles in Judaism, developing ways to include women's experiences in our religion and culture.

The cost of failing to do so was brought home to me some years ago when my children and I attended a traditional service in California after having become used to egalitarian services at home. When we left the California synagogue, my daughter Emily, then about eleven years old, was close to tears. She said, "Did you see the women? They seemed to want to pray, but their lips didn't move. They didn't know the words."

Honoring mothers is, I fear, one of the slowest things to change, but the dawning awareness of the sexism in Judaism—and of its poignant consequences, as Emily saw—is cause for some optimism.

A black man told the following story (Staples, 1986). As he walked down a street in a large city one night, he saw a white woman walking ahead of him. She heard his footsteps and turned around, saw him, and sped up. He realized to his horror that she was afraid of him because he was male and because he was black. But he felt helpless. What could he do? If he had called out to her or had run to catch up with her to reassure her, he would instead have frightened her still more.

This is parallel to what occurs when Jewish feminists raise issues about the dishonoring of women in Judaism. We are often treated as other than what we are. Recently, some men in a congregation hissed in response to a pro-woman, feminist comment I made during a *d'var Torah* discussion. It had not been an anti-male comment, just a pro-woman one, but that did not prevent them from hissing.

If asked, I feel sure that they would say they were just joking. In fact, they grinned as they hissed. But no one of either sex hisses when pro-male or traditionally male or sexist comments are made. I am an adult and a feminist who has often been derided for my feminist remarks; but I wonder, do hisses at me inhibit and silence my daughter and the other girls and women of the congregation, not to mention the boys and men who might be of like mind? If the hisses are not in jest, then feminists are being treated like the black man in the story, as threats, when we do not wish to harm or to threaten. If the hisses *are* in jest, then feminism is being treated as a joke.

The black man's reaction also resembles the helplessness mothers sometimes feel. If we know that by being Jewish mothers we are assumed to be overpowering in the home but powerless outside, either oversexed or undersexed—depending on which part of the

Torah or which novel by which Jewish man we read, we feel ashamed and apologetic. We allow the images of ourselves as guilt-inducing, masochistic, trivial, not worthy of reverence and honor, to inhibit all that we do.

The fifth commandment promises us happiness and fulfillment if we honor our parents. Jews of both sexes need to honor our mothers as well as our fathers. In failing to honor women, we fail to honor mothers, and in failing to honor mothers, we fail to honor all women. Because women and girls all are daughters, and many of us are mothers and nurturers, we must honor our mothers or we cannot honor ourselves and each other. And men who cannot honor their mothers will have trouble genuinely honoring the women they hope to love and the daughters they hope to cherish.

REFERENCES

Arcana, Judith (1986). *Every mother's son*. Seattle, WA: The Seal Press.
Baum, Charlotte, Hyman, Paula, and Michel, Sonya (1976). *The Jewish woman in America*. New York: New American Library.
Caplan, Paula J. (1989). *Don't blame mother: Mending the mother-daughter relationship*. New York: Harper and Row.
Caplan, Paula J. (1993). *The myth of women's masochism*. Toronto: University of Toronto Press.
Caplan, Paula J., and Hall-McCorquodale, Ian (1985). Mother-blaming in major clinical journals. *American Journal of Orthopsychiatry, 55*, 345 – 353.
Miller, Jean Baker (1987). *Toward a new psychology of women*. Boston: Beacon.
Plaskow, Judith (1990). *Standing again at Sinai: Jewish memory from a feminist perspective*. New York: Harper and Row.
Siegel, Rachel Josefowitz (1987). Antisemitism and sexism in stereotypes of Jewish women. In Doris Howard (Ed.) *Dynamics of feminist therapy: Treatment, theory, and ethnic issues*. New York: The Haworth Press.
Siegel, Rachel Josefowitz (1988). Women's "dependency" in a male-centered value system: Gender-based values regarding dependency and independence. *Women and Therapy, 7(1)*, 113 – 123.
Staples, Brent (1986). Just walk on by. *Ms* (September), pp. 54, 88.
Surrey, Janet (1985). The "self-in-relation": A theory of women's development, #13, *Work in Progress Series*. The Stone Center, Wellesley College, Wellesley, MA.

Chapter 6

Backwards and Forwards in America

Sandra Butler

My mother is upstairs in the kitchen as I write. She is sweeping the kitchen floor, her arthritic hands holding tightly to the broom, as much for her own balance as for the task at hand. She is visiting for three weeks and we spend much of our time together sitting at the kitchen table, talking. We review our lives over rye toast, ginger marmalade, low-fat cottage cheese, and perked coffee. Later in the day, we continue with iceberg lettuce salad and mark each nightfall with a festive glass of wine. We offer our memories to each other, so different still, of my growing up, her mothering, our shared parallel years.

Every morning of my childhood began backwards. I sat on the closed toilet cover facing the pale green tiled wall, as my mother stood behind me in her blackwatch plaid bathrobe, preparing my hair for the day. She brushed the unruly morning tangles, then, with the sharp point of the comb, made a perfectly even division down the back of my head and began the painstaking process of creating two absolutely exact braids fastened with a firm snap of the rubber bands that were saved for that purpose on the bathroom doorknob. It was a ritual of containment, binding the thick, wild explosions of hair that would fly in all directions if they were not bound. My blouse was carefully tucked into my skirt, my elbows carefully tucked below the table, my voice carefully modulated. Gender was the daily practice of containment.

I was not just a girl, but a six-year-old girl in America. The America of the 1940s, a decade of living in the greatest country in the world. A country which won the war because of the courage of our boys. A country that, along with some other countries from far away, stopped the bad people that the daily papers called "Nips" and "Krauts." I read *Photoplay* and *Modern Screen, Life magazine* and *Ladies Home Journal* for information about how big girls dressed and acted. I listened to the radio every night to hear the stories about grownup lives on *Lux Radio Theater.* The articles about manners and conversational tricks were for the white girls and boys of America. None of them were about Jews. Jewish movie stars changed their names and their noses. I studied carefully, because I wanted to be like Ruth Roman, Ida Lupino, or Jane Greer—a bad, uncontained girl.

My coloring books had their own American version of ethnicity. There were three colors for girl's hair—brown, red, and blonde. Blonde was best. The blonde was always the most popular and sought after by the boys. Red was like Susan Hayward. A spitfire. Tempestuous, easy to anger and to tears. The brunettes were second best to the blondes. There was never a plain blonde, but lots of plain brunettes. I thought I was a plain brunette. Everyone, including me, was white. None of these lessons were lost on me. I was learning to be a girl in America.

I was also learning how to be Jewish in America. Except for very old grandparents whom you loved, Jews were dead people who had lived in places called *shtetls*. They left, after saving their money carefully, and came to America on ships. Then they worked hard and continued to save their money and brought over all the rest of the family or, at least, as many as they could. Now, here in America, they were called greenhorns. Once terrified girls and boys hiding in root cellars, then scholars and tradespeople, now they were not quite Americans; they spoke with a funny accent, ate peculiar food, worshipped in alien ways, and huddled together in neighborhoods that consoled and reminded them of their histories.

My history was shaped by the Grimes children, who were briefly in my grammar school class. They were both blonde, blue-eyed, slender and graceful, and belonged to the country club. We drove past it often. I would lean forward in the back seat, hoping the gate would be open and I could get a peek inside, but I saw only a small marker on a high fence with square letters that announced The Country Club. I was left to imagine the winding driveway, the terraced clubhouse, the men and women of impeccable breeding, drinking martinis and riding horses. This was where real life was, the life of the magazines, movies, and the newspapers. It wasn't good to be a Jew, so being Jewish carefully, according to the rules—non-Jewish rules—was the best you could do. This meant learning how well-bred Gentiles dressed, set their tables, and raised their children. When my mother was sixteen and got her first job, she was determined not to marry young but to go to business like Rosalind Russell. She began to ready herself for a life of private homes, graceful table manners and witty conversation, so she, and now, by extension I, could go forward.

Class marked how and where we practiced being Jewish. Poor, nonassimilated people went to small, dark buildings called *shuls*. The men and women sat apart from one another, wore heavy woolen clothing and held to the old ways. These Jews were scornfully referred to by my parents as "backward." Working-class people went to temple, but we, the newly minted middle class, went to synagogue, whose very architecture assured my parents' choice, soaring, as it did, to unimaginable heights like America itself. Our rabbi was never "controversial" in his sermons, but left his prosperous congregants feeling self-satisfied about having the advantages of living in the best country on earth and remembering the mitzvah of planting trees to support the brave people, our brothers and sisters, who were building the state of Israel.

Only once, when I was eleven years old, did I have an intimation of something greater than the well-rehearsed exercise that was suburban Judaism of the late 1940s. My parents, brother, and I, all wearing our new clothes, my mother her fur, attended the High Holy Days services. The rabbi delivered a booming sermon that I didn't understand, the cantor completed the *Kol Nidre* prayer and, surprisingly, left the *bima*. As the service continued, two of the synagogue elders hurried down the center aisle to ascend the bima and whisper to the president of the congregation. Our rabbi rose and walked slowly to the microphone. The cantor was dead.

He had completed the holiest of all prayers, left the bima, and fell over dead. "God allowed him one more year," the congregants all agreed. "It was God's hand, surely," they said. This experience of God as someone with a precise sense of timing frightened me. This meant he was watching, allowing his chosen people—for I had learned that we were chosen, especially if we acted well—to complete what they were supposed to and then die. This meant there was something I was supposed to do. This meant I would die. My family never spoke of it after that day, yet I always tried to leave my homework a bit incomplete, just in case God was watching.

Class distinctions shaped how and what we ate and how and what my mother cooked. Roast beef not pot roast. Lamb chops not kasha. Tea in cups not glasses. Tablecloths made of linen not oilcloth. My parents' generation of assimilating, upwardly mobile American Jews were careful to have no slippage. Nothing of the old ways. In both my grandmothers' apartment houses, the lobbies were filled with the smells of browning onions, baking pies, simmering stews and soups from all the kitchens above the central stairwell, the odors blending in welcome. The importance of having a private home was that you didn't have to smell other people's kitchens—or your own. There was always an open bottle of Air-Wick on my mother's windowsill to absorb the odors of food. My mother never cooked fish when we were growing up and certain foods were saved for the times of year when the windows could be open to "air out" the room. Kitchens didn't smell. Having a kitchen smell of cooking was going backwards.

When my brother and I were called to the table, we used good manners and didn't interrupt each other or talk when grownups were talking. We ate everything on our plates because of the children, always very far away, who didn't have food. Several times a year, we drove to New Jersey to visit my mother's parents. I remember the tuneless humming of my mother's mother, my Nannie, who, as I perched at her kitchen table, would make backwards food. In one white enamel pot were chicken feet and unborn eggs and in another prunes and raisins. While I ate a kaiser roll with whipped butter, she told me stories of "before." My Nannie would never let me help. "Time enough for you to be in your husband's kitchen when you're grown," she would say fondly. As she chopped and stirred the unfamiliar foods, she told me stories about growing up in Poland, eating potatoes and turnips, stories about sharing beds and blankets with her brothers and sisters, stories meant to remind me about how good life was in America, and how lucky I was. And implicitly, how grateful I was supposed to be.

Sharing beds and eating potatoes sounded like fun though, and I loved the backwards food much more than the forward kind. Backwards food didn't require table manners; you just picked it up and ate it, even making smacking sounds to show how good it was.

Sometimes I heard my grandparents talking in very quiet solemn voices about something called "the camps." They said unimaginable things about live bodies being stacked among cords of wood and ignited, Jews being marched to the edges of pits they had dug themselves, then shot as they stood, soundlessly, at those edges. When I asked what kind of camps they were talking about, they wouldn't answer except to assure me that camps were something that had happened very far away and not to worry because such a thing couldn't happen here. I did worry though, because their descriptions of mass murder felt much more dangerous than the killing of one bad person at a time that I had seen in an Edward G. Robinson movie at the Circle theater. And I knew that when I got just a little bigger, maybe when I was seven, I was going to have to go to camp.

My grandparent's kitchen floor had black and white octagonal tiles that my grandmother washed religiously every other day after breakfast. Just underneath the gleaming coal stove was a splash of what I had been told was borscht that had spilled years before, leaving a dull stain that always looked to me like blood. Images of the Czar, the Cossacks on horseback, the camps, jumbled in my mind, leaving behind my growing suspicion that the red stain had something to do with being a Jew.

Being Jewish in America meant being cosseted by protective silences. I was not to know the history that was being made, even in the moments of the end of World War II. I was the eldest and the only daughter of a woman who had unquestioningly absorbed the American dream. The dream that one can invent oneself, remake oneself with sheer acts of will and determined forgetting. I was learning to go forward in America, the country where everything was possible, where one could remake oneself, one's history, one's very Jewishness.

I was to be Jewish but not a Jew like my grandparents. My brother was to have the bar mitzvah, although I was a better student and he hated reading. I was to live in a Jewish neighborhood, marry well to a Jewish boy, have children and live a Jewish life. No accented speech, old-fashioned ways, hand-me-down clothes and values. We were Americans—Americans who happened to be Jewish. Being Jewish was simply an unquestioned given. The task was to become the right kind of Jewish. Not a "dirty" Jew, someone who called attention to him/herself, who acted or spoke badly in front of the Gentiles. Not a commie or a slumlord, not a gambler or someone who did anything to go "backward," or bring a bad name to the Jewish people.

By the time I was thirteen, I knew that there were generic girl rules that had to be followed carefully as well. Let the boy take the lead. Discuss what is of interest to him. Be smart, get good report cards, but don't be smarter than the boys. Ask questions, but careful ones, and not too many and only in certain situations. I followed the rules carefully. Married well. I became the mother of two daughters, now safely yet another generation away from the terrors of Eastern Europe. I worked very hard to follow all the rules for Jews. For girls. For women. For the white middle-class culture of urban America in the late 1950s.

By 1960, after both my daughters were born, I decided that a more ecumenical approach to religious observance would serve them better than the Judaism of my childhood. We had *Chanukah*, the girls giddy with the pleasures of finding eight nights' worth of presents. And Christmas. Not an apologetic Chanukah bush, but a tree with popcorn and cranberry ropes and presents next to the yellow plastic water basin that contained the tree. We decorated Easter eggs and hid the matzo on Passover. I wanted my daughters to live in all of America, not the constrained, rule-driven world of Jewish-Americans following the endless practices of careful cultural, religious, and gendered assimilation.

I was divorced in 1963, the first in my family and in the lives of everyone we knew. It was a *shanda* and my family was terribly angry and ashamed. I had failed in my attempts to be a successful adult woman. It was a great shame not to have kept a husband to take care of me. A divorce was, still then, unimaginable. My daughters and I moved into a neighborhood in Greenwich Village.

Within a few years their school PTA chapter split in an angry debate in the citywide struggle about the value and danger of busing black children out of their neighborhoods to white schools in surrounding neighborhoods versus gathering funds to upgrade existing neighborhood schools. I found myself, for the first time, aligned with radical Jewish mothers and some fathers, who were in support of the black parents' insistence on busing their children. It was the first stirring of my pride in this different kind of Jew. There were no Jewish activists in my childhood, no political discussions. That was for Christians. You can't change City Hall, I had learned. Life is not fair, I had been taught. You need to work to make it fair, I was learning.

I was restless and eager to participate in the world exploding around me. It was a time of the civil rights struggles in the South and the North, of the beginnings of anti-Vietnam activism. I got a job as a secretary in a dental office, a set of skills that served to support me and my daughters for the next twelve years, and I threw myself into the passions of American life. I demonstrated. I attended meetings. I handed out leaflets. I rang doorbells—all after work and with my young daughters beside me. Each meeting, whether it had as its focus antiwar activism, school busing, civil rights, was filled with Jews— the kind I had been kept from. They were verbal, passionate, outraged, engaged. I was faced with questions about what it meant to be a Jew. No longer the Jewish wife and mother I had been trained to be, I was becoming another kind of Jew, the kind I was warned to stay away from. I was becoming the Jew my parents feared.

It wasn't until 1970, when I saw an announcement for a consciousness-raising meeting and sat in a circle for the first time with other women quite unlike myself, that I began to have a sense of my own oppression as a woman, and then later, nearly ten years later, as a Jewish woman. I began in the decade of the 1980s to see the limitations, the proscriptions, the diminishment that characterized so much of my early socialization. They had been everywhere, those lessons. I had learned them in my home, on the radio, from the comedians ridiculing mothers-in-law, princesses, avaricious women; in the teachings of the synagogue, in the absence of teaching in my secular schools. I began to engage yet again with the process of unlearning and relearning. Of shaping my own questions and my own answers.

Now, in the America of 1996, I know that not just hair, but skin is red and yellow, brown and black. Now, in the America of multicultural activism, of antiracist theorizing and practice, I stumble and bump up against that girl of the 1940s—that eager, watchful giraffe of a girl. How hard she tried to become a Jewish American. How attentively she apprenticed herself to those who promised to show her how to live, how to think, how to pray, how to understand herself and the world around her. She, like her grandmother, her Nannie, wanted to be a real American, the right kind of Jewish, the chosen wife of a good man and mother of a boy and girl, both brunettes, neither plain.

Now I sit in circles of women, listen, speak, read, re-think, examine my privilege and my oppression. Now it is a different America. Now, in the America of 1996, I live as a feminist, a Jew, a lesbian, an activist, a radical middle-aged woman. This means, in part, that I struggle to understand the ways in which the practice of gender, the practice of class, the practice of Judaism, the practice of white privilege has shaped and distorted my life and the lives of other women. Everything I was so carefully taught in the 1940s must now be unlearned. The tight bindings of gender, the three colors of hair marking all the difference that mattered, the careful predictability of religious practice have utterly changed in the past twenty-five years. I will never again have the sureness of meaning that shaped my childhood. Things seemed immutable in America then. No longer. Meaning shifts just as I feel it in my grasp. Sometimes I am exhilarated by the complexity and layered nature of meaning now and, at other times, I grow overwhelmed and depleted.

I go upstairs to have a cup of tea with my mother who is pretending to be reading in the living room, but I know is waiting for me to climb the stairs so we can continue to talk. Writing about Judaism and feminism, I feel the rich complexity of such a different America, and I want to tell her, this old woman, my mother, who holds tightly to the certainty of what she labored so hard to learn. The right and wrong ways to live, to think, to act, to be a Jewish woman in America.

We begin, as we often do now, with the obituaries. "Gone," my mother calls death. "Martha is gone," she begins, holding up the paper to confirm her words. Another in a series of diminishments.

The population in her world shrinks every month. I use the opportunity to tell her how death is a part of my world also. About how, now in America, death has a language. A psychological language, a political language, a spiritual language. I tell her that with the breast cancer epidemic, with AIDS, death has become a part of daily life. Ordinary catastrophic life in the America of the 1990s.

"I know. I know. This is not the first time people died by the hundreds of thousands. Died too soon," she pauses remembering the newsreels, the stories, the Europe of the 1930s and 1940s. "It's nothing new, that children and young people die before they're supposed to. I just never thought it would happen here."

I tell her that death is no longer a hushed, muted silence, punctuated by wailing, then a shuddering silence. Death is a field of study. So is loss. Even narratives of the elderly, as they are called, is now a form. Procedures are emerging to engage the end of life. Hospices, living wills. We have never spoken of this, my mother and I. She has simply told me that her "wishes" are in the safe-deposit box and she expects I will follow them.

She sits, looking puzzled, waiting for me to continue. I talk about how so much is new, unfamiliar, changing. How feminists are developing forms to honor life and death, forms that have emerged to witness and comfort the women and men of 1996. Forms that emerge from a faith that as feminists, as Jewish women, we can create what we need. She listens attentively and I describe the *Yitzkor* service shaped by a group of my closest Jewish women friends.

Eight women attended the Kol Nidre service together. At its completion, we all rose to leave, and I was holding my breath, as I always do on that night. God is watching, and I still try not to be finished. The next afternoon, after the *Yom Kippur* morning service was completed, we all moved from the synagogue to regather in my living room. We eight women created, for the first time, a service to mourn the dead, name our losses, articulate our grief, prepare for the closing of the gates and the New Year. We needed to embed this most holy day in the reality of loss, the insistence of responsibility, the demands of commitment and the joys of our connection. We began the Yitzkor service led in the prayers by the most learned of the group, a convert to Judaism. We sang, we chanted, we prayed, we talked, we witnessed, and we held one another in our arms. Each of us found our own and the traditional words to speak what was in our hearts, to ourselves, to each other, and to God. A circle of Jewish-American women, all feminists, some secular and political, others with a daily Jewish spiritual practice, punctuated the ancient prayers and chants of that most holy service with our dailiness. Our grief about parents, children, choices. Our grief, individual and collective. Our efforts to evaluate. The sounds of our Jewish women's lives.

As I described the afternoon service, my mother interrupted, "How can you do that? You just can't make things up. Things are supposed to be the way they're written, the way they have been done for centuries. You just can't call yourself a Jew and make it up. There is a right way to do things. An appropriate way."

"Appropriate" described everything when I was a girl in the America of the 1940s. There were appropriate ways to sit and eat, to talk and dress, to catch a ball and talk to a grownup. Appropriate ways even to pray.

"And that's not all. In the first place, your need to talk about everything is something I never had. I am private that way. I know what I feel. It isn't necessary for me to say it in front of people. Some things are just private. I am loyal to the people I love. There is supposed to be a sense of privacy in a family. Not to talk over every little thing with strangers outside. I could never do what you do."

Stung, I answered sharply, "Ma, it isn't necessary to compare and evaluate everything. I'm just telling you the ways we do ritual. Your way can just be different. Not better. Just different." She continued pensively, as if I hadn't spoken, as if I weren't even in the room with her.

"I remember when Nannie died I couldn't sit there in New Jersey while they were sitting *shiva*. They didn't sit shiva. They were having a party. Platters of food, people stuffing their faces like they had never eaten before. Sitting there laughing, talking. As if she wasn't dead. I made Daddy take me home. Being there with all those people, strangers, made me feel even more lonesome. I wanted to be quiet in my home to mourn for my mother."

"I know Ma, but some women find that gathering and talking about the person who is gone makes them feel better, closer to the person. Can't it just be that you don't like it? That you never wanted to do it? Not that people who do it are wrong?"

But, as I impatiently swept butter onto my baked potato, she began to weep. "Maybe I'm talking about me. I wonder what will happen when I die. Are you going to sit with your friends and talk about me? Tell things about me?" Before I had a chance to reply, she balled up the napkin and continued, "I think sometimes that my life would have been different if I could verbalize how I'm feeling the way you do. I just can't do it. Something inside me can't. It's just a different time. Nowadays, women verbalize about things we never did. Maybe, if I had been able to verbalize, I wouldn't have kept so much inside myself." She settled heavily in the chair and blew her nose in the napkin, signaling an end to the conversation.

Now, the kitchen returned to its spotless order, my mother's yellow rubber gloves drying on the edge of the sink, I settle back in front of the computer to write about being a Jewish American woman in transition. About the multiple ways in which my life is surrounded by women. About how I say things that my mother feels are disloyal. About how I wrote two books that told private things to strangers. Things about sexual abuse, and things about dying. And living with dying. I feel the weight of my mother's limited choices growing up in the America of the 1920s and 1930s. Limited opportunities for balance. I want so much for her—all that I take for granted. All that my generation of Jewish-American feminists have created. I want for her the way she wanted so much for me when I was a girl. Wanting such different things. I want to respect her capacity to change and respect my hunger to be known by her. I want to find the words that will allow me to do both at this time in our lives at the end of the twentieth century in America.

This morning, as I was pouring her coffee, she said, "When I'm gone, you're the only one I'll miss."

Frightened and trying to lighten the moment, I replied, "How can you miss me if you're gone?"

"I make up a story," she said. "Doesn't everybody make up a story they can believe in?"

"Yes, Ma, they do," I said, taking her in my arms.

Now I have a Jewish cookbook and am trying to find the recipes my mother never wanted to learn. Now I attend a synagogue and try to read the transliteration without understanding so that my mouth creates the sounds of the ancient words that link me through thousands of years of Jews. Now I have a lace tablecloth, a wedding gift given to my mother nearly sixty years ago, that I use for feminist seders. Now every important event in my life is marked in some way by a circle of women. Now I am going forward and backward, creating, like my grandmothers before me, old forms into new. Some remain intact and others need alterations, like the top quality cloth she shaped and reshaped until it fit the next grandchild.

Now I understand that there is no finishing, even if God is watching. Now I see how the daily practice of faith—political faith, religious faith—is my only certainty. Bringing forward, looking backward, blending like the stews of my grandmother, imagining like the dreams of my daughters. Finding my footing, keeping my balance is only achieved in each moment. It is the work of my life.

Chapter 7

Personal Reflections on Being a Grandmother: L'Chol Dor Va Dor

Rachel Aber Schlesinger

MY GRANDMOTHER

My maternal grandmother lived with us. I learned from her that grandmothers have great power. They represent a relationship that, like a parent's, demands respect and provides love but is different. *Omamma* was a "queen," she kept religious standards high, passed on a sense of family history, and told wonderful stories. She helped give us a sense of who we were and what we stood for. Our family had religious and family traditions. We were a matriarchal family. The men were important and respected, but the names and the stories were those of the mothers.

The family stories began with my great-grandparents, the rabbi and *rebbitzin* of Luebeck. They had twelve children. My great-grandmother greeted the birth of each child, and indeed every family occasion with a poem, a *Tischlied*. In quiet moments she wrote a book of poetry for the young Jewish bride, stressing the family and religious roles of Jewish women. This book of poems was still given to my older cousins upon marriage. Before the Second World War, the lives of these women and the poems held commonly understood meanings.

I was able to carry out this research with the help of a grant from Canada Multicutural Department and the Centre of Jewish Studies at York University. I want to thank Sarah Taieb Carlen for conducting some of the interviews with Sephardi women in French, and for her help with this project.

My grandmother was the oldest of eight daughters. In her later years she wrote her memoirs. Even in this religious family the important items that she remembered were elegant balls, clothes, and meeting her husband. She lived in the age of romance, and saw her early years in these terms. She was also deeply religious and supervised the early religious teachings of her grandchildren.

Tragically, she was widowed as a young woman. Her life in Germany was devoted to social service activities; her home was filled with interesting people. Upon her death I found correspondence from Bertha Pappenheim dealing with rescue activities for Jewish women and children. Omamma spoke English well and came to America by way of Portugal in the 1940s. Once here, she divided her time between living with her two surviving children, my mother and my uncle. She did small jobs, was a companion to others, and baby-sat, yet this work never diminished her queenly status in her eyes or in the eyes of others.

MY MOTHER AS GRANDMOTHER

I was able to understand my mother in her role as a grandparent because of the influence of my grandmother. Both women were unique; daughters and wives of distinguished rabbis, they had a strong sense of self, of Jewish values, and of family *Yehus*.

Mutti's world changed with the Nazi era. My mother's stories were told not to her children who experienced the events she recounted, but to her grandchildren. Since I was the youngest of her children I didn't remember these experiences, but my children told me Mutti's stories. Here is one of the stories.

On *Krystallnacht* in November 1938, the synagogue in Bremen was destroyed and my father, the rabbi, was taken to a concentration camp. My mother, known by Jew and non-Jew in this middle-sized port city, worked for his release and that of the other men taken that night. Each day, as the story goes, she went with her three daughters to the Gestapo headquarters to ask when the men would be released. One day she was told that they would be sent home on a midnight train, but she did not know which night. Every night, at midnight, she walked to the railway station to see if my father would be coming on that train. Every night, she heard footsteps behind her as a Gestapo officer followed her through dingy parts of town. That did not deter her.

Weeks later, after this routine was followed each night, my father did indeed arrive on a train. Mutti turned around at the station. The footsteps behind her had stopped. She looked up to see the Gestapo officer salute her and my father. He had been following her each night for her protection. That is the kind of devotion my beautiful mother inspired.

Mutti believed in the power of the individual, and the vital role of the woman in the family and in the community. She was a deeply committed Jew. Her religion, her vocation, and her belief system were holistic. I know that her grandchildren loved her, respected her, and understood her. My son told me, "Mutti was unusual. She really believed in what she believed in!"

MY OWN EXPERIENCE

Now I am a grandmother. I am a living ancestor! My stories will be different, I live in another land, in another time. I wonder if any of us can transmit to our children's children the tastes, the smells, the environment, the understanding of the values that shaped us.

What do I want to pass on to my grandchildren? I find it easier to ask "how," than to pinpoint "what" it is I want to transmit. Like my grandmother I tell stories, sing songs, and recount family history. If my sisters and I have pictures, we put them on the walls. We use the ability to name to perpetuate memories and names. Those of us who were born in other countries speak in our mother tongue. We use language to recall roots. We model our religious practices and holiday observances. We convey our oral traditions in the kitchens of our homes. As our grandchildren get older, we share secrets often not told to our own children.

The bond between grandchild and grandparents may be the strongest, and of the longest duration, next to the parent bond. Can grandparents transmit values, or is this too difficult due to the age gap between the first and third generation, differences in life experiences, and competition from outside agents of socialization?

IMMIGRANT GRANDMOTHERS

For the past few years I have been talking with Jewish grandmothers, asking them about their perceptions of being a grandparent and transmitting their own values to their grandchildren. Let me introduce some of the women who shared their thoughts on this question.

Sephardi Grandmothers

Sara comes from Morocco. There is a big difference between her world and that of her grandmother. Her grandmother was married at twelve years of age, and was only fifteen when Sara's mother was born. The role of women in her community was important. Sara recounts that it was often the woman who urged the family to leave, either for Israel, France, or Canada. In Morocco, women lived in separate spheres, yet had valued roles. With the shift to a new country, their roles changed. The family changed from being a large, extended family living with each other to having members dispersed. Sara's family life is strongly linked to religious observance. "If you can't cook, you can't fulfill your religious obligations."

Leaving Morocco meant leaving cultural roles behind. "My grandmother's religious views, and her ways will be acknowledged in her home, but maybe not in ours. This means that while we have memory, we may not have continuity of culture." In order for a culture to survive, it must be practiced. It is not good enough to talk of the "old days," if they are not followed today.

Lena, born in Morocco, adds: "Family traditions . . . are very important. They are mostly French traditions, like table manners, classical music, French literature. Yes, in my country, it was our way." She talks about a way of life that combines Jewish and secular culture, a civilized worldview, formed by Continental culture in an Arabic environment, far removed from her present North Toronto setting.

Pina says, "I want to give them an idea of the way we lived. My father taught me wisdom; my mother's family had been in Iraq for millennia, maybe since Abraham."

Nadia, who comes from Turkey adds: "I have to tell them about our life. . . . Here, there is no Turkish atmosphere, no Turkish synagogue, no Turkish bath, no Turkish schools . . . so I have to talk about our way of life, and it is not always possible to imagine. It's like a dream."

Values grow out of a culture. These Sephardi grandmothers want to pass on respect and obedience to elders, for "they know more than us, they have a whole life behind them. Respect, it's like breathing. It comes naturally; we are born with it" (Mrs. C).

Ashkenazi Grandmothers

While Jews from Eastern Europe also had close associations with their home countries, when they talk of bringing grandchildren "home" it is to teach them what can happen to Jewish communities. It is to put the Holocaust into personal terms. Or it is to put the Russian experience into perspective.

Ada is under five feet tall, and she is a survivor—of the Holocaust, of displaced-person camps, of migrations to several countries, before settling in Canada twenty years ago. She spoke in optimistic terms about her life.

For her, her grandchildren are a miracle, the remnants of a family that is once again extended. She feels the need to transmit memories, and has taken her five grandchildren to Poland, to see the *Camps*, to show them what she has survived. She tells them how she picked up her life after the war. She returned to Poland after the war, met her husband, lived in Israel, then came to Canada.

She wants to perpetuate language, not Polish but Hebrew, and speaks it with her grandchildren. Ada models her values, she still volunteers time as a nurse's aide, and together with her husband, remains active in the community. She lives within walking distance of her children.

She finds it difficult to convey her Jewish values. "One son-in-law does not speak Hebrew; he is a Canadian, and cannot even understand the feelings of being a survivor. He tells me I spoil the children."

Mrs. Z came to Canada seven years ago; she focuses on her Lithuanian experiences. Her grandchildren do not understand why she chose to remain in a Communist country. Indeed, she had a high position in the government. She was eventually able to connect with her grandchildren by telling them about her experiences in the underground during the Second World War. She still has difficulties, since her children in Canada became "very Jewish, and I don't understand this. It was not my way."

These women are survivors—of their generation, of the Holocaust, of war. They can no longer return for a visit with their grandchildren; their world died. Many return to visit the death camps, but some women do not want their grandchildren to associate the Jewish life of their own youth only with death and destruction.

DOMESTIC RELIGION, FOOD, AND PRACTICE

In our families we model our beliefs, talk about them, emphasize what's important. Religious observance is an area we articulate, often in loud, judgmental terms. The grandmothers speak of learning, religious rituals, and observance.

Religion is often viewed from the perspective of the kitchen. Cooking for holidays, talking in the kitchen, passing on *kashrut* by doing, not by reading; these are all examples of transmitting values. Recipes are handed over from generation to generation; they are part of the oral tradition. This too is religious commentary.

In terms of religious observances and even foods, the Sephardi feel a degree of cognitive dissonance. The foods they ate at home are not common in Canada. Ashkenazi families can find familiar kosher or kosher-style foods in supermarkets; the Sephardi cannot.

Mrs. W. had been unable to follow her religion in her home country. "In Latvia I couldn't be religious. Here I want to be, but my husband is still afraid. My granddaughter helps me."

Grandmothers feel that they have contributions to make to the family in terms of ideas, responsibilities, child care, and even financial assistance. Many of them hope that they are role models, as indeed their grandparents had been to them. It is important to them to be seen as representing the old culture, providing continuity of family traditions, while still being close to their grandchildren. They articulate the values of a Jewish education, family closeness and the concept of *Shalom Bayit*. They feel a sense of responsibility to ensure this for the next generation.

These grandmothers reflected a wistfulness for times past. Singing together reminds them of their own childhood. The first contacts with a new grandchild are often through singing songs in grandmother's mother tongue. They hope their grandchildren will respect them as older persons, by means of their behavior, such as good manners. They report that their grandchildren do respect their views and opinions, often coming to them before going to parents to ask for advice.

ROADBLOCKS

Some fear they do not have a place in their grandchildren's lives now, but hope this will develop with time. Factors that impede communication and closeness include physical location, distance, family mobility, and family fragmentation.

Grandparents often have less formal education than their children or grandchildren, and some feel that this educational gap creates barriers. Others report feeling "inferior," "not modern enough." They feel inadequate because they can only transmit what is most common to their own life and experience, for example the customs, traditions, and history of their country of origin. Yet their children and grandchildren may not have a frame of reference for the information grandmothers wish to impart. So much is lost, replaced by strange new ways. Grandparents try to fit their culture into a new setting, and that is often a difficult task.

Even the words we use have changed. In Jewish tradition an older person was a *zakena*, a person of wisdom. In modern Hebrew, the terms *Saba* and *Safta* are used to denote grandparents, the father of my father; what has happened to the concept of wisdom?

SOME REFLECTIONS

Some of the grandmothers felt frustrated, partly because the changes that have taken place during their lifetimes make it difficult to transmit a sense of what was. Their own world has been transformed through transitions.

Family roles have changed and older women see their status as lower in Canada than it might have been in the old society. The pattern of immigration itself has weakened family links. The new buzzword of "individualization" undermines the sense of family and of community as well as woman's and grandmother's role in the family. Grandmothers no longer occupy the same physical space as their children and grandchildren and they fear that their domestic religion is out of their hands. Today's grandmother may really have little influence in conveying her concept of Jewish culture. A way of life has altered in a short span of time.

The grandmothers I interviewed examined the concepts of societal changes and ideological shifts. The Sephardi women spoke of open community life; some of the Eastern Europeans had belonged to the *Bund* and grown up on socialism. One needs to question if it is possible to have cultural transmission when the culture and politics have changed so drastically.

Are Jewish grandmothers different? Perhaps. This generation of women gives great importance to perpetuating the Jewish people. Older grandparents today are a generation who experienced migrations, displacements, and the Holocaust. We cherish the ability to have given birth, to survive as a people. We worry about the Jewishness of our children and grandchildren. We do have values to pass on—from generation to generation.

Can I transmit a sense of family to my grandchildren? Hopefully, yes. I can provide the smells of *hallah* baking; I can surround them with pictures of family members, of places and events. I can record voices for them to listen to; I can even use videos to pinpoint places and people. Modern technology helps, but being there, talking, being willing to listen, trying to explain our perspective, and respecting our own children and grandchildren may be the keys to future communications and continuity. Our grandchildren are not mind readers; contact, open communication, and understanding are also necessary ingredients in a relationship.

It is harder to impart religious values for eventually we each must find our own path and follow it for a time. We too change and may change our perspectives. That is what we can try to pass on—the ability to see and judge for oneself.

What do I want to communicate? I want healthy, thoughtful, creative, and caring family members—the rest is commentary.

L'chol Dor Va Dor, from generation to generation. My grandmother once told me, "listen carefully to what I will tell you . . .

then you will tell this story to your children, and they will tell it to their grandchildren."

But will the story lose its meaning? My grandmother's and mother's stories were unique, coming from urgent times and far away places. I am part of the quiet generation. While I was born in Germany and raised by European parents, I grew up in North America. I need to add my own stories to those of the women in my family.

We are links in a long chain—which of the stories will our great-grandchildren repeat?

SECTION II:
WANDERING JEWS:
LIVES FRACTURED BY GEOGRAPHY

Chapter 8

Jewish Identity Lost . . . and Found

Trudi Alexy

This is the story of a personal quest, a quest set in motion by an event that happened fifty years ago.

My family originally came from Rumania, but we moved to Prague, Czechoslovakia, when I was a baby. We lived there until 1938, the year I turned ten and Hitler marched into Vienna. My father decided it was not safe for us to stay. "Prague is next," he explained to my grandmother, trying to convince her to flee with us to Paris. She refused. "What's Hitler going to do with an old lady like me?" she asked. She later died in Theresienstadt.

Once in Paris, my parents settled in a small hotel while my brother Fredo and I attended a private boarding school near Versailles.

We were vacationing in a fishing village in Normandie late next summer when, one early morning, we were awakened by the town crier who announced that German tanks had rolled into Poland and German planes were bombing Polish cities. Everyone began to cry. I did not know that France and Britain had ageed to go to Poland's defense if Germany attacked.

"That means we are at war," Father explained.

The next day he disappeared. Everything seemed far away and unreal. I tried not to worry, but I had many questions, questions to which I was afraid to hear the answers.

From *The Mezuzah in the Madonna's Foot: Oral Histories Exploring 500 Years in the Paradoxical Relationship of Spain and the Jews*, by Trudi Alexy. Copyright © 1993 by Trudi Alexy Sternlicht. Condensed and abstracted from the Foreword and Part One (pp. 11–70) with the permission of Simon and Schuster.

When Father reappeared, two weeks later, he announced: "We're becoming Lutheran, then we're becoming Catholic. That way, when someone asks what were we before, we can say Lutheran. After that we are moving to Spain."

"What is Lutheran?" I asked.

"It's a religion. Like Catholic. Almost everybody in Czechoslovakia and France and Spain is Catholic."

"Is that why we have to become Catholic?"

"No. It's because Hitler wants to get rid of the Jews. His soldiers just invaded Poland and started a war."

"Why does he want to get rid of the Jews?"

"Just because they are Jews."

"Are we Jews?"

"Yes. But it is not safe to be a Jew, so we will hide in Spain and tell everyone we are Catholic."

"Isn't that a lie, Father?" I asked.

"Tell your daughter I don't have time for stupid questions," Father said to Mother as he walked out to take care of business.

Until that moment I never knew we were Jews. There was nothing about our life to indicate that our family was Jewish. If others knew, I was not aware of it. Christmas and Easter were part of our life as they were for everyone else around us, but devoid of meaning beyond the most obvious: they were fun-filled holiday festivities. No religious connotation was apparent.

Religion was not discussed. Neither was politics. There were no traditions or rituals, no reliable guidelines to tell me what to do, no rules that confirmed I was good or reassured me that I had not crossed some invisible line, committed some unknown crime for which some unspeakable punishment would be meted out by some all-knowing power.

Both my parents worked, and my emotional connection with them during that time remains a blur. As I grew older I felt increasingly isolated and alone. I did not know what to make of the cataclysmic events suddenly creating chaos in our lives. I had always been keenly aware of things I could not explain, events that seemed mysterious and frightening: people and pets became ill and died, anger erupted without apparent reason, friends disappeared without saying good-bye, adults acted in secretive ways, pretending nothing was wrong, vague threats lurked in unlikely places. Since no one ever offered anything comforting or reassuring to counteract my confusion, I was forced, from very early on, to find my own way to cope with the turmoil around me. My way was to lose myself in books and to create a fantasy world around the characters in them whose reality became my own.

These books revealed a world where mythological gods wielded unlimited power and meted out justice, where witches and wizards wrought magic, sainted martyrs performed miracles and heroes risked their lives for noble causes. Their stories stirred my imagination and provided me with standards of nobility of spirit to which only a child would dare aspire. I admired their willingness to suffer, even to die for what they believed. I wanted more than anything to be like them. How wonderful to be swept up in something grand and heroic! I wished I, too, had something important enough to die for.

Although the world I read about seemed no less tumultuous than the one from which I was trying to escape, its reality relieved my anxiety by providing answers to questions I did not even know how to articulate. What mattered was that in that reality nothing happened by accident, everything had logical explanations and predictable consequences. Mysterious signs and random intuitions proved meaningful, even if only in retrospect. Those who were good were rewarded and those who were bad got punished, here on earth, in heaven, or in hell. Life felt more stable; I was convinced that whatever happened, no matter how unexpected or irrational, SOMEONE, SOMEWHERE, WAS IN CONTROL. "Magical thinking" (ascribing symbolic meanings to ordinary events, investing them with mythical relevance and power) became my religion, my spiritual security blanket.

When Father announced we would hide in Spain as Catholics because it was too dangerous to remain Jews, I did not know what being Jewish was all about, anymore than what it meant to be Catholic. But I was sure what we were doing was wrong: to say we were Catholic was a lie. Would any of the heroes I had read about ever have lied about their truth in order to be safe? Of course not. They were brave and good. Father was telling us to be cowardly and bad. My protests went unheeded. I felt sure we would never be forgiven.

I remember little about the religious instruction classes we attended along with several other people going through abbreviated conversion processes. The Lutheran minister was very unpleasant and seemed in a great hurry to be done with us. The Catholic priest was kind and patient. He let me ask a lot of questions. One day I requested to talk to him alone.

"I think what we are doing is wrong. If we're Jews, we shouldn't pretend we're something else. Father says we have to become Catholic or Hitler will get rid of us. But I don't want to say I'm Catholic when I'm really a Jew. It's a lie." I started to cry. The priest put his arm around me.

"Your Father is right. You must obey him. But remember, Jesus was a Jew. He will understand."

I wasn't at all sure Jesus, or anyone else, for that matter, would ever understand. Certainly the heroes and martyrs I had read about would never understand. *They* were not afraid to die for what was right. *They* never lied to save their lives. I didn't know what Jews believed, or even what they were, but if I was a Jew, the right thing to do was to stay a Jew and not hide it or lie about it, *no matter what.*

We were baptized twice. It didn't seem to bother the rest of my family, but I felt like a coward and a criminal. I was sure I had forever forfeited the right to call myself a Jew.

In spite of this, a strange sense of wonder and peace enveloped me as we crossed the border into Spain. I did not question why I felt that way. I simply welcomed it as a good omen: Spain was sure to be a magical place where we would all be safe and where I would feel good again. That feeling remained with me despite the ominous presence of Fascist Dictator Francisco Franco, who had recently won a bloody three-year civil war with the help of Hitler and Mussolini.

For two years we lived with widowed Senora Carron in her spacious flat on the top floor of an old apartment building in Barcelona. Her maid, Pilar, took me to church on Sundays and Holy Days. I loved the light streaming through stained glass windows, the ornate altars, the choir singing hymns, and the heady scent of incense.

Fredo and I walked to the Lycee Francais de Barcelone every day. One teacher took a special interest in me. He seemed to enjoy answering my many questions. My unfamiliarity with Catholicism must have been obvious because during the many hours we spent together, he took great pains to show me a rather idealized view of his faith, stressing its mystical, spiritual side: the miracles, the forgiveness through confession, and the death of Jesus on the cross to save each and every one of us. He made it all sound fascinating and beautiful and I was drawn to the logical, clearly drawn dos and don'ts by which Catholics lived.

I had no clue, back then, how important Spain would become in my life. Not until years later did I uncover personal details of the stirring history of the "*Marranos,*" Spain's Secret Jews (Catholics in name only, baptized under duress) and felt a rush of recognition: just as my family sought to escape Nazi persecution by pretending to be Catholic, so centuries before, the Marranos had hoped to escape the Inquisition's savagery by submitting to baptism. For them, being found out meant torture on the rack and death by fire. For us and others like us, getting caught meant the horrors of concentration camps and death in gas chambers. I felt an immediate feeling of spiritual kinship with them.

However, unlike the Marranos, who had powerful traditions and spiritual laws to sustain them, and unlike the rest of my family, for whom baptism had been a mere technicality which created no moral conflict, I had nothing to help me reason away my certainty that hiding our Jewishness was terribly wrong. Thus, I salved my guilty conscience by losing myself in the pomp, pageantry, and seductive security of Catholicism. Years later, safely in the United States by then, when reality set in and the magic wore off, my guilt over surviving the Holocaust by fraud while so many others perished as Jews pursued me into my adult life.

By mid-April 1941 Hitler's hordes had laid waste to much of Europe, and threatened to invade Spain in order to get to British Gibraltar. Father's brother, Uncle Milos, who lived in New York, finally succeeded in obtaining our entrance visas to the United States, and we hurriedly sailed for America. Again we left everything behind, including my dream of remaining in Spain forever.

Before we had time to settle into our new life in New York, a Catholic refugee organization contacted my family and offered to send Fredo and me to Catholic boarding schools in New England, on special scholarships. Our parents accepted. Unencumbered by our presence, they moved into a small apartment and began to rebuild their lives in the New World.

I spent the next three years at Marycliff Academy. Until my graduation at sixteen, one part of me lived the normal life of a teenage boarding school student, the rest of me struggled with an increasingly compelling pull into a spiritual realm I had never before had the opportunity to explore. I became more and more caught up in the mystique of Catholicism, and eagerly responded to what seemed to be natural, logical solutions to all my inner conflicts. There was hope. If Jesus died for my sins, was not forgiveness attainable after all? Could everything that happened have all along been part of God's plan?

I kept my past to myself. To explain my unfamiliarity with Catholic prayers and rituals (when to genuflect, sit or stand, when and how to respond to the priest, etc.), I told everyone I had converted from Lutheran Protestantism. Nobody ever suspected the truth. I never forgot it.

As a "convert" I was given special religious instruction by Father Hannegan, the school chaplain. Under the stress of such intimacy, cracks in my story quickly appeared. I finally revealed my secret. He was supportive and compassionate, and never betrayed my trust.

After graduation I joined my family in New York while commuting to Manhattanville College of the Sacred Heart, whose full scholarship I had accepted against my parents' wishes.

Living at home, in my family's Upper West Side neighborhood while attending a strict Catholic convent school soon took its predictable toll. Far removed from the insulated life at Marycliff, where I was steeped in such a single-minded and protected atmosphere, everything felt conflicted. I was split between two antithetical worlds and spent the next three years growing increasingly uncertain about my Catholic faith. Frightened by my doubts, I knew drastic measures were in order: I decided to become a Maryknoll missionary nun. Dying a martyr's death in China would certainly be one way to save my soul.

Meanwhile, the war, which had seemed so far away at Marycliff, now screamed out at me from radios and newspaper headlines at every street corner. Stories of the extermination camp horrors could no longer be dismissed as mere rumors, and Jewish refugees were struggling to reach a safe haven in Palestine.

The shame over my apostasy, not out of conviction, but as an act of cowardice, hung over me like a dark cloud. I still saw myself as an impostor. Taking the easy way out while so many others died remained as simplistically unforgivable as ever.

Toward the end of my junior year at Manhattanville, the anaesthetic effect of my flight into Catholicism finally wore off. What had once made sense, what had felt healing and reassuring, now felt irrelevant and empty. In falling out of the Catholic Church's safe, warm womb, I had lost my purpose in life. Now nothing fit. There was no refuge in the Church for me any more, and no forgiveness. The scaffolding I had erected to support my shaky identity was falling away, leaving me with nothing solid to hold onto. Who was I really? Catholicism no longer worked for me, and I had no doubt that being a Jew had long ceased to be an option. Once again I felt I belonged nowhere.

At the ripe age of nineteen, I felt everything meaningful in my life had evaporated.

In that state of despondency I met a Jewish boy as removed from his religious roots as I, who wanted to marry me. He was leaving to attend graduate school in California and I was eager to get away from New York. I envisioned a blessedly placid and uneventful life together, providing me a secure, serene haven, far removed from all the turmoil that had consumed me for so long. All I wanted was some semblance of peace. I agreed to marry him.

My husband joined an army internship program that allowed him to pursue his doctoral studies in psychology. We bought a home and had two children, Peter and Debbie, within the first four years of our marriage. I threw myself into caring for our home and children while free-lancing as an artist/designer. Outwardly, all seemed to be going well, but had I bothered to look inside, I would have found it empty.

We lived far from any relatives and, because the Army frequently moved us from post to post, we were torn from fragile connections with others again and again. There was little to feed me spiritually or emotionally, but I did not take time to notice. Instead, I lost myself in a whirlwind of activity.

In 1958 my husband quit the Army. We returned to Southern California and fell back into much the same routine as before. His graduate school studies were replaced by years of analytic training. I resumed my free-lance designing work. We occasionally attended services at various safely nonsectarian Unitarian congregations, so our children developed nebulous religious and ethnic identities.

One day, eleven-year-old Debbie asked me an unexpected question.

"All my friends go to Sunday school. How come I can't go?"

"Because our Unitarian Church does not have one."

"But I want to go. Can we find me one with a Sunday school?"

"Why don't you try going with some of your friends, and see if there's one you like. Maybe we can arrange for you to go."

After several weekends attending services and religious instruction classes with various friends, she announced: "I have found a Sunday school I want to go to, only it should really be called a Saturday school, because that's when they have their services. Can I go?"

She had chosen a Jewish congregation! I felt a shiver and suddenly I was back in September of 1939, in Normandie, when I found out we were Jews. My daughter was exactly the same age as I was then, and the coincidence felt too significant to ignore.

When I awkwardly explained that all four of her grandparents were Jewish, her response was: "Well, if *they* are Jews, that makes *us* Jews, too, doesn't it?"

Only then did I tell her what had happened to me when *I* was her age and why I thought I had lost the right to ever call myself a Jew. In the telling, many memories I had blocked out for years began to stir. At the same time, I felt as though a hand was being held out to me, welcoming me home. Could God have chosen my daughter to bring me back, to show me I was forgiven? Could my exile really be over at last?

When I first walked into a synagogue, it felt strange. I experienced neither the awe nor the majestic presence of God that had always swept over me when I entered a Catholic church. It was easy enough to say, "I am a Jew." But inside, I still felt like an interloper, an intruder in a place I did not belong. How would I ever justify to anyone my survival by fraud, my years as a Catholic? Who would help me connect to roots I never grew, to claim a birthright which I had denied? What if I never fit in? And if I did, what if it ended up meaningless? I felt alone with my doubts, certain no one would understand. All I could do was acquaint myself as best I could with the heritage to which my newly assumed identity now allowed me access.

I attended classes on various aspects of Judaism and began to read armsful of books. But when I try now to remember what books I read, what subjects I studied, nothing comes to mind. It is all a blur, as though everything happened so fast or felt so strange I was unable to absorb it.

In reality, though I did not know it, my psychic system was breaking down. I was unable to sleep. I continued to work, but found it increasingly stressful. I withdrew more and more inside the black cave that had become my safest refuge. Every time I was tempted to reach out to something or someone for help, to ask for anything, to seek even the smallest comfort, a voice inside me screamed: "Shut up; you're supposed to be dead!"

My depression came in waves, becoming ever more unfocused, without concrete content, and dissolved into an amorphous, wordless abyss. It wrapped itself around me, dense and dark, screening out the sun, blocking out sound, clogging every pore, making every breath an effort, every movement an ordeal.

It took years of intensive therapy for the depression to become manageable. It was an uphill battle for every step gained. Today, the memory of those days has mercifully receded into the background, but it took a long time for me to learn to look at life with some measure of self-acceptance and optimism. Along the way, there were subtle signs of change, showing I was gaining insight, courage, and the resolve needed to set myself free from my self-imposed prison.

Little by little, very tentatively, I began to look for ways to reconnect to the roots from which I had cut myself off for so long. I occasionally attended services at various outreach Jewish congregations, most of which held *Shabbat* and Holy Day observances in Protestant churches because they had no synagogues of their own. It was at one of these innovative services that I first learned the meaning of the *Kol Nidre*. I discovered that because Jews so often were forced to make spiritual compromises under the threat of death, this ancient Aramaic prayer asked God to disregard any vows made under duress which concerned their connection with Him: vows of baptism and conversion, vows of denial, or vows of allegiance made on the crucifix.

It was of great comfort to me to learn that Jewish tradition, unlike Catholicism, which threatened eternal damnation, not only acknowledged circumstances under which one might be forced to make compromises that went against one's conscience, but provided an instrument specifically designed to bring about God's forgiveness. I felt this prayer could have been written for me.

After twenty-two years of marriage my husband and I divorced. My children were grown with lives of their own. At the age of forty I quit my designing job and returned to graduate school to earn a master's degree in psychology, and became a Marriage, Family, and Child Counselor, with a specialty in Art Therapy. My practice soon flourished and I developed a social life. By 1988 I knew the time had come to do the one thing I knew I had to do.

To sort out the many intertwined facts and fictions about my life, I realized I would have to go back to my childhood, to retrieve my connection to a past that seemed lost in a jumble of denials and contradictions, and to roots from which my family was cut off long before I was born. I also knew I had to begin my search in Spain, where I first experienced what it meant to hide that I was a Jew, like the "Marranos," who, for centuries, suffered the same sense of dislocation as did I, never feeling safe, forever strangers in a hostile environment where their survival depended on disguising or hiding their identities.

The more I learned about the Marranos and their stubborn efforts to maintain their essential connection to their spiritual wholeness, the more I identified with them, or perhaps more precisely, the more I longed to be one of them. They had something deep inside which kept alive their link with each other and with their heritage, even under the most dangerous circumstances. I, on the other hand, never saw myself as anything but a failed, flawed outsider during all the years I practiced Catholicism and long after I stopped doing so, cut off, forever banished from my own people because there had never been anything experiential in my own past to bind me to Jews. More than anything I longed to have what the Marranos had: a sense of "belonging."

Thus, at the age of sixty, I began my quest, my journey into my own past and into a deeper exploration of the history of the Jews in Spain, as a way of reconnecting to a spiritual core of which I was not even aware as a child, but whose lack had left such a gaping void.

That five-year-long search proved to be very healing. I spoke to many others who shared similar experiences, not only in Spain, but in several other countries, including Israel, where I felt the full magic of being somewhere where Jews were not a minority.

Since then I have attended many classes, seminars, and retreats with several fine teachers, on a variety of Jewish subjects. Last year I joined a rather unusual Jewish congregation where explorations into spirituality, meditation, and music are part of each service. We meet in a church. I am learning daily, but slowly.

It's a struggle, but I am hanging in. I have many questions and find my search for answers stimulating. It's an exciting process. What I love best about being a Jew is that I can argue with God. We have a dialogue. That more than makes up for what I miss about the Catholic mystique that so captivated me as a spiritually deprived child.

Chapter 9

Trials and Tribulations in the First Year of a "Mixed Sephardi/Ashkenazi Marriage"

Sarah Taieb Carlen

I was born and brought up in Tunisia in a very large and traditional *Sephardi* family with century-old roots in the country. Peter was born and brought up in Canada, in a small, secular *Ashkenazi* family of Roumanian and Lithuanian origin. We met in Jerusalem where I had hoped to settle after I left Paris where my family lived. A year later we decided to get married. Peter flew to Paris from Toronto, and I flew in from Jerusalem. Since it was the period of the *Yamim Noraim*, between *Rosh Hashana* and *Yom Kippour*, during which no joyous celebration is to take place, no French rabbi would marry us. Even the fact that my father was quite sick did not change anything.

An Ashkenazi new member of the family suggested we try talking to Sephardi rabbis: "Ils sont plus souples!" he said (They are more flexible). But, like all French rabbis, the Sephardi rabbis had to be registered in the Consistoire de Paris, an institution established by Emperor Napoleon I in 1809, in order to set the rules and regulations of the Jewish community in France. Time was running out and Peter had to go back to his job in a Toronto hospital by the following week. One morning the phone rang. It was Rabbi Perez who had heard about our problem and wished to perform a double *mitzvah*: to marry a Jewish couple and to give a dying father the joy of seeing his daughter married.

According to French law, no religious authority can perform a religious wedding if the couple has not previously been married by a civil servant at the Mairie (City Hall). Peter and I went to the Mairie where the Mayor married us. So Peter kept saying: "Why do we need all this headache from the Consistoire and the Rabbis? We are already married." Thinking he was joking, my parents did not pay much attention to him. One day, my mother said:

"Please, Peter, make sure Sarah is comfortable during *Kippour*" (the Sephardim do not say *Yom Kippour*, but just Kippour)," since you said it can be quite hot and muggy in October in Toronto."

"Why, what happens on Yom Kippour?"

"What do you mean? People fast on that day, so she will be fasting and with the jet lag, the new family, the new country, the fact that she just got married . . . it's a lot; just keep an eye on her!"

"Why? Why should she fast on Yom Kippour?"

Horrified, my parents looked at me with a "How could you lie to us?" kind of look, and then at each other in utter disbelief. Then my mother pronounced the sentence, loud and clear, but still mindful of Peter's feelings, she said it in Arabic:

"This one, you will NOT marry. He cannot possibly be Jewish!"

It took me all the patience in the world to explain to my parents that Peter belonged to a Reform family. This was hard for me because I was not yet familiar with this concept myself, since Sephardi Jews have not subdivided Judaism into several categories and subcategories: Orthodox, Ultra-Orthodox, Conservative, Reform, etc.

This does not mean that they are all equally religious. They are not. But they all go to the same synagogue—which is closer to an Ashkenazi Orthodox synagogue than to a Conservative or a Reform one—they pray from the same book, their rabbis go to the same *yeshivot* and it is only in the privacy of their home that they express their various degrees of belief and practice.

So, the closest I could get to a coherent explanation of Peter's family's Jewishness was that they were like Protestants in the Christian Church. But that was not a good idea.

"Who can dare change anything in G-d's words? Why do they have to have their own laws? Why do they have to have different synagogues, different rabbis who learn different things?"

My parents seemed lost and confused. My mother said, "But even his name is not Jewish! Carlen! What kind of a Jewish name is that?"

"Ma, they used to be called Kaplan, but because of antisemitism, they had to change it to Carlen."

"Oh! Kaplan, like our chief Rabbi, Jacob Kaplan!"

They looked relieved, even happy.

"But then," said my father, his eyes twinkling with pride, "he is a Cohen; you are marrying a Cohen."

"Yes," said Peter, "our name used to be Cohen."

"So," said my father, "why would anyone with the beautiful name of Cohen end up with a non-Jewish name like Carlen, and how can a Cohen be a Protestant Jew?"

An uncle, who was visiting us asked, "Forget about the father's name, Carlen, Kaplan, Cohen, who cares? The mother, what's her maiden name?"

"Steinberg," said Peter, relieved since for Ashkenazim, the name is a passport for Israel. But in my family, it caused consternation.

"But, that's German. In fact there are two German names in it: Stein, stone, and Berg, mountain," said my father. "And if it is so . . . so German, could it also be Jewish?"

"What is her first name?" asked my uncle.

"Muriel," answered Peter. Blank looks.

"Well," I said," it was really Myriam, but at school, she had to change it to Muriel."

Sighs and looks of relief. My parents could well relate to that since when they registered us at the Lycee Francais, they used to give our Hebrew names first and then our non-Hebrew ones; the French principal always ignored the Hebrew ones. But I only had one first name: Sarah. The principal said: "C'est trop oriental," (it's too oriental) and right there and then, without asking my parents or me, she baptized me Edith.

At some point, I asked my mother, "How come two of my brothers can marry French Catholic girls, and if you decide that Peter is not Jewish, you won't like me to marry him?"

"How can you dare asking such a question? Look how sick your father is. It is mostly due to the pain that first Albert, and then Simon caused him when they married Poussy and Rosie."

"But, he is always so nice to them, not just polite. He is really affectionate, warm and kind."

"Your father is a gentleman; that's his personality. He can't be nasty to them just because they were not born Jewish! But it hurts him very, very much that their children will not be Jewish!"

"But mine will be, even if Peter is not Jewish!"

"You know your father has a soft spot for you. If you marry out too, that will really be too much for him!"

These words kept haunting me. I wished I could prove to them that Peter was Jewish, but just a different Jew from most Jews they had met in Tunisia or in France. But, how? What could I say or do? What could Peter say or do? Finally, the light! EUREKA!!

"Who cares about his mother's or his father's name? He is Jewish because he is circumcised!" I said.

DEAD SILENCE. Then, as one person, they asked, "How do you know?"

"He told me that at his *brit*, one of his uncles fainted, the family panicked and Peter's father, who was a cardiologist, exclaimed: 'Oh, for G-d's sake, calm down, will you! He fainted! So what! He can't have hurt himself falling from such a short a distance!'"

Everyone laughed so much! At last I had succeeded in diffusing the tension.

Later on that afternoon, Peter asked me, "Do I smell or what?"

"Why?"

"Because they are all offering to take me to the *Hamam* (Turkish bath) in the Faubourg St. Denis."

Not wanting to hurt his feelings, I said, "Men and women should go to the *mikveh* before their wedding, but since we can't have a wedding mikveh, the next best thing is the Turkish bath. It's fun. We used to go every Thursday in Tunisia. My sister and I went with my mother in the afternoon, and my brothers and my father in the evening. We loved it!"

He went, accompanied by my four brothers, eight first cousins, and three uncles. As a Sephardi saying goes: "He who has no witness cannot be believed."

In retrospect, I think it was Peter's winning personality which made our marriage possible and the fact that the whole family had fallen in love with him.

We finally got married in my sister's apartment with thirty-six people attending, all of them known and dear to me: Peter and his brother, me, my family, and other assorted relatives. The buffet dinner, made by the women of the family, was beautiful and delicious. There were jokes, dancing and music, and it was really one of the most genuinely happy weddings I have ever been to, although totally devoid of the usual trappings.

The next morning, Peter, his brother, and I flew to Toronto. We went to my in-laws' Forest Hill home. The maid opened the door. "They are still in Florida," she said, without greeting us any further.

My First Shabbat

Shabbat, when I was growing up, was glorious. I have no other words for it. But, Friday nights at my in-laws' were like any other night, and Saturday was a regular day.

First Formal Dinner at My In-Laws

My mother-in-law threw a dinner party to introduce me to the rest of the family. It was to be a memorable experience. Among the guests was the formidable Aunt Bertie, my father-in-law's aunt, who was considered the Miss Manners of the family. It seems that she was impressed by my French table manners. She loved my French accent and my cream French lace dress, but stated "Why is being Jewish so important to her? She does not look it; she does not act it. Why not just forget about it?" I could not understand these remarks since being Jewish to me was the most natural, the most basic trait of my personality. I had never questioned it; I had never known or felt that there was anything to question. I was born Jewish just as I was born with brown eyes. I never gave much thought or attention to either.

I was told later that Aunt Bertie's dream, like many people of her generation, was to be a WASP, to be accepted in the WASP milieu of the city; therefore, while she was growing up, showing off or being proud of one's Jewish roots was a big NO-NO. When I finally understood that, I also understood how proud I had been, and still was, of being Jewish. Before Aunt Bertie, it had been an unconscious, natural pride. After Aunt Bertie, it became a conscious pride, as if I was proud of being proud.

But back to the dinner. My mother-in-law served THE Canadian dinner par excellence: before the meal, drinks and hors d'oeuvres;

and, at the dinner table: lettuce salad, standing rib roast, Yorkshire pudding, baked potato with sour cream, boiled green beans, apple pie and ice cream. The maid brought a roast cutting board, knife, fork, sharpening stone and, with much ceremony, set all this in front of my father-in-law. He stood up, took the knife in his right hand, the fork in his left and started carving. He looked proud and happy. It was all new to me and I liked it very much because there was a warm, comforting feeling of custom, of tradition, of ritual. Everyone looked at him and gave his or her order: end-cut, medium rare, rare (????) The maid passed the plates.

First slice; second slice, so pink; third slice, so red, blood was flowing from the huge piece of meat! My stomach was churning. I thought my mother-in-law's oven was out of order and/or she was a totally incompetent cook. I looked at Peter. He was relishing his thick, raw piece of meat. I looked at all of them, they were eating with obvious delight. I thought they were just being polite, and as soon as no one was watching, I quietly slipped my "end-cut" onto my husband's plate so he would stop eating this raw flesh. But he said, "I don't like end-cuts." On our way home, I was expecting him to comment on his mother's raw roast beef. But, no! Thinking he was really embarrassed, I did not say anything either.

Then, an important doctor invited my in-laws and us for dinner one Sunday, because they wished "to meet Peter's French wife." No matter how often I told people I was not born in France, but in Tunisia, it did not seem to make any difference. Many people did not know where Tunisia was anyway: "Oh! Indonesia!" And they loved Peter so much that they preferred to think of him as married to a Frenchwoman. I stopped caring.

So, we went to the home of Dr. and Mrs. McX for dinner. It was the same menu as my in-laws'—same ceremony, same ritual, and same unfortunate reaction on my part at the sight of all this blood. This time, in the car, I asked Peter, "What is wrong with ovens in Canada?"

"Why do you ask?"

I told him. He was laughing so much he had to stop the car.

"But didn't you hear my father ask us whether we wanted our meat "rare" or "medium rare?""

I thought it was an insider's joke about the "rare" quality of this huge piece of meat the maid had put in front of him.

When I told my mother-in-law about my "roast-beef allergy," she also laughed, promised to buy her meat from a kosher butcher and to serve chicken or fish more often. She also said they were dying to be asked for dinner at our place (we had moved to a students' residence a few weeks before), because Peter was always bragging about my cooking. I had dreaded that moment, but there was no way out of it.

My In-Laws' First Dinner at Our Place

I asked Peter to help me with the guest list and the menu: French, Tunisian, Canadian? He invited 14 people and strongly advised me to make a couscous, which is the Tunisian national dish and takes forever to prepare. We had only two chairs and no table. Our neighbors loaned us cushions and mattresses which we used in lieu of chairs and table.

The big D-DAY arrived. The many salads which are served with couscous, so colorful and flavorful, were on the "table" which we set on an elevated board on the floor! At 6:30 sharp, my in-laws rang the door bell. As soon as they walked in, I smelled disaster. My father-in-law immediately held his nose and my mother-in-law asked:

"Where are we going to sit?"

"Here, on these cushions, on the floor!" replied Peter.

"We are not Arabs!"

I had wanted to retort that I was not Arab either, and the only time I had sat or slept on the floor was when her son had taken me on a canoe trip in the Canadian wilderness, but I was trying to see what I could do to save my dinner party and not make things worse; besides it never bothered me when people thought of Jews of Moslem lands as Arabs. Their ignorance bothered me and the fact that they thought that being Arab is bad bothered me, but the cultural confusion did not, since the Arabs have given so much in the past to the Western world and have today a very rich culture full of old and admirable traditions.

I asked my mother-in-law, "Why is Dad holding his nose?"

"Because there is a strong smell of garlic, and it makes him sick!"

Just then, my father-in-law said to Peter, "G-d, these spices stink. Cumin smells and tastes like gasoline to me!"

So, there they were, not willing to sit or to breathe the air of the apartment. I could see they were most uncomfortable and miserable, so I said, "Don't feel you have to stay. We have to wait for the other guests, otherwise we would come out with you for dinner. If you wish, come back for dessert."

"What are you serving?"

"Mint tea and Tunisian pastry, with nuts, almonds, and honey."

"We hate honey."

After this memorable first dinner party, I always served my in-laws roast or boiled chicken and potatoes, and apple pie for dessert.

First Hanukah

My in-laws were not used to celebrating hanukah. I asked my mother-in-law to teach me how to make *latkes*, I bought a *hanukiah* and we had a lovely party on the eighth night.

First Tu-Be-Shvat

They had never heard about it. I bought all kinds of dried fruit and had a little party. By then, my mother-in-law was calling me "the mystique" because I liked observing all these holidays.

Purim

In the Sephardi tradition, husbands offer their wives gold jewelry for *Purim* every year, but the first year, the gift ought to be more substantial. I was waiting for mine with such excitement! I am still waiting. . . . But we had such a fun-filled party, I forgot about not receiving a gift.

First Pessah

I cannot describe the pre-*Pessah*, *Pessah*, and post-*Pessah* Sephardi rituals and traditions, and I must say by then, I did not expect my in-laws to know, let alone observe them. But neither did I expect to have only one seder and to see bread appear on the table after the ultrasonically fast seder in English.

First Shavuot

We were invited for a dairy meal. There was no prayer, no blessing.

My First Pregnancy and Delivery

When I was in my ninth month, I went to my obstetrician for my last visit but one, on a Friday. He told me that he was going to the cottage the next weekend, which was my due date, and if I wanted him to deliver the baby, he would have to induce me on Friday in the early afternoon, otherwise I would be under the care of his resident, whom I had never met or seen. I thought he was joking, and that night at dinner I said to Peter and his family, "My doctor is funny! He said . . . ." To my amazement, Peter, his father, and his brother, all three of them doctors, took my doctor's offer very seriously and encouraged me strongly to accept it. I phoned my mother who said, "Don't do it! A baby should come when it is ready and not when your obstetrician wants it to. What's the big deal about giving birth anyway? It's the most natural thing in the world and it is most certainly not the business of a man. What can he possibly know about it?"

My mother had had six children all of whom were delivered at home by a midwife, except for the last one, who "just came" one night as she was singing at a party. This reminded me of a scene I had witnessed as a child. It was the day after Pessah: the *Mimounah*, during which the Sephardim go out in picnics. There were hundreds of people singing and dancing in the fields, picking flowers, eating sandwiches. (Incidentally, many young people meet their lifetime companion during these Mimounah picnics.) At some point, my father and I wandered off and we noticed a fat-looking woman dismounting from her donkey. She squatted, and then wrapped her baby in a piece of cloth and tied her or him to her back, then she got back on her donkey and rode away. My father explained to me that she was a Bedouin woman who had just given birth. Since this was the only time I had ever seen anyone give birth, for me it was a rather natural event. On the other hand, however, I had formed quite a strong bond with my obstetrician, whom I trusted. And, when the three doctors in the family said, "It's better for the baby," I felt I had no choice.

The following Friday, my mother-in-law picked me up and took me to Mount Sinai hospital. It really did feel very, very strange because I had never been a patient in a hospital. I always associated hospitals with acute cases of serious diseases and here I was, feeling perfectly healthy, with doctors and nurses all around me, wearing masks, holding syringes, placing monitors on my belly, giving me a needle, and another, and then. . . . nothing. I woke up seven hours later in the Intensive Care Unit. I had been in a coma all this time apparently because of too much medication. Maybe my mother and that Bedouin nomad woman were right after all: why make such a fuss about such a simple, natural function of the female body?

And so our first son was born. While I was pregnant, my obstetrician kept telling me, "You have a girl!" So, we had a long list of girls' names, but . . . surprise. Since in the Sephardi tradition, a son has to name his first son after his father, when my father-in-law came to see the baby at Mount Sinai, I said, "Dad, we are going to call him Sidney." His expression soured: "Why do you wish me dead?" I explained to him that, in my culture, it is a great honor to be named while alive and told him that my father had been named seven times before he died, to which he answered, "Maybe, but now he is dead!" I was flabbergasted! It puzzled me that such a highly intelligent and educated man who was a confirmed atheist could be so profoundly superstitious! I was then reading the book of Amos. I loved the prophet; I loved the name, and so did Peter. Since we could not name our son Sidney, we decided to call him Amos. Aunt Bertie hated the name. I ignored her. My father-in-law was horrified: "Poor kid, such a name! Amos rhymes with anus. You'll see! He'll have hell at school, whenever a kid wants to make fun of him, he'll call him Anus."

First Brit mila

Came the day of the circumcision, the brit mila. I wanted to go home. "Oh, no, no, no, you have to wait a day or two after the brit to see if the baby is OK. You just can't leave before that." I was upstairs in my hospital bed of the maternity ward, waiting and reminiscing, daydreaming. . . . In the Sephardi communities, the brit is preceded the night before by an evening of rejoicing, praying, singing songs of praise and thanks—*piyutim*—until very late into the night. I told myself: "Nothing of the sort happened last night because they are not religious, but today, today is the brit, and they are going to do what everyone does." What everyone does, for me, is what I had seen done in the Sephardi world and in my family. On the day of the brit, the new mother is dressed in her best lingerie, fresh flowers adorn her hair, her bed is made up with a beautiful, rich-looking satin bed cover, above her headboard, reprints of specific passages of the *Zohar* are hanging, decorated with fish and hands which are supposed to fight the evil eye. The baby is dressed up in a blue dress embroidered with verses of the Torah, his crib is beautifully decorated, his little bonnet is made of blue or white lace. *Eliyahu's* chair, placed next to the mother's bed, is decorated with garlands of flowers, fresh leaves, and fragrant herbs, and on the seat is a blue or white satin cushion. The maid walks all over the house with burning incense. The ladies ululate, sing, and, in their best apparel, they sit in the mother's bedroom waiting for the *mohel*. Before the circumcision, her husband and her father-in-law come to see her. They offer her jewelry and they thank her for having given a son to the family, thus perpetuating their name. When the mohel comes, the women ululate, get up and stand between the mother's bed and Eliahu's chair to prevent her from seeing. During the circumcision, they comfort her and give her hot milk and honey. They make her laugh because she should never be sad while nursing the baby. Immediately after the circumcision, her mother brings her the baby who, so they say, forgets about the pain as soon as he starts nursing.

But . . . I hear a baby crying, a nurse walks into my room, I am wearing a hospital gown, and so is my baby. While Amos nurses, I cannot fight my tears of sadness, of nostalgia for what is no more forever.

First Rosh Hashana

Apple dipped in honey and nice dinner. No mini-seder as is customary in the Sephardi tradition.

Second Yom Kippour

It was really the first Yom Kippour, since I had spent the previous year sick in bed. Peter had decided to fast. Aunt Bertie was horrified. I ignored her. My mother-in-law was in tears. Because she thought it was my doing, I spoke to her: "Peter decided on his own to fast. I did not demand it from him. I did not brainwash him. Don't worry, he is not becoming The *Rebbe* of Toronto. Simply, he has noticed that holiday time is usually very hard on me and makes me miss my family. It's just love and caring on his part, and you should be proud of him for being so sensitive." These few words triggered what was the beginning of the most beautiful friendship story of my life which, most unfortunately, was to end so very soon and abruptly with the premature death of my mother-in-law at the wheel of her car only a few years later.

First Sukkot

No *Sukka* was built. How I missed the fun of my childhood, building and decorating the *Sukka*; eating, sleeping, playing in it and feeling so sad when time came to dismantle it . . .

First Shmini Atzeret

For my in-laws, that was????

First Simhat Torah

Ditto.

First Wedding Anniversary

My in-laws took us to a posh restaurant (they loved doing that) and gave us a fat check. I felt happy because I could tell they loved me despite our many differences, big and small, and the many cultural clashes—funny, serious, and dramatic. I loved them because the more I knew them, the more I understood them, and the more I realized how genuinely good and kind they were, even if they were not as warm and sensitive as what I had been accustomed to in my family.

I knew my experience in Canada would be different from what I had known in Tunisia, France, England, and Israel. I was not prepared, however, for the extent, the pervasiveness, the magnitude of the differences.

It took me time to realize that if I talked back to my in-laws, the sky would not fall on my head, because in the Sephardi tradition, people of the parents' generation, in particular in-laws, were owed the utmost respect. This did not necessarily mean that the new bride was a doormat, just that confrontations were to be avoided and that even though she might in principle agree to things, she could and often would do just as she wished. Obviously, the first year or so, the rules and principles I lived by were those I had been brought up with and that I had observed during my formative years in my own family: my mother was always respectful to her mother-in-law, but practically always did as she pleased in most domains.

What hurt a lot was mostly the loss of all those beautiful, old, rich traditions which, I started to realize, had wonderful therapeutic functions: The circumcision of a baby, for example, is bound to be much harder on the mother if she is alone, in an impersonal hospital room, a few floors above the aseptic room where it is taking place, than if she is in her own room, richly decorated for the occasion, surrounded, cared for, even spoiled by those she loves.

Many years went by during which a kind of religio-cultural osmosis took place: After Amos' birth, my mother-in-law started lighting candles on Friday night and celebrating more and more holidays. I always kept an ashtray on the table for my chain-smoking father-in-law, even during the religious holidays. Our sons were exposed to Sephardi and Ashkenazi Judaism, and they have grown to respect and appreciate both cultures. I hope they will pass this respect and love on to their children.

Chapter 10

The Joys of Mitzvoth

Rebecca L. Bradley

ON MY BEING A JEW BY CHOICE

I am a woman; I am a lawyer; I am a Jew; I am an American; but who am I? And how did I become who I am? Born an American female, I went to law school to become a champion for the underdog, a righter of wrongs, first to protect myself from some ill-defined danger and then, as time passed, because it felt right, because in retrospect I know I could not have done otherwise. Today, after thirty years of identifying myself in my role as a trial lawyer, I know I would have become miserable had I not followed those other dreams.

I was not born Jewish. I chose to be Jewish. Being Jewish feels right, inevitable; it is an inextricable part of my being. I have come home to my people, part of a bigger plan, far beyond my control. The exploration and expansion of my Jewishness is central to my happiness; my joy of life; the joy of *Mitzvoth*.

My journey began with an unexplained passion for the Russian language—many, many long years ago. I was captivated by the sound and dramatic melancholy of Russian music, poetry, and literature, a flowering of my childhood love for Russian folk tales. Learning Hebrew, many years later, kindled a new fire in my soul. It was not coincidental that many of the Russian songs that had been my favorites as a young girl were based on folk songs that had become also a part of Jewish culture. I frequently hear them today in Israel, sung in Russian and Hebrew . . . and other languages.

But let me try to start at the beginning and go somewhat directly to the end—or at least toward the current state of my story.

As a young child I was bright, but painfully shy—so shy that in first grade I hid under the desk from the teacher and my classmates. I did all the math problems in less than half the allotted time. But then, too shy to volunteer to talk about the answers, I would draw spirals over the answers until sometimes they were no longer discernible. In second grade I was sent to a rural Catholic school. There I learned how to get good grades in all studies, including Catholic Religious studies. But I felt like an outsider, invisible, an alien from another planet. I remember playing "Communion" with Neccos candies with one or two other non-Catholic children, shivering with fear of this strange Catholic god who liked statues and wanted us to live lives full of suffering.

As a teenager I had a special compliment for my mother—I called her "my Jewish mother," which was my way of expressing my joy at her pride in me and her acceptance of me, whatever I was involved in. She was the only one who supported my interest in studying Russian language and culture at a time immediately post the McCarthy/House Un-American Activities Committee (H.U.A.C.) era. She believed that it mattered more how one lived, how one treated others, what one did to help improve life, than what views one verbalized, or what "beliefs" one professed.

My father was an atheist who held religion to be only for fools and ignorant people. He also told me that it was a pity I was born a girl, because I was so bright that, had I only been born male, I would be capable of great things. I worked very hard to disprove my father's view of women's potential. In fact I think in some way I always knew he understood that I was very capable and that in his own way, he was also proud of me. I went to college on an academic scholarship, studied math and science, carrying a 3.9 grade point average. I made Phi Beta Kappa. Ultimately I went to law school on scholarship. For years I suppressed my artistic, more feminine side, painting, writing, dancing, acting, and doing crafts as a secret delight. Keeping my nose in the books served to keep me out of disfavor with my father and allowed me to avoid most of the beatings that my less academically inclined brother endured. The anger I felt for my father's low regard of women led me to become extremely competitive, and to look my fears in the face, many times jumping straight into the unknown *because* of those fears almost as much as because the course of action felt right. As the years passed I have gradually discovered that many of the unexplained steps along the way were ultimately part of a G-d-directed plan.

My first closeness with being Jewish seemed accidental. When I was a high school junior I was "adopted" by a Jewish family. I was madly in love with the youngest boy, Jack. The papa didn't trust me too much, because his son liked me too much, but he allowed me to listen to him pray in Hebrew and he helped me to understand that the Passover Seder was a celebration of freedom. I felt a need to learn more about this religion that seemed to talk about how one should live, and relate, and behave, instead of telling one what to think or believe.

The mother, Celia, who was a redhead like myself, taught me a little Russian; we read Pushkin together. I had spent many hours memorizing Pushkin's poem "The Bronze Horseman," about Peter the Great. In my early years of studying Russian, I was told that every Russian youth knew Pushkin's **Медныы всадник** ("The Bronze Horseman") and how very important it was to memorize that poem. I was reciting it to Celia one day, when tears suddenly started slipping down her cheeks and she told me a most amazing story. At the time of the Russian Revolution, in 1917 or thereabouts, she was a beautiful, buxom young teenager, fleeing on a train from the Ukraine with her family and other Jews. Their train was stopped by Russian soldiers and she was separated from her family. She spent a terrifying night with the young soldier guarding her. She knew she would be raped, perhaps murdered. As the soldier, no more than a boy himself, came closer to her, she burst into tears and started reciting "The Bronze Horseman." Caught off guard, the boy-soldier also started crying and recited the poem with her. They spent the night discussing Russian poetry and literature and in the morning she was allowed to continue her trip unmolested.

When I graduated from high school, with enough honors and scholarships to make any parent envious, my own father, who thought that education was wasted on girls, hardly acknowledged me: "You'll just get married and have children." Jack's family had a big party in my honor. I had a small kitten in my pocket, and in the middle of the party the kitten awoke and crawled out. A woman from Argentina, a survivor of Hitler's death camps, saw the kitten and came over to pet it. Amid tears she told me of the night when she was so cold, so depressed and miserable she was ready to give up and die; G-d sent her a small kitten like mine to crawl up on her breast and warm her heart—to keep her alive. The next day the Allied forces came and liberated the camp, and she never forgot the kitten G-d had sent to save her life. At that point her husband came over and said in a hoarse whisper: "Masha, we don't talk about that." I knew almost nothing about the death camps, but I had heard whispers. I was afraid to ask more at the time, but immediately developed a passionate interest in trying to understand the Holocaust.

This experience had a profound impact on me. From that moment on I have felt that I was a part of the Jewish people, ready to stand up against injustice and, if necessary, to die with my people. Formal conversion did not seem to be necessary to me, however, until I experienced some major life changes in the mid-1970s. In 1976, my husband, two children, and I moved to Boulder, Colorado. Two weeks later, five days before my thirty-fifth birthday, my mother was killed in an automobile crash. Her death blasted a huge hole in my moral and ethical life support. My marriage was not healthy, although it gasped its way into the late 1980s before it was dissolved. My children and I began attending the local Reform Synagogue and in 1979, my eight-year-old daughter, Morgan, asked when she would become Bat Mitzvah.

We were not the only members of the Congregation who were not *Halakhicly* Jewish and Morgan had been regularly attending Sunday School and Holiday celebrations. We baked *hamentashen* for *Purim* and attended *Passover Seders*. I was learning how to keep *kosher* from my housekeeper, who had been raised in an Orthodox Jewish home. I then determined that we needed to have a *halakhic* conversion to be legally what we were already committed to spiritually and socially.

My son, Douglas, was less interested in study, although he enjoyed the social events at our synagogue. Because his father was not Jewish and Douglas was already thirteen, he did not participate further with Morgan and me in our preparation for Halakhic conversion. I have always felt a little sad that I did not actively pursue Judaism sooner so that Douglas would also have had the opportunity to choose Judaism.

In 1980 I began seriously studying Hebrew with a group of people I knew from our synagogue, and in 1982 I undertook the final formal stage of my conversion to Judaism. With my daughter, then age eleven, who was determined to become Bat Mitzvah at the age of thirteen, we went through a joint Halakhic conversion, with *mikvah.* When I heard the voice of my beloved Rabbi Daniel Goldberger, together with two of his colleagues, within earshot but out of sight, prompting us to say the *Shema,* my heart grew warm and tears of joy ran from my eyes into the water of the mikvah. Morgan was more down-to-earth. She already knew she was Jewish and was not so happy to be cold and wet and facing a one-hour winter's drive home.

That week my Hebrew classmates, with whom I had then been studying weekly for nearly three years, had a surprise party for me with a cake that said, "To a nice Jewish girl." There is a Jewish belief that there really is no such thing as a convert to Judaism, only a person whose ancestors had been detached from the Jewish people in some past generation, whose soul, *neshoma* had finally found its way home. I had come home.

When I visited Jerusalem, with just enough Hebrew to read the Prayer book, I went to The Shrine of the Book. There, as I bent over the ancient parchment, looking at the text penned 2,000 years ago in the archaic script, I tried to decipher the letters. Pain-stakingly I decoded "alef, tav, heh, shin, mem." . . . Suddenly the meaning came as a flash of light! I recognized the words את השמם ואת הארץ "et ha shamaim v' et ha aretz", . . . for in six days G-d made "the heavens and to the earth." The music we used to sing these words in my synagogue sounded in my head. The rest came more easily. וביום השביעי שבת וינפש "U-vayom ha shevii, Shabbat vayi-nafash." "And on the seventh day He rested and refreshed Himself."

It was an awesome moment. I was standing alongside the anonymous scribe in the Judean desert, 2,000 years ago, bent over and reading the words as he wrote them. I was there at Mount Sinai, in the shadow of Moses, ready to receive the Ten Commandments. I was rooted in history, rooted in G-d. This G-d was my G-d; this history was my history; these roots were my roots. I sat on the cool bench for a moment and became more calm. I belonged; I felt my mother's arms again around my shoulders and I was permeated by her warmth. "You are my daughter" she seemed to be saying to me and I could feel her pride in me. I was home.

BOULDER ACTION FOR SOVIET JEWRY

I felt deeply about the Jews of the Soviet Union, who carried the label JEW in their passports and identification papers, and who were maltreated and oppressed because they were Jews. They were denied the freedom to join their fellow Jews, to become a spiritual and physical part of the Jewish People. From some time in the late 1970s I had been involved with Soviet Jewry support groups. At first I did little more than write letters to Jews being refused permission to emigrate from the Soviet Union, and letters to Soviet and U.S. government officials asking for help for these people. I began to review and upgrade my use of the Russian language in order to communicate with Jews and officials in the Soviet Union. I bought tapes of Russian and Hebrew and for years drove around in my Volvo listening to verbs being conjugated in both languages.

In the mid-1980s, I began a new adventure that has not yet played its final scene. For over twenty-five years I had studied Russian language, culture, and history; then Hebrew and Jewish culture and history. None of these studies were directly related to my life as a personal injury trial lawyer. But at long last an important purpose for my life began to focus. Because of my knowledge of Russian I was asked to join as a cofounder of Boulder Action for Soviet Jewry (BASJ), to travel to Russia, the Ukraine, the Caucasus, and Central Asia in search of freedom-seeking Jews with whom to connect and offer my help. Four of us, two judges and two practicing lawyers, spearheaded a group of Jewish activists to develop an entity that became Boulder Action for Soviet Jewry to help these Jews escape from their oppression. At that time, Boulder, Colorado, had formed a Sister City relationship with Dushanbe, in far-off Tadzhikistan, in the Central Asian part of the former Soviet Union. I was an active member of that group. It planned a trip to the Soviet Union with Dushanbe as the ultimate destination. I was asked to go on the trip because of my ability to read, write, and speak the Russian language. My companion, Roxanne, was to go with me because we felt that two women would be less threatening to the Soviets than would men, and since we could share a room without raising questions, we would be able to move around outside the official itinerary without upsetting or disturbing the rest of the group.

Through contacts with Israelis who had family remaining in the Soviet Union, BASJ had a list of Soviet Jews who were desperate to escape to freedom. We networked with a number of groups like ours from all over the United States, Canada, and England. From this network we had much information about "Russian Jews," the Jews from the western part of the former USSR. However we knew almost nothing about the Bukharan Jews of Central Asia.

Before Roxanne and I left for the Soviet Union, we were briefed by others who had established contacts with Jews in Russia, the Ukraine, and other European areas of the USSR, and they taught us what to do to avoid accidentally violating Soviet laws or compromising the safety of those we were trying to help. It was all very "cloak and dagger." An elaborate system of substituting numbers in our checkbooks for names and addresses and messages worked well, but it played havoc with my checkbook balances and I had to close my account and open a new one after my return. We were given names, addresses, telephone numbers, and detailed instructions about how to contact the Russian Jews. Sometimes we had detailed descriptions of family members and specific items of clothing, food, or religious items being requested by them. But when we asked about the Bukharan Jews, we were told "Go, find out, and tell us. We have no experience there."

In Russia, our fear level was so high that we stopped up several toilets in Moscow, shredding and flushing all but the most condensed and coded of messages we had received from Jews living in the USSR. Our biggest fear was that we would be strip-searched at the time of our departure. We were all in a sweat every time we went through an airport, because a well-known news reporter had just been set up. He was given a message written in Russian to forward to a friend, arrested, and held in jail for some time before he was released.

In fact we had reason to think we were the target of conspiracy. As we approached the synagogue in Moscow at 8 Akipova Street, two young men tried to engage us in conversation. We were carefully nonresponsive. Shortly after they left, an old woman approached us and tried to get us to take a letter written in Russian. Because of her odd demeanor and the fact that she started speaking English before either of us had even opened our mouths, we were immediately suspicious. We remembered the fate of the news reporter and firmly declined, speaking clearly into an imagined microphone hidden under her coat. As we walked away we observed that the two men who had approached us earlier had now joined the woman. All three of them stood and stared at us, scowling with terrifying unknown significance. My heart stood still.

Otherwise, our travels through the Russian part of the Soviet Union went pretty much the way we expected. On a dark, rainy day we donned dark glasses, met Boris in the subway, and accompanied him to his family's small apartment. We walked up the stairway in silence so the neighbors would not hear any English or foreign accents to raise their suspicions. We gave Boris's family kosher food, a raincoat, and film for a camera. Once, carried away by emotion for the plight of a mother who had no overcoats or winter boots for herself and her two small daughters, I gave her an expensive gold Star of David from my neck. I knew she could take it to Israel when she was allowed to emigrate, or, more likely, sell it for money to buy food and clothing in the meantime. The same scene was played out in each Russian City with minor variations.

CENTRAL ASIA AND BUKHARAN JEWS

Dushanbe is a city in Tadzhikistan, one of the former Soviet states located immediately to the north of Afghanistan and on the western border of China. The people there looked quite different from those in Russia. Many of the Tadzhik Islamic women wore traditional bright-colored costumes—dresses worn over pantaloons that showed underneath, usually of different patterns and colors from the dresses. Many had mouths full of flashing gold teeth, worn not because of needed dental work, but to show their wealth. The women and girls all had very long, thick black hair, and surprisingly thick black eyebrows. Most of the women disappeared at sundown, leaving the men to occupy the numerous teahouses one saw everywhere. The men dressed in a variety of ways, some with almost European-type suits, some with Asian-style robes; many wore square bright-colored hats. The Jewish men wore the same style hats as *kippot*.

Roxanne and I had been provided with three telephone numbers of *refusenik* families in Dushanbe. We followed the directions given by our advisor, which by now had become routine, and walked several blocks away from the Intourist Hotel to a bank of sidewalk telephones. The traffic was fast and noisy. My throat clamped shut, and I tried to swallow, fearing that I would not be able to carry on a conversation in Russian over the noise. I thought of tricks I had learned to get over stage fright when I acted in plays in college; tricks I tried to calm myself at the beginning of a trial before I had begun to develop a rapport with the jurors. I knew if I did not get a good grip, my memory, my vision, and my hearing would fade, and I would have trouble remembering the meaning of simple Russian words. The sun had set but I was sweating uncomfortably. I felt that with my height and my red hair I stood out to all, visible as an alien invader up to no good. I expected any minute to be accosted by another local Communist leader, and questioned—or worse.

I had to laugh when I remembered the first such character I met in Dushanbe, who had tried to chastise me for taking Polaroid pictures in the farmer's market. I was taking pictures of the vendors, especially those who were very old and had wonderful faces to photograph with the fruits and vegetables they were selling. I also had focused on the young women with little children, giving most of the pictures to the subjects or their parents. We were having a great time, getting to know each other, when a man came up to me and told me I could not take pictures. He wanted to know where my man was—to keep me in check as were all women in Central Asia. In his culture it would be unthinkable that a husband would not be close by to control his woman's behavior.

As we walked to the telephones Roxanne sensed my fear and kept asking me if I was afraid. I lied to her, pretending to be ever so cool. We were like two competitive sisters. Roxanne could merge; she was little, dark-haired, and born Jewish. On the other hand, I was the one who spoke Russian, and it was my second trip to the Soviet Union. She was usually so in control that I couldn't help a small twinge of satisfaction when she openly expressed her fear of "this terrifying land."

The first two telephones did not work and I lost four of my precious few kopecks. I finally realized that I had to stand in the *long* line to find the phone that actually worked. I had wondered why Soviets always stood in one long line at a bank of phones when there were two or three other phones not being used. It was finally my turn, and I dialed the number with a trembling hand. One number rang and rang without an answer. The second was answered by a woman in Russian, saying loudly, "They moved away! You have the wrong number." With my last two kopecks I was able to reach Liza—a name Roxanne had been given by her sister who lived in Israel. Liza patiently listened as I explained in Russian that I was "a friend from the West," our code words from the briefings, and asked her to meet us at the synagogue.

Liza was small, dark, shy, perhaps fearful. Yes, she had wanted to emigrate and go to Israel in the past, but now she had "changed her mind." When pressed, she admitted that the real reason for the change was that she would not go without her older son, who had been drafted into the Soviet Army and was ineligible to leave for five years. She now wanted only to be allowed to visit her dying mother in Israel. This was denied to her. Liza invited me to her home and we walked rapidly a long distance. At the last minute she asked me to wait, ducked into a neighbor's house and then introduced me to Maya, "who spoke a little English." Maya introduced me to her husband and her two children. After a brief conversation, she excused herself and spoke excitedly on the telephone to her sister, Alla, who was persuaded to join us.

Alla, who had taught English to both Russian and Tadzhik-speaking students at the foreign language school in Dushanbe, arrived with a flourish, and announced in a loud, clear voice in English that emigration "was no problem." All who applied received exit visas. The new policy under Gorbachev was to allow everyone who wanted to leave to do so. "We have everything here. We need nothing here." When I pointed out that her neighbor, Liza, was not allowed to go to Israel, she said that was different—"because of the army." All of these new friends, within minutes of our first meeting, shared their most intimate, and possibly dangerous, secrets with me, their "Jewish sister from the West." This identity obviously meant to them that I was invulnerable to

Soviet dangers, powerful, capable of single-handedly saving them from the antisemites and bearing them safely to any part of the free world to which they desired to go. Roxanne was impatiently asking that every word be translated into English so she wouldn't miss out on the conversation, and I had great difficulty switching back and forth between the two languages. My temperature rose and my pulse quickened. I felt like a fraud! What if I got people killed?

The father of Maya and Alla was a good Party man, well-educated and with a number of privileges. I did not find out until over a year later, when Alla and her family came to live in Boulder, that she had discovered only on his deathbed that her father spoke Hebrew and had studied as a rabbi. Because of his Communist Party membership both Alla and Maya and their families had very nice homes, beautiful furniture, Czechoslovakian china and crystal, many art books, lovely Persian rugs on the walls and floor. We were entertained with caviar, vodka, wine, fresh fruits, and wonderful foods of great variety and quantity. Gifts of silk, amber, and art books, as well as cognac and canned fish were given to us by these new friends.

David and Alla, with their son, Ilya, drove us home in their car, parking directly in front of the Intourist Hotel. Alla said they had been granted permission to leave and they were trying to decide whether to come to Israel or the United States. Alla was concerned because she did not want to part with her sisters and she was distressed to leave all of her nice possessions behind. She had not yet told her sister, Maya, that they were leaving. She indicated that she would not leave at all but for her sons' determination "to be free." At length Alla said she believed they would come to Boulder.

Nine years ago I first wrote in my diary about that trip, ending with the comment: "Many of these things are curious. Why had Alla not told her sister, Maya, about their imminent departure? Why did they park right in front of the Intourist Hotel, seemingly unafraid to be seen with a visitor from the West as were the Jews in Russia? Were these Asian Jews really free from discrimination as Alla had so emphatically declared? . . . If and when they do arrive here, many of these perplexing questions would perhaps be answered, and we would certainly have some insight into future additional contact with the Jewish community of our sister-city, Dushanbe."

Upon my return from that trip I was ablaze with the desire to help Soviet Jews to be free, eager to welcome them if they came here, but ever so unaware how this one trip was to forever change my life. I felt as if I had been hibernating for nearly fifteen years at the time I took that trip. My resignation to eternal unhappiness in my suffocating marriage—and the near abandonment of my once youthful burning passion to be of some significance to the world before I died—came to an end. My mind cleared and I was free. By giving a small gift of love and hope to a few of my people I was given to understand the meaning of "freedom" in my heart and mind.

For months after I returned I spent night after night writing and rewriting my report on the trip; speaking to anyone who would listen to enlist help in freeing those who had asked me for such help. Trustingly, touchingly, I believed that I actually had the power to do something to save these people from their oppression. And the miracle was, that by combining my energies with others who also wrote, spoke, called the USSR and demonstrated, we did have such power! In the period of approximately two years after my return from that trip to the USSR, over two dozen families with whom we personally connected were allowed to emigrate.

As I interacted with these new American immigrants, so happy to be given their freedom to make their own decisions and futures, I felt I was seeing America for the first time. I traveled to Boston for the first time in my life, seeing it through the eyes of Russian-speaking Jewish immigrants, who told everyone who would listen that I, Rebecca Bradley, their most beloved *sister* from across the seas, had single-handedly freed them from Gorbachev's land and opened the doors to their new free motherland. In Boulder, where I lived, my new family cooked for me, had parties in my honor, asked me to advise them on education for their children. Suddenly I was all-wise! It was a terrifying experience for me. I felt dishonest. Soon I would be discovered and held up to ridicule for my pretensions! But, miraculously, that never occurred. I gradually lost touch with most of my "new-American" friends, as we all got on with our lives, but with some I became closer than family.

As a result of my work with Soviet-Jewish dissidents and my ongoing relationships with Russian-speaking Jewish immigrants in the United States, I feel I have gained far more than I ever gave, and learned much about being Jewish. To my great surprise, I became a much better lawyer than I had been in the past. This was in part due to new Russian-speaking Jewish immigrants who knew of my work and referred clients, but primarily because I just grew and became more competent in the art of human problem solving.

IMMIGRANTS IN AMERICA: THE GURZHIEV/LEVY STORY

"My mother told me G-d sent you to Dushanbe." Reuben Gurzhiev, whose face showed at the same time sensitivity, pain, and a wisdom beyond his twenty-one years, spoke quietly through the late hours one night in his clear but accented English. He looked straight in my eyes with his lovely dark eyes, and spoke of his impressions of this country, his country now that "was his dream" for so many years.

He began with a story of how a gang of eight to ten Tadzhik and Russian boys would typically surround a Jewish boy on his way to or from school, taunting him by calling him a Jew and trying to intimidate him and humiliate him. No matter what the Jewish child would do, they would then beat him, sometimes severely. Reuben, his younger brother, and all the Jewish boys he knew experienced this type of primitive antisemitic intimidation, which stopped only when a large enough opposing force could be assembled. "When I first experienced this type of attack, I was only a child. I didn't understand then. But I soon came to understand what it would be like to live my life and raise my children in that part of the world as a Jew, and that is why it was my dream to come to America."

He then told a long and terrifying tale of his difficulties when he was in Russia studying in college. "I was one of only two students in a college population of 26,000 who refused to join Comsomol, the Communist Youth Organization." Because of this refusal, a great effort was made by the Communists to force him out of college and into the Soviet Army. "The environment for Jewish boys in the Soviet Army was not good anywhere, but because I was from Tadzhikistan and spoke Persian, they would have sent me to

Afghanistan." Only his calm demeanor and intelligence allowed him to avoid this fate and remain in college until he could emigrate.

Reuben, at the age of twenty-one, was the self-appointed leader of this family of Bukharan Jews, in their efforts to migrate away from the religious and intellectual restrictions they faced in the Soviet Union, living under Communism and among poorly educated, primitive and violent Muslim Tadzhiks. Reuben has said that July 4th is now his "Passover," his "birthday." We spent their first July 4th in America playing games, horseback riding in G-d's beautiful mountain meadows, watching the sky alight with fireworks. This leader who came from that dark land was like a child one minute, like a wise man the next.

"Gurzhiev" was not Ruben's real name. It means "Georgian" in Tadzhik language. Reuben and his family have now changed their names to "Levy," a name that signifies their pride in their identity as American Jews.

The fall of the year the Levy family arrived in Boulder was in some ways even more beautiful than the summer. Not so hot, the clear blue skies and yellow aspen leaves delighted our eyes as my new adopted family and I spent hours driving to Colorado Springs, to Vail, to Aspen, to Estes Park, Las Vegas, Los Angeles, San Francisco; to Santa Fe and Taos. As I look at the pictures of the park in Santa Fe, with the blue, blue sky, the colored leaves, the red peppers, the street singers; as I wear my turquoise jewelry or look at the paintings or listen to the music we bought there, I remember with a kind of pleasure/pain, how perfect was that brief time when this family, and Reuben in particular, was so sure of a wonderful new life and new freedom. They attributed wonders to me. They credited me with everything good that was coming in their lives, through lengthy Russian toasts made at countless gatherings in my honor. It made me blush with pride and embarrassment.

Our "New Americans," as we in BASJ called them when we threw welcoming parties for them, came to learn very soon that life in the United States also presented many difficulties, stresses, and disappointments, and required much hard work and effort to adapt—but that is another story.

Two years after the first Gurzhiev family moved to Boulder, Colorado, the remaining family members were forced by increased violence and the impending fall of Communism to emigrate also. With the help of the Levy family, we were able to help numerous other Bukharan Jews from Dushanbe to emigrate and settle in Israel and America, including some forty families who chose to come to Colorado.

After 800 years, these people made a major migration from Central Asia in order to seek religious and political freedom. It is an awesome feeling to have been a part of that movement. Every time I read my notes from that trip I am amazed at how my life changed with a trip to the other side of the world. I am a different person, having been given the gift of trust from my new family of Bukharan Jews, who, to this day, continue to tell me and tell others that I "saved their lives" by taking their hand and traveling with them from oppression to freedom.

Reuben has worked for my law firm for several years now, and hopes soon to pass the Colorado Bar, and eventually to become a partner in my law firm. He just completed his legal studies and graduated from the Denver University School of Law, my alma mater, which makes me feel very proud. He and I made a fearsome team, first fighting to get him into the law school; and then fighting to stay the course until it was complete, simultaneously starting my new solo law practice and making it a success. Unfortunately, I was too ill to attend his graduation in May of this year. After eight years of working and waiting for this great occasion, I, who am rarely ever sick, was unable to attend.

Reuben said he thought of me and, in his imagination, proposed a speech that was something like a Russian toast:

> I had a dream when I was thirteen years old of becoming a lawyer in America. This dream of mine triggered a move for my entire family. Yes, this move was coupled with my family's need and desire to seek freedom from political, religious, and intellectual limits that were intolerable to us, but my personal priority was to become a lawyer in America; a lawyer being the symbol of having the power to help people, and the desire to do this in America having been fueled by what I saw as the injustice of the Soviet Criminal Law System. It was not an easy road. In addition to realizing my own personal dream I

knew, because I brought them here, I needed to be always aware of my duty to help family and relatives, many of whom were struggling to survive this immigration. The years of support of friends, especially my friend Rebecca, has made this dream come true.

All the years of encouraging him to believe in his dream of becoming an American lawyer is now bearing fruit. The years of struggle in which I shared so many of this family's dreams makes their joy in becoming educated, professional American citizens my own success. These are the joys of mitzvoth.

All my life I had wanted to do something to improve the world, something to prove myself as a good Jew, something to definitively counter—at least in some small way—Hitler's Holocaust and Stalin's horrors against the Jewish People. With the first step—in the mikvah—I had given back two Jews in the place of the lost six million. Now, while I could not cure the ills of the Soviet Union, maybe my life's purpose was to take one family by the hand—and help lead them to a better life.

I know in my heart that my natural talents, my nurturing female nature, and my religious and professional goals are coming together. It is good to be a Jewish-American woman lawyer.

Chapter 11

In Search of Eden

Pnina Granirer

Like many other Jewish women who were born in Eastern Europe, and who have lived in a few different countries, I am essentially an uprooted human being. This is not a complaint, but simply a statement of fact. The curious aspect of this situation is the often heard remark of how lucky I was to have lived in various countries and to be able to speak several languages. While I, always carrying within myself a feeling of otherness, a shadow of a stranger's presence, yearned time and time again to belong in the deeper sense, that of language and culture, of children's songs and games played in early childhood, of schoolmates still close, of words which trigger memories in people who grew up together. All these elements bind a generation with invisible bonds and a sense of belonging. But the faint perfume of the outsider will always cling to me, a burden as well as a gift.

Since one cannot change the cards one has been dealt, the game has to be played with the hand one has. All in all my deck was a good one. Looking back I see how fortunate I have been and I am thankful for that.

I was born in Romania, in 1935. My family was not religious and only marginally traditional. We were, in fact, secular Jews, although with a strong awareness of our Jewishness. How could we forget it during the dark years of the war? Our family was extremely fortunate to live in one of the rare towns where there were no life-threatening experiences. Not so in many other cities. Members of our family who lived in Iasi for example, had to flee, barely escaping the *pogroms* in that city. Even for us, should the war have continued for even one more month, we would have joined the bitter fate of many of our people. Fortunately, King Mihai of Romania was the first to sign an armistice with the Russians on August 23, 1944. For us the war was over.

During the late 1940s I joined Gordonia, a Zionist youth organization. I remember our huge elation and joy when the State of Israel was declared in May 1949. I still have the jubilant poem I wrote for the occasion, enclosed in a small book of poems with faded blue covers.

Eventually my father was forced to flee the country for political reasons. Being a Socialist who refused to join the Communist Party did not sit well with the authorities. He managed to find his way to Israel, smuggled aboard a Yougoslav freighter. Our fervent wish was to join him there.

This impossible dream became a reality when, in August of 1950, we succeeded in leaving for Israel due to a new policy allowing a large number of Jews to immigrate. This was made possible by the American Jewish Joint Distribution Committee (JOINT), an International Jewish aid organization, which paid substantial amounts of money to the Romanian Government in exchange for passports.

And so, at age fifteen, I arrived in the country I considered my true home: Israel. During the twelve years I lived there I learned to speak Hebrew, finished high school, spent one year in the Israeli Army, got married, completed four years of the Bezalel Art School, and bore my first son, David Eran. These were difficult, but exciting years, sometimes frustrating and sometimes full of satisfaction.

I desperately wanted to be a true Israeli, going as far as reaching the decision, together with my husband, to speak only Hebrew at home, although up to that time we had spoken Romanian. But only after we left Israel did we realize that the acceptance we craved had not been forthcoming. For the *Sabras*, the Israeli born, I would always be a Romanian, someone who spoke with an accent. This became apparent to me only after my arrival in Canada where, in spite of feeling different, I felt more accepted as an immigrant.

I did not come to North America with the intention of settling. It was to be a temporary move, until a job became available for my husband in Israel. But this was not to be. After spending three years in the United States, we came to Canada, still hoping for an opening of a job at the Hebrew University in Jerusalem. Finally, during our fifth year away from Israel, while living in Montreal, a job offer came. By then we had been living in Canada for two years. We were now faced with important decisions which would affect our lives enormously. After a short visit to Israel, we took the great leap, deciding to stay in Canada and return to Vancouver.

As a Jewish woman coming from Israel, I felt very different from the rest of the Canadian Jewish women I met. I was less concerned about my Jewishness: As a secular Jew, my former Israeli identity was enough for me; I did not feel I had to prove my Jewishness in any other way. Being an Israeli meant identifying with a country I had lived in and a passport I still carried. I was perhaps closer to an Italian or Greek immigrant in this respect.

The fact that I considered myself an artist was another reason for feeling different. I tried my hand at some of the usual activities most women were involved in, in spite of not being interested in these. This "double life" was to be mine for a very long time. I had one foot in the middle-class world my family belonged to, while I yearned to plant the other in an artistic milieu.

As time went by I realized that there was some tension between the Canadian Jews and the Israeli immigrants. I sensed an underlying resentment from the local Jews toward the Israelis for having left Israel and resentment from the Israelis toward the Canadian Jews for their attitude of nonacceptance. I found it rather ironic to see a different version of the situation I had found on my arrival to Israel. Now it was the turn of the Israelis to undergo the immigrant experience. Not having been totally accepted in Israel in the past freed me from too great a dependency on seeking belonging to the Israeli groups in Canada. I was free to be Canadian and to be myself and it felt good.

The decision to stay in Canada had not been an easy one and it was not lightly taken. In fact, throughout 1965, the first year we spent in Vancouver, I experienced tremendous longing for Israel, in spite of the natural beauty surrounding me. I particularly missed the physical place, the land, the historical connection, and the language, if not the people. I discovered that the ties which bound me to Israel were a sense of identification with a place, a feeling I had never had about Romania. To this day I have a sense of wonder and awe thinking of the miracle of Hebrew, a 3,000-year-old language, coming back to life. The wonder of the survival of the Jewish people still amazes me and I get a thrill each time I think of all the places which still carry the same names as in the Biblical stories.

Having said all this, in spite and because of this longing, I realized that deep within I was angry. I was angry with Israel, as one is angry with a lover who lets down his beloved. I was angry because this country I had come to with all my love had not returned it, had never really accepted me as one of its daughters. Perhaps I should not blame the country, but rather its people and the difficult times associated with the birth of a new nation. Now, a few decades later, I understand that my expectations were unrealistic, that this is the way of the world. Differences isolate people and newcomers are not taken in gladly. This is the reason they tend to live in ghettoes of their own making, for safety and comfort.

The need for acceptance in Israel is probably higher than anywhere else, due to the way the country came into being, its idealistic start, and heartrending history. But the idealistic model does not fit human behavior in the long run and hence the disappointment.

And so, in 1967 I was an immigrant for the second time, not for idealistic, but rather for economic and pragmatic reasons. I have a very simple and clear-cut philosophy concerning immigration: Once the decision is made, an immigrant should do whatever he or she can to fit into and contribute to the adoptive country. I was grateful to have been accepted into Canada and felt particularly privileged to be able to live in Vancouver. I wanted, as I had in Israel, to be part of the society which had taken me in.

There was, however, a substantial difference between Israel and Canada, which had to do with identity. Israelis have a very strong sense of who they are, an almost fierce and self-centered feeling, which is expressed constantly everywhere. One cannot say the same for Canada. The need to find an identity is still at work. Therefore there is less pressure on new immigrants to blend in, and due to the policy of multiculturalism, they are accepted more or less the way they are. They are encouraged to keep their culture, rather than asked to abandon it entirely.

Upon our return to Vancouver, our son David was in second grade. Until then we had sent him to Talmud Torah, the Jewish school, in Vancouver as well as in Montreal, thinking that we would go back to Israel where the study of Hebrew was necessary. But now we had to make a long-term decision. As secular Jews, religion was not an important aspect for us. Moreover, we had noticed that the Talmud Torah school had a very strong educational thrust toward identification with Israel. At this point, we decided that we did not want our son to grow up with a split personality. We wanted him to be Canadian, to feel Canadian, and not to experience the feeling of guilt so many Jewish people have for not living in Israel. We opted for the neighborhood school and left the teaching of Judaism and Hebrew to after-school classes.

I could not say whether my Jewishness had anything to do with the fact that, in spite of desperately wanting to spend more time at my art, I did not put my children in daycare more than two hours, a few days a week, and this only after the first two years. It most probably also had to do with economics, since I was not earning enough money to justify the expense. In fact, I really enjoyed seeing my sons grow up. My second son, Dan Michael, was born in 1968, in Vancouver. Not only did I delight in each new word, each new gesture, and each new evidence of intelligence, but I also drew inspiration for my work from my children. During the time they were quite small I created numerous works with children as subjects. One of them, a monoprint of my older son David at age two, was accepted for the 1969 cover of the UNICEF calendar and is now in the collection of UNICEF. Due to a remark of my younger son Dan, I embarked upon a whole series of mixed-media drawings exploring the magic of childhood.

One of the images that kept appearing in this series was the circle and the egg, as the place where all creation begins. I inserted in some of these drawings the Hebrew word *B'reshit*—In the beginning—and it became a series. I do not consider myself "a Jewish artist," but rather an artist who is Jewish, and similarly I would not want to be labeled "a woman artist," but rather an artist who is a woman. Yet once in a while Jewish elements would appear in my work, as well as elements which might be described as "feminine." After all, we express who we are, and my work mirrors my own personality and experience.

For quite a long time I did not take myself seriously enough as an artist. I understand now that my feeling that what I was doing was not important enough had to do with the fact that there was no money value attached to it. In our society people are valued for their earning ability, although I was aware that a male artist was taken much more seriously, even being poor. In my time "real" artists were mostly men. The romantic image of the totally obsessed, starving artist was quite accepted, excluding, of course, women. I accepted this since this was the reality of our time. However, my whole perception about myself as an artist changed from the moment my work started selling.

My interest in ancient cultures, mythology, and archeology has also greatly influenced my art. I firmly believe that who we are is a sum total of the generations preceding us, their wisdom and their folly, their art and their myths, their achievements and the many destructions inflicted by them upon the world. Being Jewish and having lived in Israel gives me access to the Old Testament in the Hebrew language and a sense of belonging to a very ancient people distinguished by a continuous, uninterrupted presence in history.

Perhaps it is this fascination with the past which was the catalyst for a 1981 work I called *The Trials of Eve*. These twelve mixed-media drawings and twelve accompanying poems were published as a limited edition book (Granirer, 1989, 1993) and won the Alcuin Award for book design. In 1993 the book appeared in softcover. The work also appeared in a film by the same name, by filmmaker Gretchen Jordan-Bastow (1990).

At the time, I felt the need to read and document myself on the subject of feminism. There were many questions that I wanted answered, information I needed in order to better understand my own doubts and deep feelings of injustice regarding women. Although I, personally, could not complain of any major instances of discrimination, there were small incidents which disturbed me. During childhood I used to fantasize about being a boy and travel-ing the world, or doing things that only boys could do. Later, walk-ing through the Orthodox Quarter of Mea Shearim in Jerusalem, I used to make fun of the large posters describing exactly how a virtuous daughter of Israel should be dressed. I was even called "whore" by small boys on the street, because I was wearing pants and a sleeveless blouse. Nevertheless, there was bitterness and resentment in the laughter.

While exploring these issues relating to history, mythology, and feminism, I embarked upon *The Trials of Eve,* a work which was to explore and point out the status of women in our society. For this I went back to the very beginning and chose the story of Adam and Eve as the vehicle which would enable me to express my opinions. I believe that the interpretation of this myth has shaped and defined the gender relations in our society for 2,000 years.

The process was intense and lasted a whole year. During this time I learned a great deal; this exploration changed my perception of women, of myself, and of some of the cornerstone precepts of Judaism.

Since the creation of *The Trials* was such a major endeavor for me and had such important repercussions on my life, I shall elaborate on it in some detail. The work consists of 12 mixed-media drawings on paper, 30"/22," and twelve poems. It is designed as a play in three acts, revolving around Eve's trials and tribulations. The protagonists, Adam and Eve, are wooden marionettes, symbols of human beings without race, almost sexless, and given to manipulation. The snake is replaced by Cannibal Birds, West Coast Indian mythological creatures, which imply inner drives rather than outside temptation. The drama opens, of course, with the first act. It is a set-up. The tree, center stage, is there, but not to be touched. *"Who is this God who sets the trap for his own creation?"*

Further images take the viewer through "Adam and Eve Tempted by Cannibal Birds," "The Framing of Eve," "The Trial," "The Sentence" and so on. There are historic, artistic, and religious references throughout the work. While designing each piece, I did a great deal of thinking and reading.

The conclusion I reached was devastating for me, both as a Jew and as a woman. Although there had been previous attempts in history to take power away from female goddesses, it is the story of creation and the enshrining of Jehovah as the one and only God in the Old Testament, by my own people, that essentially established patriarchy as the new order. The new God was all male and had taken over all the attributes normally associated with female goddesses, such as procreation, compassion, and healing. The Christian Church later on refined and completed the process, relegating women to a totally subservient position toward men.

Having completed *The Trials,* I reflected upon the consequence upon my beliefs. It became clear to me that whatever doubts I harbored in the past about the existence of an omnipotent entity were now confirmed and validated. God, as a caring power, interested in the particular fate of each human being is, as far as I am concerned, a creation of the human mind, seeking to assuage its fears in its need for reassurance and comfort. On the other hand, I am in awe of the overwhelming mystery of the Universe and cannot help but marvel at its creation. It is, however, an uncaring Universe, concerned only with survival.

Human nature being what it is, the invention of the Hebrew God was, in great part, an attempt to introduce moral laws into a society which had none. These constitute the most important and lasting legacy of the Jewish people to the world. But I cannot accept the temperamental God of the Old Testament and I find the idea of praying to him quite useless. The only power I respect and bow to is that of Nature. In short, I can say that I identify as a Jew, but I see God as part of a fascinating mythological past.

Now, entering my sixth decade, I am painting a series of works I call *In Search of Eden.* I now know that the Paradise we all long for is gone forever. We have to plant our own gardens and create our own Edens within our small worlds. The angels we yearn for and wish to believe in are, in truth, ourselves. We are the angels; it is in our power to recreate Paradise if we only try.

REFERENCES

Granirer, Pnina (1989). *The trials of Eve/Les epreuves d'Eve.* Vancouver, BC: Gaea Press.

Jordan-Bastow, Gretchen (Producer) (1990). *The trials of Eve: A filmmaker's vision/Les epreuves d'Eve: La vision cineaste* [film].

Chapter 12

Family Memories and Grave Anxieties

Susan Weidman Schneider

Across my desk at the *LILITH* office comes an announcement that a Jewish community center in the Bronx will transport elderly Jews to visit their relatives' graves in outlying cemeteries. The project strikes me as a *mitzvah* both original and thoughtful. So why does reading about it make me anxious?

I'm comfortable with graveyards. In Winnipeg, Canada, where I grew up, attendance at funerals was not an experience denied the young. We had many opportunities to witness our elders' grieving and sadness up close. While death itself could never be demystified for me, at least its rituals and ceremonies were familiar.

The family plots in the Shaarey Zedeck synagogue in Winnipeg are landmarks to me. Of those I especially like, the biggest and oldest is the Weidman one—on the right as you enter the large, ornate metal gates, at what had once been the edge of town and is now on route to a suburb.

When I visited one rainy fall day recently with my cousin Sheila (our two young children, like a scene from some French art film, running around among the tombstones in the mist), I realized that nearly every row holds surnames which call out to me from my own family's mythology. The name of the man who played Disraeli opposite my mother in a university production in the 1920s. The name of a business partner who cheated my *zayde* out of his dry-goods business. (Zayde recovered financially, but not emotionally.) All the old Jewish merchant families rest here; most of their children became professionals and turned away from commerce. The grandparents—and even some parents—of the kids I'd known in high school.

This cemetery is my version of *Our Town*. My father's and mother's parents are here, and uncles and aunts. And my father, too, who was buried here when I was seventeen.

My father and my maternal grandmother both died in November of my first year away at college, so I suppose graves were a natural subject for my mother and me after that. My mother always punctiliously and ardently tended to the graves of her parents, worrying about what kind of flowers my *bobbe* would like, and reminding my brother and me—before Alzheimer's quieted her concern—that she had arranged for "perpetual care."

The Winnipeg gravesites would be enough, you'd surmise, to explain why I go on red alert when I read about visits to cemeteries. But Jerusalem ones are lodged in my consciousness as well. My father's grandparents decided, in 1904, that it wasn't enough to have come from Russia in 1882 to settle their children safely on the Canadian prairie. *They* were leaving for Jerusalem (the move spurred, family legend has it, by my great-grandmother, who told her husband that the children were settled, so they could leave for the Holy Land). They planned to die there, and did. Their graves are on the Mount of Olives, the headstones still intact at my last visit. (Cousin Joanie carries around their row and tombstone numbers in her address book under "G" for "graves.")

When I first visited that famous Jerusalem cemetery 18 years ago, I'd never known my great-grandmother's first name. On her tombstone was carved *RAKHEL, ha ishah ha 'kshara*—Rachel, the kosher wife. My heart leapt. We had given our older daughter the name Rachel—only because of its biblical associations, we thought, but that gravestone in Jerusalem revealed its deeper association.

Perhaps all of this connectedness helps to explain what bothers me about cemetery visits now that I'm in my middle years. When I, too, left Winnipeg, and later married a New Yorker and had three children, it didn't occur to me that my mobility would present a special problem: Where will I be buried?

I don't want my final resting place to be in Queens, or New Jersey, or Long Island. I want to be snuggled up with Weidmans and Zagrabelnas in the frozen soil of Winnipeg's North End. Or at least with that earlier Rachel. But if I die first, what will my husband do?

Born in Brooklyn and raised in a New York suburb, will he join me? And is Winnipeg too far away for the children to visit?

My worries are surely shared by others with lives similarly fractured by geography. Even when husband and wife are from the same place, what about their children, who may have been raised far from the family homestead in, say, Columbus or Tulsa or Birmingham? And what about my pal, divorced twice, who confesses that she felt betrayed when she found out her two closest friends had bought double gravesites with their husbands, without even asking if she'd like to be buried nearby?

I want guidance on burial. In the world to come, my soul will be free to go wherever it desires or deserves. But in this world I need to decide where to rest my bones—which will be, I hope, much wearier by the time I'm ready to relinquish control over them in the grave.

SECTION III:
THE JOURNEY HOME

Chapter 13

Really Jewish

Jane Marie Law

On August 23, 1991, I underwent the formal process of converting to Judaism. The day was the culmination of a commitment I had made nearly ten years prior to that August morning. In the late 1970s, I became interested in Jewish ethics and ritual. As I read and studied, I saw in Judaism a religious system that I felt would allow for the deepest expression of my own spiritual nature. By the early 1980s, I was intent on conversion. There was no Jewish man in my life urging me to convert, although this is the assumption people repeatedly make when they discover I am a convert. I was motivated to take this step by a profound sense of identification with Judaism, and an inner attraction to Jewish religious life that I am still unable to fully explain in rational or intellectual terms. My more spiritually inclined friends consider this long search an act of divine influence. My cynical friends suggest I read too many Isaac Bashevis Singer stories. I consider it a process of coming to peace with my own spiritual and ritual inclinations. In this short article, I would like to discuss the related issues of how I am often asked to narrate my experience of conversion to Judaism, and what I feel to be the tensions that conversion and the rising profile of converts to Judaism raise in the larger Jewish community. Converts, unlike people who are born Jewish, are often required to explain their Jewishness, and the structure of asking converts about their decisions to convert has become one of the avenues for the exploration of a range of charged and sometimes painful issues in contemporary Jewish life.

In 1982, while I was a doctoral student in the History of Religions at the University of Chicago, I went to see a rabbi about conversion. I had been told that I would be discouraged, and indeed this was the case. But the content of this rabbi's response had a great deal of wisdom in it. He said, "Right now you are having a romance with Judaism. Conversion is a marriage, and there really is no divorce. Wait ten years, and see if this is really what you want to do. If you want to convert then, you will have thought about it and I will be happy to help you prepare for conversion."

Nearly ten years later, I took the decisive step of going through the formal ritual introduction to Judaism. The morning of my conversion in 1991, I got up, took a shower, and went to the synagogue with my husband, who incidentally was born Jewish. After a *Beth Din* at the local synagogue, attended by three rabbis, we proceeded to a nearby lake, which served as the *mikvah*. Prior to entering the lake, I went through the elaborate process of preparing for the mikvah by carefully cleansing my body. Following my immersion, we returned to the synagogue, where I recited the affirmation of my identification with the Jewish people before an open ark, in the presence of the rabbis who had officiated at the conversion, and my husband. The whole affair began at 8:30 in the morning. By 10:30, we were home, and the formal beginning of my identity as a Jewish woman began. While the morning had been meaningful and beautiful, there was nothing earth-shattering about the event. No angels had appeared to me on the road, urging me to adopt a new religious identity. The gates of heaven did not open and shower me with blessings, or if they did, I was oblivious to it. I did not feel faint, nor was I overcome with deep emotions or a profound sense of a great change in my life. I felt no urge to give testimonials, and had no investment in seeing other people follow the path I had chosen. I had not expected any of these remarkable experiences, so characteristic of conversion experiences in some other major religious traditions. And I did not experience them. Going to the mikvah for the first time for the purpose of conversion was the beginning of something. But I felt that at a deep and spiritual level, a major yearning in my life had been settled and now I could get on with the business of having a Jewish household and living my life as a Jew. This was something I had longed to do for over a decade. That night after my mikvah for conversion was Shabbat, and I lit candles with my husband, something we had done for over a year. On this night, I lit candles for the first time as a Jew. It felt normal and right.

Although I have no regrets whatsoever about my decision to convert to Judaism, it would be wrong to suggest that it has not been without enormous ramifications in my life, most of them very positive and enhancing, but some of them troubling. I know, and my conversations with other converts support this, that making a decision to convert often constitutes a dramatic change in one's relationship to one's own birth family and friends, and entrance into a murky new category called by any number of names: *ger tzedek* (righteous stranger), Jewish convert, Jewish proselyte, Jew by choice. No one seems to agree on what to call us. We are hyphenated Jews.

My husband was raised in a nonobservant Jewish household in a largely Jewish section of London. He and I have created a Jewish home, where we observe the Sabbath and the festivals and Holy Days. We ushered our children into our lives with Jewish rituals of circumcision and naming. We keep kosher and are involved in our local congregation. Being Jewish is an important part of our own identities and that of our family. Neither of us consider ourselves to be zealous, but the Jewish calendar sets the cadence of our family life in a way that we enjoy. Although my conversion took place a little less than five years ago, my self-identification as a Jewish woman is a natural and inalienable part of my existence. While I am often made aware of being "differently Jewish" than my husband, I do not feel any less Jewish. The biggest difference I notice is that while my husband is never asked "Why are you Jewish?" or "How are you Jewish?" I often find myself answering versions of that question several times a month. The frequency with which I am asked this question has not diminished in the last five years, but retains a sort of dull constancy. People are curious about why I would make such a decision, one that has clearly had enormous ramifications in my own birth family and my life. They want to know how I feel about the role of women in Judaism, and how I, as a feminist, could convert to a system that has many oppressive aspects for women. Sometimes, the same people ask me the same questions on several different occasions. I have wondered what is behind their questions. What do they want to know? Am I some sort of a zealot? Am I nuts? Do I simply want attention? Am I some sort of an impostor? Can I really be a feminist? Do I know something they don't? People ask about my conversion for different reasons, based on their own relationships to Judaism and their own life histories. Other converts say that the same thing happens to them, and with equal frequency. Being asked about being Jewish is in many ways one of the ongoing defining events of a convert's Jewish identity.

Over the last several years, I have unconsciously developed a variety of answers to the many different shadings of the same question that I am repeatedly asked: "Why did you convert?" Here I am reminded of the joke that opens the book *The Joys of Yiddish* (1968) where the simple sentence "Two tickets for her concert I should buy?" can have entirely different meanings depending on which word in the sentence is emphasized. The same goes for this simple question about conversion. I have long versions and short versions, funny versions and deeply spiritual versions, versions for Jewish audiences and versions for Gentile audiences, versions for my birth family and relatives and versions for my husband's family and relatives, versions for Jews who hate Judaism and versions for non-Jews who hate Jews, versions for Jewish women and versions for non-Jewish women, versions for observant Jews and versions for non-observant Jews, and other versions that I have yet to classify. Some of these versions have had an airing, and some of them are just sitting in there, still in fragments, waiting to be told so I can piece all the meanings together. All of them are an authentic reflection of some facet of my decision to become Jewish. But none of them tells the full story. And all of them are continually developing, becoming more nuanced as I grow older.

I considered myself a little bit strange, having all these versions of my reasons for choosing to become Jewish. As an historian of religions, I have a professional interest in the role of narration in how people construct meaning, and I was a bit disconcerted to find such a lurid example so close to home. But as I have gotten to know more people who have made the same choice to become Jewish, and all for widely varying reasons, I have discovered that this process of creating a history for oneself out of one's own experience is quite common. In fact, this is something very commonplace for most people. Our stories about our lives are the webs upon which we survive intact. Being a convert to Judaism means joining a people for whom

History is an especially charged mode of experience. Although I have thrown in my lot with this people and their history, I have to find ways to have a history, too. And these tellings of the conversion experience become part of a process of history creation.

But the most important reason I have so many stories is because I get asked the question so darned many times. It is a little bit like having people know you can play the violin. You are likely to get asked to do so at parties, and so you develop a repetoire to keep from having to play the same piece over and over again. But all of your pieces are music, and you genuinely can play them all. Just so with my stories. They are all true. They all happened to me. It is just that some are more suited to certain audiences than others.

In many religious traditions, personal accounts of powerful religious experiences frequently share common elements. And often the legitimacy of the experience is judged by whether or not certain key features are present in one's story. In my own exploration of Jewish convert narratives, I have noticed a series of overlapping constraints which govern what can and cannot be considered part of one's personal history of becoming Jewish. These constraints, in turn, are unconsciously communicated to converts through this process of being continually questioned about conversion. In a very real way, being questioned about conversion is an important dynamic in identity formation for the convert, but it also allows the Jew by birth asking the questions to delineate his or her own Jewish identity in contrast to that of the convert. But what is most interesting about the kinds of questions I am asked is what they reveal about the tensions in American Jewish life today. In a very real sense, the convert becomes a resident outsider upon whom a number of anxieties can be projected, and this projection is accomplished through the somewhat ritualized quizzing about conversion experiences and decisions.

What kinds of questions am I often asked, and by whom? The most striking feature of my questioning about conversion is that I am most often asked to discuss my conversion by total strangers whom I meet at dinner parties, seders, weddings, breakfasts, synagogue functions, etc. In spite of the fact that it is a very personal question, it seems that the likelihood of being asked about my conversion is inversely proportional to how well a person knows me. The most common phrasing used when people ask me about my conversion goes something like this: "Did you convert because your husband is Jewish?" This phrasing usually draws out my story of my own religious attraction to Judaism, and stresses the independence of my decision to convert. I find I am most often asked this question by Jewish parents who have an adult child who is involved with or has married someone who is not Jewish. Behind this question, I sense that the parents are really asking themselves whether or not it is possible for a convert to become "really Jewish," and my narration becomes a means for them to explore their own feelings. Often, I am consciously aware that my unfolding story represents either someone's deepest dream for a child's partner, or their worst fear. I find these contexts to be the most uncomfortable, because clearly my presence in a situation is a reminder of the charged issue of intermarriage, something that has often caused great pain in families, feelings many families try to deny lest they appear old-fashioned or intolerant. It also points out a reality that many people only partly recognize: often the presence of a convert in a Jewish family creates a whole new set of problems concerning Jewish identity in the family. Converts often have a genuine enthusiasm for Jewish observance, and this enthusiasm is often greeted with tension and even scorn in a comfortably nonobservant Jewish family who would still nevertheless prefer that their child married a Jew. So while on the surface a convert may seem like a solution to the problem of intermarriage, often people listen with only slightly veiled horror as I describe the fact that my husband and I keep kosher and observe Shabbat and the Holy Days. "Will my kid become so *frum*?" they worry inwardly. "What pressures will I then feel about observance?"

The question as stated above, "Did you convert because your husband is Jewish?" is also a direct expression of the suspicion that a convert cannot really have been attracted to Judaism for spiritual reasons. Incidentally, conversion to please a potential marriage partner and his/her family is the reason rabbis most often give for refusing to help someone through the process of conversion. It is simply not a good enough reason to take on the yoke of Jewish observance. But the phrasing of this question directly asks me if this was my reason for conversion, and is the most common question I am asked. I am not offended by this question, in spite of its potential for being construed as rude.

The other group of people who often ask me that question "Did you convert because your husband is Jewish?" are non-Jews who have assumed that I am not Jewish, and who must suddenly deal with my chosen difference. To many of them, the subtext to the question is "Why ELSE would you convert if not for your husband?" Choosing difference is a problematic stance in the dominant society, and a rational explanation of my decision to become different must be found. Doing so to please a spouse somehow gets me off the hook. With few exceptions, outside this context, I am rarely asked about conversion by non-Jews. But often converts are the targets of veiled antisemitism. I once met a highly educated man who said to me (after he had consumed several beers to be sure), "I don't dislike Jews who were born that way. They can't help how they were born. But it is just plain weird to convert." He spoke for more people than himself, I have found.

I do not often feel the legitimacy of my Jewishness openly called into question in settings when I am asked about my conversion by Jewish parents of adult children. Recently, however, I had an experience that was bluntly to the point, and which raises another question about Jewish identity.

I was at a seder, and in between courses, we were discussing the meanings of the readings that were in our *Haggadah* and how place informs identities. A pleasant middle-aged woman sitting across from me asked me where I was from.

"Montana," I replied.

"Montana? There can't have been many Jews in Montana. What was it like growing up Jewish in Montana?"

I explained to her that I had not grown up Jewish, but had converted in 1991. Because conversion is nothing unusual in our community, I was surprised at her response. I was also, perhaps, unconsciously gearing up to sort out which response would be called for in this lighthearted but intellectual setting.

"So you aren't really Jewish then! My daughter married a man who also isn't Jewish, and they talked for a long time about his conversion, but then they both realized that you can't become something you aren't, and so in the end he just remained a Catholic. I don't understand how anyone can think they can become Jewish. You just can't. You are either Jewish or you aren't. My daughter and her husband are very happy together, and they accommodate their differences very well."

This comment, naive and thoughtless in its assumptions and implications, was not intended to be malicious, and I did not take it as such. This woman was simply expressing openly a view of conversion that many people hold privately, namely that converts are people pretending to be something they are not, going through the motions. And the irony of this barbed criticism is that precisely because Judaism is a ritually based religious tradition, people who convert to Judaism develop a Jewish identity by *going through the motions.* I develop a depth to my Jewish experience by lighting candles and washing my hands and saying *kiddush,* and going to the mikvah, and reciting blessings on certain occasions. And Jewish prayer is an act of worship that involves one's entire body. Judaism is a verb, and we are Jewish by what we do. And I learned to do these things much by being shown how to stand, use my hands, handle ritual objects, cook, and set a table for a seder or braid *challah.* I learned to go through motions, and as I have done so, the inner meanings of these motions have become available to me. I have learned the meaning of the academic dictum concerning ritual: ritual is its own means of cognition. I know what I know of the inner meanings of Judaism through what I do.

Here, again, is another issue confronting a convert, something of a Procrustean bed of identity, meaning, and tact. Those who are born Jewish are Jewish whether they set foot in a synagogue, observe the Sabbath, say a blessing or not. A person who has converted to Judaism is not afforded that same luxury of slack observance. I stood before an open ark and promised to keep a kosher home, circumcise my sons (should I be blessed with sons) and observe the commandments. When I do not do so, I feel like I am breaking a promise I made to myself, to G-d, and to the Jewish people. Yet if I am too observant, I look like I am being holier-than-thou or a poor imitation of Jewish life to some of my born-Jewish friends. If I am not observant, or pick and choose my way through observance based on what I like and find convenient or pleasing, I am a hypocrite, in spite of the fact that most Jewish people approach observance in this way. A

Jewish relative once said to me angrily, "How can you call yourself a Jew? When you don't want to go out on Shabbat, you claim religious observance and refuse to go. But when there is somewhere you absolutely need to go, you seem to forget all about Judaism and ride in a car on Saturday." I did not point out to her that she could be describing most Jewish people I know. In short, many converts feel conflicting messages about their observance. If we are too strict, we are impostors and zealots. If we are as relaxed as our born-Jewish friends and family, we are being hypocritical.

My most uncomfortable experience mediating these levels of observance and the boundaries between Jew and non-Jew came one summer when my in-laws were visiting my family home in Montana. My in-laws do not observe Jewish holidays at all, and feel uncomfortable with our level of observance. Wearing *kippot* and saying *"Shabbat Shalom"* seems foreign and even embarrassing to them, although they are deeply involved in Jewish social causes and clearly their lives have been shaped by Jewish ethics. My own birth family, a nonreligious combination of Norwegians and Scots, do not know what to make of candles and blessing and kiddush, but are oddly intrigued by all this ritual. Something about it is beautiful and even a little bit exotic to them, yet they are also uncomfortable with the fact that I have chosen to be different from mainstream white America. They secretly hope we will be "invisibly different," ostensibly out of a concern that I not suffer at the hands of antisemites, but also because of their own subtle embarrassment that I am a religious person. Since we always light candles on Friday nights as a family, I lit candles and my husband and son and I recited *kiddush*. My daughter watched from the womb. My mother asked my mother-in-law, "What do you make of all of this?" meaning with her question, I think, "What does all of this ritual mean to you?" My mother-in-law replied, "I am amused by it" meaning, I think, "I am amused that my daughter-in-law is going through all these motions." My mother-in-law heard my mother expressing concern about my ritual actions, and my mother heard her respond that it was all amusing. I think neither of them were having the same conversation, and both left with more misunderstandings than they had had before, but I felt as if I were a microcosm of contemporary Jewish observance. The confusion, ambivalence, and intrigue about

Jewish observance is a powerful force in Jewish life, one which is able to both destroy and create meaning, depending on how it is handled. This issue lurks below the surface in Jewish families with little observance. When a convert comes along and starts "lighting candles like a real *yenta*" (to coin an expression I was once told), this issue can explode, and needs to be confronted.

Dealing with the fact that as converts, we often have a better formal Jewish education than our non-observant Jewish friends, is a difficult balancing act. The presence of a moderately Jewishly educated convert (which is what I consider myself to be) highlights the charged reality that many Jewish people are ignorant of their own Jewish heritage, and it is the very presence of the convert that allows for an expression of this deeply worrying reality. But the reasons why converts often feel a pressure to be well educated about Jewish issues, and to voice their education, are varied. One reason concerns a part of the job description few converts read in the fine print at conversion: Many of my non-Jewish friends feel it is safer to ask me their list of "Things You Always Wanted to Know About Jews but Were Afraid to Ask" than to ask a "real Jew." So I often find myself in the uncomfortable position of being an ambassador for the Jewish people, asked to typify 5,000 years of Jewish life, ritual, and experience based on my own five years' experience and limited study. Many converts say they are often placed in the same role, and it is one of the many reasons we often feel such a pressure to have a solid education in Jewish ritual life. The irony is that converts are often teased about trying to be "more Jewish than the real Jews," a barb that is often aimed in fun at converts but rarely received without a great deal of inner pain.

Another issue I am often asked about my conversion concerns the role of women in Jewish ritual and life. The question usually goes something like this: "How can you convert to a system that allows for an unequal and oppressive treatment of women?" Almost without exception, the questions about this are asked by Jewish women who are either estranged from Judaism or who are struggling to find meaning in a system that can be very oppressive to women. This is an intriguing question to me, and I must admit that like other Jewish women, I am struggling to find the answers to this question. I feel that there is the potential for deeply meaningful expressions of feminine spirituality in Jewish ritual, including the family purity laws and the *mikvah*, but that these meanings must be claimed and created by discourses led and developed by women in communities. I find this to be very challenging and even exhilarating, and feel that this is an exciting time to be a Jewish woman. I also admit frankly that I have no room for a community which refuses to count me in the *minyan*, and so have little contact with Orthodox circles. I am aware, however, that the state of Israel may not allow me the right of return, in spite of my strong commitment to my Jewishness, because I had a Conservative and not Orthodox conversion.

Because these questions about the role of women in Judaism usually come from vibrant and committed women, I have rarely found these questions to be anything but very welcome invitations to lively discussions. But the prevalence of this question indicates another fissure in the fabric of contemporary Jewish life.

The other question I am often asked about my conversion is a somewhat friendlier inquiry, one which invites a thoughtful response from me. It is usually phrased something like this: "What was it about Judaism and Jews that made you want to convert?" I have found that my response to this question depends on a number of unconscious factors. First of all, are the people asking me this question hoping for a certain answer or afraid of the wrong one? Second, does this question afford the asker an opportunity to explore his or her own feelings about Judaism and what can be attractive about it when seen from a new perspective? This question points to another role that converts play in Jewish society. It is often remarked by those who are not lamenting the marked rise in conversion that throughout Jewish history, converts have brought a great deal of new life to the religious community. I certainly believe that this is the case. Converts have a great deal to offer. This particular question is an open-ended invitation for me to express what it is about Judaism that I find spiritually enhancing. These questions more often lead into satisfying discussions of inner issues of spiritual practice and growth, in which I feel that my religious experience is being considered and respected. It is in this vein that I think converts have the most to offer to contemporary Jewish life. It is worthwhile to discover what a person coming from the outside finds engaging and deeply meaningful about Jewish life.

I have recently had to stop and ask myself: Why do I feel really Jewish? How did I get this way? What process has led me to feel Jewish? What situations challenge that sense of identity? In this article, I have been less interested in telling the story of my conversion to Judaism than in talking about the new ritual of asking converts for their life stories. There is a direct relationship between how people who have chosen Judaism, the majority of whom are women, tell their stories about their own conversions and how the larger Jewish and non-Jewish communities experience their altered status.

It would be naive to conclude a discussion of the issues of conversion to Judaism by simply calling for greater tolerance for and acceptance of converts within the Jewish community. It goes without saying that people who choose Judaism feel a need to be accepted as equal Jews, and allowed to develop their relationship to Jewish worship and practice in an accepting and nurturing community that does not regard them with suspicion and derision. And it also goes without saying that converts have special needs regarding their construction of Jewish identities. We face different stresses throughout the year, and have unique challenges in our relationships with our birth families. All of these issues need to be stated.

But more important, there needs to be an open recognition in the community that the issues converts have come to symbolize are in fact real issues: What DOES it mean to be a Jew in the 1990s? Is being Jewish a religion, a culture, or an ethnicity? How does a religious system held together by ritual practice survive in a religious climate which so denigrates ritual action as empty, merely traditional, and even old-fashioned? Can Judaism survive the threats of assimilation and intermarriage? Are women being alienated anew from Judaism as the more Orthodox voices of Jewish life reclaim the center of the discourse? Should Jews become an "invisible minority" and assimilate even more? Converts are in many ways the lightning rods for these vital questions.

Like most converts with whom I have spoken, I welcome discussion about my conversion, and find few of the questions I am asked rude or unpleasant. Many of us find these "narrative moments" to be odd but creative parts of our Jewish lives. These narratives will be the most creative for the Jewish people as a whole when we learn to embrace this dialogic process as an expression of the larger process of Jewish identity creation. All of us—Jews by birth and Jews by choice—need to ask ourselves the question: How do we become *really Jewish?*

REFERENCE

Rosten, Leo (1968). *The Joys of Yiddish.* New York: McGraw Hill.

Chapter 14

You Don't Know Me
Because You Can Label Me:
Self-Identity of an Orthodox Feminist

Norma Baumel Joseph

I am a Jew
a Female Jew
an Orthodox Jew
and a Feminist

It is not always easy to be a Jew. It is difficult to be a woman, demanding to be an Orthodox Jew, and always a challenge to be a feminist. But that is who I am. In many ways men and women have tried to disempower me; even to disown me. The Orthodox world would rather I resigned or disappeared: The feminist world does not believe I can exist. Characteristically, feminists frequently felt that I was too Jewish. Jewish feminists found that I was too religious, and Jews in general decided that I was too feminist. Each part is an Otherness; each term marginalizes and alienates; each category contains a complex entity.

At a Feminist Jewish conference in Jerusalem in 1988, I made the following statement: "You don't know me because you can label me." This declaration was captured in the film *Half the Kingdom* (Zuckerman, 1989). I admitted then that I have contradictory and

Parts of this chapter were developed for the "Regina and Irving Rosen Jewish Studies Lecture" at Queen's University, November, 1995. It was a dialogue with Rabbi Elyse Goldstein, called "You Don't Know Me by My Title: Self-Identities and Modern Jewish Feminism."

clashing feelings; that my life is not one seamless harmony. It is difficult to be a practicing feminist and a practicing Jew. I am a controversy unto myself. And too much to handle for many.

But there is more to the disclaimer. As I viewed the film in the editor's room, I was shocked by my own anger. What had set me off? Those raging words were spoken in Israel, at the First International Jewish Feminist Conference. I was feeling ostracized in the one place where I had looked for acceptance and inclusion. Instead, I was pigeonholed and disparaged. Jewish feminists had tried to manipulate me. And that made me angry.[1]

People frequently tell me that it is not possible to be a Feminist Orthodox Jew. What am I? An oxymoron?

I am who I claim to be: Orthodox, Jewish, Feminist.

I used to refuse those categories, refuse to be called Orthodox or feminist; I am a Jew, I would say. Unimaginatively I would strive for simplicity or escape—so that people would not prejudge, deciding they knew all my opinions just on the basis of those words.

In the initial stages of making the film, *Half the Kingdom,* the participants gathered in Toronto for a short preview clip of baby Sarah's naming ceremony. During the question and answer period a number of women lined up at the available microphones. They wore *sheitels* (wigs). They were angry because there was no Orthodox woman in the film.[2] They maintained that I do not and cannot represent Orthodoxy because I am a feminist. I responded that I was Orthodox; that is part of how I practice religion, of how my parents raised me, of how I raised my children, of who I am. I told them that they cannot take that away from me. Although I made no claim to represent all of Orthodoxy, neither could they.

Regrettably, that was not a unique experience. The film grew out of a conference on Jewish women. There, too, I was not allowed to raise my voice as an Orthodox Jew. The rabbi of the community insisted on a "real" Orthodox woman being on the panel. I was somewhere else in his classificatory system. I must sadly tell you that in this regard my life has not changed so much. Feminists still refuse to see me as a real feminist like themselves; and Orthodox Jews disown me quite readily. Just recently, in two Canadian cities, I was informed that the rabbis in Orthodox congregations would not allow me to speak because they deemed my orthodoxy suspect. And

I was not even speaking about feminism. Years ago, one rabbi had written that Blu Greenberg (a well-known Orthodox feminist author, see Greenberg, 1981) and I were dangerous Jezebels. Just as many of his colleagues, without ever having spoken to me, listened to my lectures, or read what I wrote, he "knew" what I stood for and condemned me.

Unexpectedly, his slander made way for me in certain feminist circles. If I was "dangerous" in the eyes of an Orthodox rabbi, then I might be okay for the feminists. The entire experience troubled me greatly but left me with a great Purim costume.

Predictably, many people have avoided confronting the complex issues of feminism and religion by hiding behind stereotypes. Hence, my disclaimer that I am not known by my titles. Yet I must admit, in many ways I am. I am a professor with a doctorate, a grandmother, orthodox and feminist, community champion and challenger, legalist and social activist. These labels do give an intimation of who I am. I have fought too hard for some of those titles to avoid proclaiming them. But they do not contain nor define me. Moreover, I keep changing. Self-identity is that very difficult yet necessary step in proclaiming oneself, of naming and believing and behaving and growing.

To be sure, the struggle to be an Orthodox Jewish feminist is painful and radical. To pursue a feminist vision within a traditional community is essential. It requires an examination of the roots of that traditionalism, an understanding and appreciation of its history: a commitment to it while, at the same time, arguing for a transformation of it. Significantly, it also necessitates personal patience and persistence. This is not easy. Moreover, the struggle is not just one of access, of insisting on inclusion. Nor is it limited to convincing others of the correctness of one's vision. The struggle is also within oneself. Since as an Orthodox Jew I enthusiastically value that traditionalism and the vitality of the religious community, I worry about the audacity and power of my claims. What right have I and how do I know I am right? How can I welcome new interpretations without losing my legacy? How can I make my vision authentic without completely vindicating or shattering the tradition? How can I support that tradition and community? Must I? How does it support me?

Thus, the need to stay within and find a community has been very trying. The *aggadic* (nonlegal rabbinic narratives) story of Honi, the rainmaker and Jewish Rip van Winkle, reveals parts of this dilemma (*Talmud Bavli, Ta'anit* 23a). Honi sleeps for seventy years. When he wakes up, nothing is familiar. The changed physical environment, however, is not his problem. Rather, he is perturbed by the absence of his friends and the disappearance of his community.

I would like to tell the story of Hana, not Honi. I know that there were women "miracle" workers in our past, with interesting experiences and imaginative stories to tell. But my literature is missing. In the Talmud (Ta'anit 23ab), there is a suggestive story about Honi's grandson, Abba Hilkia. He and his unnamed wife prayed for rain: her prayers yielded more clouds. Was she a rainmaker like the illustrious Honi? So the first part of the problem is trying to restore women to the tradition; to find women's voices in history. But doing that requires careful reconstruction. As a feminist, I worry that we do not gloss over the androcentrism of the text nor the patriarchal hegemony of the community. As a Jew, I want to reclaim the tradition with men in it too. As an Orthodox Jew, I worry about distinctiveness and authenticity. As an Orthodox feminist, I want to restore the tradition, all its laws and rituals, to women too.

The other aspect of the story that is appropriate here, is the desperate search for community. When Honi wakes up he says to God, "*O Hevruta, O Metuta!*" Either (give me) companions or death. And so he dies! He could not survive without his community. Neither can I. That search for community as part of my self-identity has been the central facet of my struggle.

In the second chapter of Genesis, God makes the pronouncement that "it is not good for the earthling (*ha'adam*) to be alone" (2:18). The story has many layers of meaning, including a vision of human heterosexual coupling. But it also has been understood as a metaphysical articulation of humanity's need for a social environment. This declaration suggests both a descriptive and prescriptive pronouncement on the part of the Creator. Humans need humans in community. Religious feminists have been seeking communal acknowledgment and acceptance in both the Jewish and feminist worlds.

Certainly, many Jewish women have not been engaged in the feminist struggle. They have remained satisfied with their role and place in community. There are also many who have not struggled with religion at all; women who have simply dismissed Judaism. Then there are those who have felt tinges of unease, but have buried them in the quest for inclusiveness and survival. Others valued religion but could not find their place or peace within the Jewish world. They either converted or created new visions of spirituality and sacrality. But in the last twenty years there have been an increasing number of religious women like myself from all the denominations, who have struggled with the tradition, believing in its integrity, while refusing to surrender their agency and convictions. The strain to stay within is combined with the drive to transform, but not destroy, the tradition. Furthermore, we strive for acceptance because imbedded in the feminist pursuit of individuation is the search for community.

Hegel wrote that the human community is a series of individuals who do not lose their uniqueness in community (Knox, 1967). Rather, they connect with each other and sustain each other through membership in the social unit. Thus, life in community confers upon the individual obligations and privileges, rights and responsibilities. By performing them, not only do I sustain my community, but I am sustained by it. For me, feminism is my challenge to be a responsible Jew, with all the obligations and rights of the tradition. That is why my Orthodoxy fits so well with my feminism. My quest is to be more involved; to give more because I am capable of giving; to demand full participation in Jewish life as a fully obligated adult Jew. I was thrilled to hear these ideas vehemently challenged, supported, and dissected at the February 1997 International Conference on Feminism and Orthodoxy which gave over one thousand Jews a chance to voice our religious and feminist concerns.

The transformation of Judaism has certainly begun (Joseph, 1995). There are avenues and venues for female participation in all sectors of the Jewish world. The traditional world has also been enriched by the innovations. The most prominent accomplishment is the Jewish education of female Jews. The growing exploration of Jewish law and texts by women is impressive. There have also been major shifts in female ritual participation and levels of communal leadership.

Nonetheless, there is more to accomplish. I am still seeking a Judaism that acknowledges my individuality and a feminism that accepts my religiosity. There are two arenas in which I have been politically active that reflect this dual problem. For many years, I have worked with agunoth, women who cannot obtain their Jewish divorce. Their trials and tribulations are tragic. That *halakhic* Judaism is the means through which some men can torture and extort their shadow wives is deplorable. Everything I believe in is challenged by the system as it now operates. No righteous person can be satisfied with or justify this state of affairs. My activism in this sphere originates from both my feminist commitment and my understanding of the religious ethic of justice and human responsibility in Judaism. My knowledge of Jewish law fuels my sense of outrage since I know of the law's flexibility and responsiveness to human affliction.

That same combined motivation has propelled me into another campaign. In 1988, at the previously mentioned conference, I helped organize the first women's prayer group at the *Kotel*. Since then, I have had the privilege to work with women from all sectors of the Jewish spectrum, as a Director of the International Committee for the Women of the Wall. We have been continuously seeking our rights to pray halakhically as a group of women with *Torah* and *tallit*. From court to commission, the Israeli government has continuously delayed and denied us our rights to full participation. Distressingly, feminists in Israel and North America have also attempted to marginalize us.

There is much to do. I am an Orthodox feminist Jew. I accept the burdens, glories, complexities, and ambiguities of that existence. I wonder where I will be accepted and in what ways I will change. After making the film, many strangers approached me and said: "I know you." Well, they do and they don't.

NOTES

1. Interestingly, after the session things changed radically. Many of us decided that we wished to express ourselves ritually at the Kotel. We went there to pray and unknowingly became the central media focus of the conference. This led ultimately to a long battle in the Israeli courts, still pending, for the right of women to pray with *Torah, tallit,* and voice at the *Kotel.*

2. It is interesting to note how many times women criticized the film because it did not represent their particular perspective. It was as though they expected one

film to depict all female Jews. How ironic, since it is feminism's basic contention that we are not all the same, not reducible to one generic type.

REFERENCES

Greenberg, Blu (1981); *On women and Judaism: A view from tradition.* Philadelphia, PA: The Jewish Publication Society of America.

Joseph, Norma Baumel (1995). The Feminist Challenge to Judaism: Critique and Transformation. In Morny Joy and Eva K. Neumaier-Dargay, (Eds.) *Gender, genre and religion: Feminist reflections.* Groton, NY: Wilfrid Laurier University Press.

Knox, T. M. (translator) (1967). *Hegel's philosophy of right.* London: Oxford University Press.

Zuckerman, Francine (Director) and National Film Board of Canada and Zuckerman (co-producers) (1989). *Half the kingdom* (film). Montreal: Kol-Isha and Studio D.

Chapter 15

The Journey Home:
Becoming a Reconstructionist Rabbi

Elisa Goldberg

I am in the gynecologist's office. I am on the table, staring at the ceiling and trying hard to imagine I am somewhere else. The woman with the speculum begins to ask me questions. "What do you do?" I am studying to be a rabbi. "Oh, how interesting. What made you decide to become a rabbi?" I stumble for an answer. She continues, "I didn't know women could become rabbis." "We can't; I am actually a man in drag." She doesn't believe me.

In truth, the Reconstructionist and Reform movements have been ordaining women for twenty-five years and the Conservative movement for over ten. As in most other professions, women are only now moving into positions of leadership. The visibility of women rabbis is further complicated by the fact that many Americans still think that rabbis are men with long beards, and that Judaism has not changed in 100 years.

I am often asked why I want to be a rabbi, and I struggle to find my answer. Perhaps that is because my reasons for becoming a rabbi change every day. I want to be a rabbi so I can change the world; so I can show the wider world the beauty, wisdom, and richness of the Jewish tradition; so I can be a part of making Judaism alive and fulfilling to Jews today. I want to embody and teach the best my tradition has to offer, serve God, and honor my ancestors by playing an active part in the continuity of our history. I want to be a rabbi, because I cannot imagine anything I would rather be.

Four years ago I began studying at the Reconstructionist Rabbinical College. I went to rabbinical school for all the right reasons and for all the wrong reasons. I went to explore the richness of our heritage so I could one day teach others. I also became a rabbi because I longed for community, because I wanted the legitimacy of the title, the sense that at last I knew "enough," and because I relished the shock value of being a lesbian rabbi.

I believed that I had something to offer the Jewish community; that I could transform my story, my return to Judaism, my passion, into a voice that could call others into our tradition and could enrich the tapestry of Judaism. I have found the process both rewarding and frustrating. I found shapes of being a rabbi that I never imagined, and found new parts of myself called into being. At the same time, I have been disappointed to find that being in rabbinical school does not alleviate my sense that I do not know enough and that I am an outsider to my own tradition.

Judaism is the home I left, the home I felt alienated from. It is also the home I have returned to, the home I have built with my own hands. It is the place where I have been able to make meaning and have found healing. It is the home where I hear the voices of those who have come before me and to whose conversation I add my own voice. My desire to become a rabbi grows out of my own experience of seeking a home for myself and wanting to open the door to others who are looking for their own place to call home.

While growing up, two powerful poles defined Judaism for me: family and antisemitism. I grew up in a family whose members had a strong cultural awareness of ourselves as Jews, but little education or community in which to root that awareness. Judaism meant our extended family and the clannish connection we felt to other Jews. Because my parents wanted to leave the communities of their childhoods for the country, my brother and I grew up in areas where our name, faces, and dark skin reminded us how different we were from our fairer-skinned classmates.

My family history comes through its women. When I was a child the women in my family were almost mythic—large and beautiful, with superhuman appetites and abilities; they ran businesses and harnessed wild men. An illustration: my mother has an ornate porcelain vase that she keeps in her living room. She had always told me that my *Bubbe* Esther, my maternal great-grandmother, had brought it over from Europe. One day it dawned on me that this could not be true, since my *Bubbe* Esther came over as a young girl, dirt poor and illiterate. She probably had no food to eat, let alone a fancy vase.

I called my Bubbe to clarify the story of the vase. My Bubbe was a strong woman who wore high-heels with gold lamé pantsuits, and was famous for the size of her rings. She considered herself a modern woman, and had run from the poverty of her childhood with a vengeance. She loved her mother, whom she described as "Old World"—a woman who kept kosher and lit *Shabbos* candles, but was a demon at the poker table.

My Bubbe laughed when she heard the story about her mother and the vase, and she quickly set me right. The vase had been a peace offering from her father to her mother. My great-grandfather was a bootlegger who disappeared for weeks at a time to tend to the gambling halls he ran. This time, he had been gone for an unusually long period. He had stolen the vase from a brothel in order to appease my great-grandmother. Such are the family heirlooms in my mother's house; such are the oral traditions of my family's Jewishness.

As a child, part of what I learned about being Jewish was that we needed to resist Christianity and be vigilant against antisemitism. Every year our neighbors invited us to help decorate their Christmas tree, and every year I refused. I felt a sense of obligation to defy the pleasures of this forbidden holiday, even though I was fascinated by its beauty. I read books about the Holocaust and drew diagrams of where I would hide out if the Nazis came to get me. My experiences were subtle—not the brutal violence inflicted on many other Jews in this century. Yet, they reminded me of my difference, and the necessity to preserve my heritage from encroachment, whether violent or subtle.

My family's members fit many American stereotypes of *Ashkenazi* Jews. They were dark-skinned, into money, loud, and close-knit. My own pale complexion, quiet ways, and disinterest in material things made me feel like an outsider to my own family. When I was a teenager I was embarrassed by what I saw as the shallow and materialistic values of the Jewish community in which I grew up.

I learned that there were delicate lines that could not be crossed. You were either on the inside or the outside of Judaism; and I always felt on the margins about to fall outside. Judaism was an arbitrary collection of inherited meanings that someone else created and handed down. If one stepped outside of them, Judaism dissolved. The only value of Judaism was the connection to the past.

My connection to Judaism waned during high school. My spiritual search lay outside of the Jewish community. Like many teenagers, I developed a thirst for transcendent experiences and a desire to reach ultimate truths. Art was my passion. I was moved by the act of creating, combining form, texture, and color to give shape to my ideas and feelings. I studied meditation and movement, and gained an understanding of the well of spirit that lies within my body. At fifteen I became a vegetarian; it was my first attempt to pattern my life after my beliefs.

After my first year of college, I went to Israel to live on *kibbutz* to escape my life and indulge an interest in communal living. Israel had much more to teach me than that. There I met my cousins Dan and Herut. Dan was a member of the leftist Mapam party and had fought in Israel's War of Independence in 1948. Herut had been raised on a *moshav*, had been a vegetarian her whole life, and was passionate about her work as a botanist. They shared housework, worried about the moral implications of the occupied territories, and had a library filled with books about Eastern philosophy. They were the first Jews I had ever met who lived out their convictions. They represented to me new possibilities for Jewish life.

Dan and Herut invited me to spend Yom Kippur with them. It was their family tradition to gather their children and grandchildren and drive from Tel Aviv to Jerusalem on Yom Kippur day. We went out for a falafel and tabouli in the Arab quarter, and I am sure they would have ordered *treif* if there had not been vegetarians among us. I loved this approach to Judaism; you only retained what was meaningful, broke the models that did not work, and built new ones. Israel was an incredible experience for me in that way; it opened a door to a living, meaningful, and livable modern Judaism.

After six months in Israel, I returned to University and came out as a lesbian. Coming out is an exciting time as one reveals hidden parts of oneself, abandons old roles, and attempts to move toward wholeness, self-acceptance, and love. Coming out challenges a person to question other aspects of her life and search for truth. Stories of coming out are basic to the lore and culture of the lesbian community. "Coming out of the closet" is a metaphor which describes not only my emerging identity as a lesbian, but as a Jew, and most recently as a person who believes in God. Ultimately, being part of the lesbian community inspired me to explore my identity as a Jew.

At first, being a lesbian made it hard to find Jewish community in Ithaca, New York. I was a baby dyke with a buzz cut and a healthy dose of attitude. Needless to say, I did not fit in with the students at Hillel or my housemates at the Jewish housing co-op. I moved into an anarchist housing co-op and met other like-minded Jews through my work with feminist, lesbian, and antiracist groups on campus. It was news to me that there was a history of radical Jews and that Jews had played significant roles in many social justice movements. I learned about Emma Goldman, Rosa Luxembourg, and the many Jewish women who, like them, had fought for social justice. I was encouraged by their stories, and it is in this arena that I began to find my own Jewish voice.

I organized a seder with a group of Jewish women I knew from feminist, lesbian, and anarchist circles. It was an unlucky potluck where nobody brought food, but everyone brought a bottle of wine. We relished our own outrageousness as we read from a lesbian-feminist *haggadah* and told stories far into the night about our liberation. This was a dizzying first experience that allowed me to own Judaism and realize that it could be fun, meaningful, and exciting. That evening, I discovered that Judaism had something of value outside of being a tradition which must be preserved. It had intrinsic value; it was a gift to offer the world. This was a moment of breaking down boundaries, validating our experiences, and liberating new forms.

Later that spring, a large rally for U.S. Divestment in South Africa had been planned on campus. There had been tension on campus between blacks and Jews, and feelings were running high. Some friends and I decided to bring together a group of Jews active in the Divestment movement to march with a banner that said "Jews Against Apartheid." At first the African-American students thought we were a counter-protest, and then, as they recognized our faces, it became clear that we were allies. Our feeling of fear turned into gratification and pride as we stood together as Jews for a progressive cause, visible and radical and making the connection between antisemitism and racism.

I transformed these experiences into my work for the next few years. In my political work, I was very "out" about being Jewish. Much of this came from my encounter with the politics of identity that were such a major force in my women's studies classes and on the campus in general. These courses challenged me to know who I was and to claim my place in Jewish tradition. As I read lesbian writers, especially women of color authors including Audre Lorde, Gloria Anzaldua, and Barbara Johnson, who were looking at their own traditions, affirming the crossings of boundaries and celebrating their unique perspectives, I felt encouraged to claim my own Jewish experience as authentic. I read the works of Jewish lesbian authors including Evelyn Torton Beck, Irma Klepfisz, and Melanie Kaye/Kantrowitz and felt less alone. The work of these women helped me ease the tension between being a lesbian, a woman, and a Jew. I was grateful to the women who went before me, who mapped out this territory; it allowed me to reach places that we could not have dreamed of a generation before.

In my senior year, I found a resting place, a way to be Jewish that felt like coming home. Three other women and I formed a Jewish Lesbian Torah study group. We called the group Lentl, because we thought the movie *Yentl* would have ended better if Barbara Streisand and Amy Irving had ridden off together into the sunset.

Our first project was another feminist seder. We made our own haggadah, sang songs, and enacted rituals to express our journeys as Jewish women and Jewish lesbians on this evening of liberation. We sang and celebrated well into the night, and this time there was even food.

From that passionate experience grew a group that was to be my community until I left for rabbinical school two years later. We met every Shabbat and studied the *parasha* (the weekly Torah portion). We consulted traditional commentaries, but mostly we responded through our own experiences. We made it a challenge to find the hidden meaning in the text; a grammatical slip would become a long commentary on gender parody: Judith Butler Meets Rashi. We studied for hours, going over the text in microscopic detail. The women of Lentl encouraged me to bring my whole self to the tradition and struggle to make it work. Soon we were meeting on Friday evenings for raucous Shabbat dinners filled with song and laughter. We gathered for holidays, designing rituals for each other and celebrating our passion for Judaism. It was in this group that I finally felt I had found my place in Judaism; in this community I was neither too Jewish nor too lesbian. Being part of Lentl gave me the courage to claim my place in the wider Jewish community.

It is within the context of Judaism that I have been able to heal the broken places I carried into my adult life from my childhood. One such example happened when I returned to the small Massachusetts town in which I had lived as a teenager. My mother, brother, and I had moved there after my parents' bitter divorce.

The year we moved I turned twelve, and my parents insisted that I celebrate a *Bat Mitzvah*. I was unprepared to participate in the service, both emotionally and practically. My tutor tried to convince my parents to cancel the event, but they wanted to prove that life was "back to normal." On that dreadful Shabbat, I stood in front of a congregation I did not know, mumbled half-learned Hebrew words, and waited for the ordeal to be over. My parents held separate receptions for their friends and families, and I spent the rest of the weekend shuttling between them. It was an awful memory that epitomizes the pain of those years.

Two years ago, I returned to western Massachusetts to spend a week at a yoga retreat center, unwinding from my second year of rabbinical school. I arranged to take Shabbat off even though I had no specific plans.

Toward the end of the week, I decided I wanted to go to *shul*. The only open synagogue in the entire county was the synagogue where I had been Bat Mitzvah. As I walked through the vaguely familiar doors the building felt much smaller and the people more friendly. As I donned my tallis and sat down among the thirty congregants, I felt a sense of destiny or fate that had drawn me to return to this place. I was offered an *aliyah* by a smiling woman; instantly, I was transported back to the age of twelve and filled with memories of shame, sadness, and disappointment. For the second time ever, the walls of the sanctuary heard my name called out. This time, I rose and walked confidently toward the *bimah*. I sang out the blessing in a strong, clear voice. As I walked back to my seat, smiling faces and welcoming hands offered me familiar words of "*Yasher Koah*," good job. The scared, hurt twelve-year-old had finally claimed her place as a woman among the Jewish people. I was able to return to a place of much pain and confusion and transform it into a beautiful, meaningful place where I now belonged.

When I applied to rabbinical school, I envisioned myself as a cultural worker, who would bring out the gifts within Judaism in order to inspire Jews to come together. I hoped my rabbinate would be a position from which to work for social justice. I wanted to be a rabbi who used my position to struggle for progressive causes within the Jewish community and represent a Jewish voice within the progressive world. Since then I have come to understand that I cannot live a life of ethical action without a personal spiritual practice.

I have found myself back in my earlier spiritual quest looking for the stillness and deep waters within. I have entered into prayer in new and wonderful ways and I have found myself in a personal and profound relationship to God. I can say for the first time that I believe in God. God, to me, is not just the pleasing image of what makes life meaningful or the process that occurs when people come together. I believe in a God who is beyond me and other human beings, who reaches out in love and compassion.

Lately, I have found meaning for myself in saying prayers of thanksgiving. In using liturgy as a poetic way to express inner thoughts and longings, I am moved by the power of its centuries of use and the beauty of its words. Prayer is a time to contemplate, to quiet the outside world, and to focus on what is important. I have learned that prayer is all of these things, and it is also a time to reach out to God and to wait for an answer.

One of my entryways into Judaism has been text study. I wanted to know the stories of my ancestors and hear their voices. I wanted to know the texts from the inside out, so I could own them and find within them lost stories of women. I used to find the texts offensive and problematic: their masculine God language made them inaccessible to me. Now, I enjoy engaging with the problematic aspects of the texts; I find myself more tolerant of things that are offensive in the tradition. Perhaps this is because I feel more at the center of the conversation; I am not afraid that some man from the second century is going to push me off the page.

Although I still maintain my desire to work for justice, I have become aware of the many different possibilities open to me. I have worked as a nursing home and hospital chaplain and gained insight into the spiritual needs of people facing illness, death, and loss. I am attracted to pastoral counseling, supporting people through times of heightened search for meaning and desire for God's presence. I find it rewarding to be able to offer others support in times of crisis.

As I have gained more confidence as a leader of ritual, I have begun to enjoy its rewards. It fills me up to have helped a couple choose the exact words with which to describe their commitment to each other, to shape prayers to allow a mother to say goodbye to her dead teenage son, and to officiate at the Bar Mitzvah of an eighty-five-year-old man. I have woven myself and my sense of the sacred into the lives of the people with whom I have worked, and I have been richly rewarded.

All around me are rabbinical students and rabbis changing the nature of the rabbinate. They are reaching out to Jews beyond the synagogue and community center. They are affirming the search for meaning and spirituality within Judaism and encouraging others to express their Judaism in innovative and creative ways. There are rabbis exploring the connections between Judaism and other spiritual traditions through yoga, meditation, chanting, and self-awareness. Other rabbis build relationships between Judaism and music, drama, dance. There are rabbis teaching feminist Bible classes and others lobbying for the environment. Innovations in the content and structure of Jewish education are shaping a new generation of Jews. Synagogue rabbis are creating communities of seekers who share leadership of ritual and civic duties. The role of the rabbi is changing in response to the needs of the Jewish community and in doing so is enriching the texture of Jewish life.

It is time for Judaism to turn its focus outward and share the gifts of our history and traditions with the wider community. I admire the Christian clergy who create shelters and soup kitchens or speak out against poverty, violence, nuclear weapons, or for the environment.

As much as I enjoy studying to become a rabbi, I have encountered difficulties and disappointments I had not anticipated. Becoming a rabbi has not lessened my feeling that I will never know enough about Judaism. In addition, my personal struggle to belong is intensified in the Jewish community by the prospect of being in a central, visible role.

One of the most difficult aspects of being a rabbi is having to deal with all that people project onto us. How I greet someone in a restaurant (and what I choose on the menu) may affect their view of rabbis, Reconstructionism, or all of Judaism. I feel that I am expected to be more observant, knowledgeable, spiritual, compassionate, and available. To some, I am the template into which they place their feelings about Judaism, their love and interest or their pain, disappointment, or ambivalence. If I do not live up to these expectations, I risk being another "bad experience" in Judaism.

I am overly cautious about who I come out to about being a lesbian, a feminist, and politically progressive. My own fear of being rejected has been reinforced by the lesbian separatist who told me I had sold out to the patriarchy because I believe in God; by the Orthodox rabbi who said I was an abomination, worse than a Jew for Jesus; by the kindly Catholic man in the hospital bed who was so disturbed that I did not believe in Jesus that he threw me out of the room.

From the moment I heard of the Reconstructionist movement I was heartened by its resonance with my own beliefs, experiences, and visions of Judaism. Mordecai Kaplan, founder of Reconstructionist Judaism, defined Judaism as "the evolving religious civilization of the Jewish people." The movement affirms that it is Jews that are central to Judaism, not law nor tradition; that Judaism will be strengthened through its connections to the wider world, not threatened; and that the survival of the Jewish people is at stake in the reconstruction of Judaism. As Reconstructionists, we seek to make Judaism relevant and exciting while maintaining a connection to tradition. The movement emphasizes creative revaluing of ritual to include new meanings, and building communities with democracy and pluralism at their roots. Because of its members' work to draw people in and not define people out, the movement leads the Jewish community in its commitment to the inclusion of lesbian and gay Jews, intermarried couples, and people previously alienated from Judaism. I am at home with the movement's commitment to equality for women, the integration of feminist vision, and the development of female leadership.

Some days I feel that becoming a lesbian rabbi is the most natural combination in the world, and other days I worry about whether this mixed blessing will keep me from finding a job when I graduate. One of the reasons I decided to become a rabbi was because I believed my perspective as a woman and as a lesbian could help transform Judaism. Allowing the perspectives of women and lesbians to change the shape of Judaism expands Judaism's possibilities and creates a more dynamic community. I have heard the criticism that feminists and lesbian and gay Jews are creating factions within the Jewish community. I work for feminism and gay and lesbian rights because we are part of the Jewish community, and deserve inclusion and because our inclusion is a valuable contribution to the growth and vibrancy of Judaism. It is a move toward wholeness and inclusion for everyone and toward a more complex and stronger Jewish community.

Becoming a rabbi has led me down many roads I would have never taken and enabled me to synthesize many strands of my life. In what other profession could I be a teacher, community organizer, spiritual leader, counselor, and instigator? I envision a rabbi as a midwife, bringing her knowledge, experience, and compassion to another's side. A midwife provides the shell, the structure, for the unfolding of life. The midwives of the Bible, Shifra and Puah, defied Pharaoh in order to deliver the children of Israel and ultimately bring liberation from slavery. This is the type of rabbi I hope to be, guiding and nurturing others toward a fruition of their Jewish selves.

Chapter 16

Becoming Jewish

Brenda Lynn Siegel

For my generation, being a Jewish woman is much easier than it was two generations ago. Although I am unable to escape the prejudices, I am not nearly as afraid as my grandparents were. Judaism is a much more accepted religion as a whole in America than it used to be. However, the combination of being a woman and a Jew has been challenging. I have experienced both prejudicial remarks against Jews as well as extreme interest in my religion. I have never been able to experience simply being normal. There is not a day that goes by that I don't hear at least one remark about my religion. I generally shrug it off so as not to give these antisemitic remarks the worth that they are meant to have. I don't think that people realize the seriousness of these remarks. I consider myself to be a fairly liberal Jew. I was taught growing up that this religion was important to understand because of the cultural aspect, not the religious.

I was taught how each generation of Jews has been persecuted in some way, but I never thought that this would have to be a worry of mine. Then one day when I was a freshman in high school, I was in world history class and my friend and I had been joking around with each other and I looked down at my paper and there were Nazi signs bordering my paper. My best friend had not realized that what she had done was simply not acceptable. She did not know how much it would hurt me. After class my teacher, she, and I all sat down and discussed it. Finally she understood where the root of the problem was. Just two days later my brother got into a physical fight with one of his friends because his friend was picking on Jews. That year I was forced to hear comments such as "Jew bag" and "KIKE!"

screamed down the hall at school to me. Eventually, I learned that these were just kids who did not know any better. They did not know that they would be hurting somebody's feelings; they thought they were just making a joke. They had not been taught, as I was, that everybody has their own beliefs and that it is not OK to pick on them.

"OVEN RIDER!" This was the ultimate insult. This was said to me by a boy who is black. I was surprised to hear him use this terminology toward me, because I thought that being a minority himself, he would know what it was like to be insulted by such a derogatory term. I also did not understand where it was coming from. This was the day that I learned that there are people out there who will simply hate you for what you are. These people have a lot of anger toward society and by taking it out on the majority they will only get an insult back. However, if they take it out on someone who is experiencing the same level of pain, they are successfully hurting someone else. By doing this they justify their own pain.

This insult also grabbed me because it was the first insult that was not based on a stereotype, but an actual historical event. It really hit home because I was compelled to think of the six million Jews who had died in World War II. I was forced to think of what it must have been like to be my grandmother, running from the Nazis. Until I visited Berlin this summer I had not realized that I did indeed have quite a few connections with my grandmother.

In anticipation of going to Berlin I had prepared myself for many old Nazis making antisemitic remarks or even hurting me. I was prepared to be on the lookout. I had this ingrained fear because whenever I thought about Germany, I thought about Nazis, and World War II. The reality, however, was that Germany had become much more liberal in its beliefs. We saw graffiti written all over the walls criticizing the Nazis. By the end of our trip my fear of Berlin was greatly lessened. This was because I had been on a number of tours that educated me both about past events and about how Germany progressed. Each of these tours taught me from a different perspective both about Nazi Germany and about the new liberal Germany. There were two tours that had the biggest effect on me. One was given by a lady whose father had been a victim of the Nazis, and another by a man who gave city tours.

The woman who gave us the tour spoke German, so my cousin and I were left only with my grandmother to translate for us. We were still able however, to see the expression on the woman's face while hearing the translation. These expressions were often of horror and despair, almost as if she were reliving what she knew about Nazi Germany. We saw everything, from the buildings where the Jews had fled many years ago to the synagogue where guards stand even to this day to protect the building from antisemitism and Arab threats. Each new piece of information caused an incredible tension. There were points throughout the tour when I felt as though there was some piece that I was not getting from the interpretation that my grandmother was giving. After much thought, I realized that I was indeed getting all of the information; the piece that I was missing was within me. I was missing all of the experiences that I had while growing up. I was throwing them away as unrelated, when the truth was that all of this information, everything that happened to me, would later help me to understand what I had learned on that tour that day. I realized as the tour went on that although I was not getting the story from the perspective of the woman who was giving the tour, I was getting a perspective from my very own heritage. I was not only learning about the concrete events but also the pain that my family went through generation after generation.

After this tour was complete we sat down to share what we had experienced. My grandmother stated that she experienced a certain level of pain, probably because she was seeing some of what her parents went through the first time they had to run. In addition, she was probably imagining what it would have been like if she had not escaped from Europe in time. She expressed that she was very lucky to have been able to escape. She was glad that her parents were wise enough to leave, because many people in that time period did not believe that it would get as serious as it did. Her parents had been forced to flee before and did not doubt that terrible things could happen; therefore, they left Europe. I grasped all this from listening to my grandmother both when describing her feelings and from the feeling in her voice when she was translating the tour.

My tour with the young German man evoked a new emotion. I was able to learn from him the view that a young person in Germany may have of the Holocaust. He taught us the ways that Germany had changed. This was where my grandmother and I may have differed in opinion. I experienced this tour as a teenager who had to deal with both the issue of learning and remembering the Holocaust, and trying to move on from it. My grandmother experienced this as an adult, who had to leave Europe when she was a teenager because Hitler was beginning his massacre. She was hearing it as a woman who wanted to make sure that it was not forgotten, so that it would not happen again. The part of this tour that really hit home happened at the end.

The young man discussed with us the possibility of erecting a large memorial of the Holocaust in the middle of Berlin. He told us how a competition was held to determine the best design. The one that won was huge. He felt that not only would this monument take up too much space, but also it did not serve its purpose. The memorial was intended to remind people of the horror that took place in Nazi Germany. This young German felt that even if it accomplished this purpose, it would make Berlin a city of sadness that could not be revived because the memorial would always be a constant reminder and a focus. The focus then would not be educating the people of Germany that prejudice is wrong. The other problem that he envisioned with this monument was that it would give people an excuse not to see the real landmarks, such as the death camps. In his opinion, these were the reminders that would have a real effect on the people who had not been around to know that much about the Holocaust. He thought if the monument was put up then people would think that they would know enough, but the truth's that you will never know enough until you have seen the terror of the actual monuments, the ones that were made by pain.

My grandmother felt that this was an excuse because the tour guide did not want to have to remember or learn about the Nazis. She believed that a person could have the monument and then also go to see the historical monuments. I understood this as well. However, being a Jew born two generations after the Holocaust, I knew that it would not be a monument that would teach those who were not there the importance of not allowing prejudice to rule their lives. It takes actual evidence to hit you as hard as is necessary. I also understood his view that this monument could very easily make Berlin a city of misery and depression. There is already so much evidence in Berlin of the Holocaust; there may be a need for more positive progress rather than negative progress.

After visiting Berlin, we visited Holland. I think this may very well be where I learned the most about the Holocaust. While in Holland we visited Anne Frank's house. My health was taken away from the moment I walked into the house. I entered and climbed a staircase, so thin and steep that I could barely walk up. The first section that I entered was the office; I was facing the bookcase that concealed the stairs which led to the place where Anne and her family hid for two years. I walked through a series of tiny rooms, one of which was Anne's room. The wall was still decorated the way that the young girl had left it. Looking at it, I saw exactly the kind of things that my friends or I might have used to decorate our walls when we were thirteen or fourteen. As I looked at these walls, I was terrified. It made the Holocaust even more realistic, because I knew that I was standing in the room of a young girl who had been taken away and killed in this awful war. It was as if I were standing in the room of one of my friends at home who had just been killed.

After we left Anne's room, we squeezed into the room that led to the attic; it was absolutely impossible to fit into. However, the little latch was left open so that we could get the full experience of the claustrophobic environment of the attic. We then merged into a room that was full of selected pieces of the Diary in its original form. Seeing the handwriting and the original paper made the Holocaust even more realistic. As we pushed through the crowds of people trying to see this exhibit, there came a point when we just had to get out of there. This again reminded me that not too many years ago there was a young girl who had stood in the same room, thinking the same thoughts—only she was not allowed to escape.

Thinking that we had finally finished this mentally exhausting tour, I started down the stairs. When I reached the bottom of the staircase, I could hear the sound of the film that was playing; it would murmur horrible acts while showing pictures to document each fact. As the film was playing I glanced around. In each direction I faced another frightening picture of the leftover bodies of Holocause victims or the camps themselves, and I began to realize the extent to which these people had been tortured. Until we eliminate all prejudice, occurrences such as these will continue to happen. These pictures of bodies of skin and bones piled one on top of one another, or incredibly sick women lying in agony, are images that will never leave my mind.

Upon returning to the hotel, I heard my grandmother's view on the Anne Frank house. "Wow! Huh, girls?" was the first thing that she said. I did not think that it had taken her breath away as it had mine. From her description of the house I got the impression that although it was just as intense for her, it was intense for different reasons. She described how stuffed up and crowded the house was. She said that she could not imagine having to hide in that little house for two years without being able to open a window or take a walk or just leave. I think that while maybe for us it had perhaps been very realistic because we had never seen the evidence from inside a victim's house before, but it was so real for my grandmother because she knew that she could have been Anne Frank if her family had not escaped in time. I think that she was feeling what it could have been like if she had stayed. Had her family not sensed that what was already bad would get worse, then she, too, could have been thirteen years old, hiding in a small area, stuffed in with no escape. When she saw how small those spaces were she felt almost claustrophobic, as though there was just no way to escape.

For the majority of my life I have lived in a nonthreatening environment. My biggest problem was those little statements such as kike and oven rider that were screamed down the hall to me by kids who did not know anything different. I never knew what it was like to really be in danger, to fear for my life. I only had to fear having to fear for my life. I learned as a young child that I must always be prepared to leave because if I am not prepared and I am ever threatened, I will have to stick around until it is too late to escape, as many Jewish women did in Europe in the 1940s.

Upon returning from Europe I began to prepare for what became one of the most important experiences I ever had with my religion. All my life I had been one of the few Jewish women in my school. I could not really share my religion and heritage with anyone. Being at Emerson College has been a great experience, because I have had the opportunity to share my religion with other Jews of my generation. I have also been able to learn more about my religion that I was not taught as I grew up. This experience at college has allowed me to grow comfortably into my own beliefs.

When I arrived at Emerson I discovered many Jews at many different levels of belief. One of the first people I met was a boy who had been Orthodox all of his life and who now practically refuses to identify with his religion. He was simply worn out by the way religion had been pushed on him. Finally he was given a chance to make his own decision and he ran. In sharing a friendship with him, I learned a lot about my religion—both negative and positive. I learned about why we do certain things in certain ways as well as the problems with our religion. Never before had I met an Orthodox Jew, I had based my feelings about my religion on how our family celebrated it. When I learned of the hardships that this young man was forced to face while growing up as an Orthodox Jew, I began to understand how someone might run from it.

Considering all that I learned from home, my trip to Europe, and school I formed my own beliefs. I have discovered that I identify most with the culture of Judaism. I cannot identify with the religion as it began, but with the Jewish people as they have grown since it began. It is my history and heritage that draws me so close to my religion. I am interested in learning more about the religious aspects of Judaism although I don't believe that I will ever identify with the religious side of my religion. I have discovered that I do not need to be religious in order to feel accepted. All Jews are drawn together by having experienced and overcome persecution, and without every one of us we would not have survived. I have concluded within myself that my religion is so special because of its history. Although many events were designed to defeat us, none have succeeded. I think that is why people of two generations ago—people such as my grandmother—do not run from the religion. They know that it takes each and every one of us to provide the strength that has been there in the past, that strength that has kept the Jewish people alive.

Chapter 17

How Jewish Am I?

Hannah Lerman

I have been asking myself this question all my life. Am I Jewish? What does it mean to be Jewish? These are variants of the same enigma that I have wrestled with throughout my life. At different times, I have had different approaches and different answers. Ordinarily I did not know what being Jewish was.

I was born into an atheistic Jewish household. My father was probably brought up in an Orthodox family in Russia. After he came to the United States, he became active in the Industrial Workers of the World, an early radical socialist union organization within the labor movement. My mother, born in the United States of Polish parents, had grown up and accepted what probably was a Conservative Jewish tradition. I offer these thoughts tentatively, because my parents' respective religious backgrounds were never directly discussed in our household. What I learned about their backgrounds, I learned indirectly.

My father told me once that he had stopped my mother from lighting the Friday night candles immediately after they were married by telling her that the smoke hurt his eyes. There were no religious ceremonies of any kind in our household. I did not attend a *Passover Seder* until I was an adult. My mother, during my childhood, did, however, maintain a *kosher* kitchen. She knew that both my father and I ate whatever we wanted when we ate outside the house. We lived in a lower-class Jewish neighborhood, so much of that was Jewish delicatessen. A non-Jewish friend once told my mother that I had eaten bacon and eggs at her house, expecting that my mother might scold me. Instead, she asked incredulously, "Hannah ate eggs?" because I wouldn't eat eggs at home. Although I have never observed the dietary laws, I also have never become accustomed to having butter or mayonnaise on a meat sandwich.

I did not get a Jewish education or religious education of any kind. We observed neither *Chanukah* nor Christmas. I was very aware of Christmas, however, as it was portrayed in stores, public decorations, etc. I felt very left out of the celebratory feelings I read about and encountered at school. At first, I had no idea what Christmas or Chanukah was. Probably because my family did not have much money and I knew somehow that I was not part of Christmas I often had sad, needy, left-out feelings as a child during that holiday.

When I was about ten years old, I had a friend whose family was quite religious. For about a year, because of this friendship, I went to services, to Sunday school, and after-school Jewish school despite my father's quite obvious but unvoiced disapproval.

Our apartment was in a Jewish neighborhood in the Bronx. I knew a few Catholics—mainly lapsed Catholics—during my child-hood, but few Protestants of any denomination. One of my best friends in high school was part of an Irish lapsed Catholic family. I greatly enjoyed and anticipated participating in one of her family gatherings in which there was a lot of music and dance.

My extended family was small, consisting mainly of my father's sister and her family, and my mother's aunt and her family. No one I knew on either side of the family was anywhere near my age. They were either at least ten years older or ten years younger. I think this played into how much I liked visiting my friend's family at Easter or Thanksgiving or Christmas. Nevertheless, I was Jewish, although I wasn't sure of what that might mean.

I was my father's daughter because I could discuss ideas with him. He always seemed so wise. Since he continually put my mother down verbally in many ways, so did I, at least in my mind. Only later did I recognize the contradictions in my father's seem-ingly clear ideological view of the world. Once, my father asked me how I could be such a close friend with someone who was Catholic. I don't recall how I answered. I do remember being amazed that he could ask me that particular question; it did not fit my image of him. Also, after we had moved, when I was eight, out of a neighborhood that was becoming predominantly black, my father told me of his regret in acceding to my mother's wish to move out of a now black neighborhood. Nevertheless, he had agreed to the move.

It was always assumed that I would go to college. In orientation at the start of college, I recall the representative from Hillel saying that there was a place for all Jews in the organization, including atheists. That made no sense to me at all. I had never been affiliated with a Jewish organization and had no sense of my identity as a Jew besides the foods I was accustomed to eating.

My first real awareness of Israel came with the Israel-Arab war of 1956. All I knew was that Israel had attacked, apparently making the first move. That seemed wrong. I knew a bit, not much, about the Holocaust and Zionism. The main sense I had about both Judaism and Israel was that they maintained a higher moral stance than others did. My father, by the way, always refused to believe that the Holocaust had occurred. I think it was one of the first things I really disagreed with him about, despite our intellectual arguments. He also did not believe in nationalism and was therefore anti-Zionist and against the establishment of Israel as a Jewish state. As another example of the contradictions in his life, after he retired he worked part-time for the Bonds for Israel Corporation.

Throughout my teenage years, my mother and I had had arguments about whom I should marry. She would say that I should marry my own kind, meaning a Jew. I would answer that I would marry my own kind, meaning whomever I felt compatible with. In my senior year of college, I met and married a man who was not Jewish. He had been raised as a Presbyterian in Norfolk, Virginia. He was, however, ferociously atheist. At the time, I called myself an agnostic. We had atheist-agnostic arguments throughout our three- and one-half-year marriage, something that seems eminently silly in retrospect. When I decided to marry a non-Jew, I enlisted the aid of my father. I told him first so that he could help me tell my mother, which he did. The next thing I can remember is an angry telephone call from my mother's aunt, criticizing me for wanting to marry someone who wasn't Jewish. At some point afterward, however, she called back to apologize.

Once, my husband and I attended a cousin's Bar Mitzvah, as did my parents. It was the first time I ever saw my father attend a Jewish service. I knew it was a sign of great respect that my mother's family called my father up to read during the service. Although he first put the *Tallis* on backward, he read the Hebrew well. This was one way I knew he had had strong religious training. I also knew that his sister, my aunt, was very much involved with Jewish women's organizations connected with her synagogue.

A year and a half after we married, we moved to East Lansing, Michigan, to attend Michigan State University for graduate study, I in psychology and he in physics. In my experience of Michigan, there were no people who were Jewish except in the Psychology Department. These were Jews like me—Jews by cultural tradition but not connected at all to Judaism as a religion. Little that seems remotely connected to me as a religious or even potentially religious person occurred during my graduate school years, except that I couldn't easily get kosher pickles or bagels, which I love, in the Midwest.

After I had received my PhD and was working in my first job in Topeka, Kansas, I began attending a Unitarian congregation. For a time, I attended regularly and appreciated the services but could not bring myself to officially sign the rolls and actually become a member. Although I had never been affiliated with synagogue or temple during my lifetime, I knew I was a Jew. I still did not have any clear idea of what that really meant. In my own mind, if I enrolled as a Unitarian, I would somehow be giving that up. I even gave a talk on aspects of folk music as part of one Unitarian service. I also discovered that many people who attended Unitarian services had been born and raised Jewish.

After I moved to Los Angeles, I lived for fourteen years in a neighborhood that became progressively more and more obviously Jewish identified. In addition to restaurants springing up that sold kosher Mexican food and kosher pizza, I saw families walking past my house on their way to services on Saturday mornings. They were dressed in their best. The men had long black coats and wide-brimmed hats; the women wore long, loose dresses and wore something on their heads too. It took a while before I remembered that Orthodox women covered their heads in public and also remembered the reason why they did so. As the years passed in that house, I grew progressively less and less comfortable as I walked around on Saturdays in my usual T-shirt or sweatshirt, jeans or shorts. I came to fear, knowing that it was irrational, that someday I might be stoned. When, for unconnected reasons, I moved to a more diverse neighborhood in 1991, I breathed a sigh of relief.

At two different times, while walking down the main local thoroughfare, I saw notices taped to the door of a Jewish temple. One time, the notice involved a complaint against something that had been printed in *The Los Angeles Times*, inviting people to attend a burning of that newspaper. I could hardly believe what I saw and looked at the notice over and over again to be sure of what I had seen. The other notice, at a different time, discussed what was seen as an increase of antisemitism in the United States generally and Los Angeles specifically. It advised that everyone keep their passports current so that they could leave the United States quickly should it become necessary. My blood ran cold when I read this.

During these years, I had only one direct experience that I would call significant. One of my friend-colleagues, who had grown up in a Protestant home, felt an affinity to Judaism and had converted. She invited me to participate one weekend in a Jewish women's encampment group. I spoke to them and facilitated their speech about what I knew—empowerment for women in a general sense. I came away from that weekend feeling accepted and knowing that I could be a Jew in whatever way fit me, an idea that had been very shaky in me before this experience.

It became painfully apparent to me during the last year of his life that my father had never fully integrated his movement away from Judaism. My parents lived their last years in a Jewish retirement home in Los Angeles' most Jewish neighborhood. I helped them find such a place at their request. They both were most comfortable among other Jewish people. Shortly after my mother died from a sudden heart attack in 1980, my father began to refuse to eat. He was fearful, he told me, that the people in the home were poisoning him because of his anti-Israel views. He began to wish to die and, I believe, willed himself to do so. He died suddenly, approximately one year after my mother's death, without any apparent illness as the cause.

In 1981, for the first and only time, I visited Israel in order to attend an International Sex Roles Conference. The impact of this experience began before I got onto the airplane. For El Al airlines, each and every bag was opened and inspected for security purposes. This was long before U.S. airport security was bolstered. On the plane, the attendants were not female stewardesses but burly men. This also was for security purposes, but it seemed somewhat funny to see them handing out food trays. I sat next to a woman who was returning to Israel after visiting her son in the United States. She had been born in the United States but had made *Aliyah* to Israel. She tried to persuade me that this was something that I should also consider doing.

I was stunned during my entire visit by how familiar the people looked. Eventually, I figured out that most of the people I was seeing had the same Eastern European background that I did and that their physiognomy was familiar and made me feel comfortable. I was also extremely impressed with how small Israel was, and how significant religions of all kinds were in its history. This was especially true in Jerusalem, where I found that several different Christian sects had jurisdiction over different parts of one single church building. When I saw the Wailing Wall and the Moslem mosque that stood behind and above it, I despaired of the possibility of any end to the Middle Eastern strife between Jews and Arabs. I was especially affected by Masada and Yad Vashem, although in fundamentally different ways. A tour of Masada impressed me with the ingenuity with which everyday living was managed by my ancient ancestors who had lived in and defended that mountain fortress.

Going to Yad Vashem, a memorial to the Holocaust, felt like a holy experience. I was face to face with this historical event, something that I had not fully experienced before. The feeling was similar to one I had experienced earlier when I visited Pearl Harbor. The emotional impact was much stronger, however, at Yad Vashem. In both places, I felt the weight of responsibility for the tragedy of senseless deaths, because I am a member of the human race which can do such horrible things.

After the conference, I took a bus to Beer Sheba, making sure, on the advice of my cousins who lived there, to arrive before sundown as it was Friday. It was this bus trip, of approximately four hours, that particularly impressed me with Israel's small size. My destination was almost at the other end of the country, but it took less time to traverse Israel than to travel by land between Los Angeles and San Francisco. I also saw how prominent the presence of soldiers was as our bus was searched after various stops. The trip was a difficult one for me as I speak neither Yiddish nor Hebrew. I did not leave the bus to purchase food because I feared that I wouldn't have been able to learn when it was leaving again. I learned too that no buses ran on the Sabbath. My cousins were not particularly religious, but Israel's laws and customs certainly are.

My cousin, a nuclear chemist, lived with his wife and several sons in an apartment which they owned. The rooms were tiny and the space at a premium, but they put me up for two days. I heard his wife rail against the new Jews in Israel, those arriving from Africa and Asia, whose customs and manners she did not share or like. I had one conversation with my cousin that particularly impressed me with the difference between his life and mine. It had begun with my talking about my recently purchased dog who was meant to be a watchdog. My cousin, who had been raised on a *Kibbutz*, told me about the two watchdogs at the Kibbutz, one who located intruders while the other held them at bay. This was very different from what I meant by watchdog! My dog was only meant to bark and notify me about possible intruders, not fight them.

At the very first meeting of what became the Feminist Therapy Institute, which occurred not very long after my trip to Israel, I began to understand something about the relationship between Judaism and ethics. The Feminist Therapy Institute's interest in ethics was evident at the very first meeting, especially in Laura Brown's presentation. I had never before heard a Jewish woman speak with a background in and specific knowledge of Jewish ethics. She applied this to feminism and psychotherapy. As a result, I began to learn something I didn't know about my own background. I am very appreciative to Laura for alerting me to the fact that there was cultural continuity and history behind my own interest in ethics.

I am still not very knowledgeable about the Jewish religion or even Jewish customs in many areas, but this was the first time I recall having encountered the Jewish ethical tradition directly. I have often been slightly embarrassed about the lacuna in my knowledge of Jewish lore in general. I recall a feminist psychologist who had been a Catholic nun asking me and another Jewish feminist psychologist what motivated our activism. She kept referring to God. We two vehemently shook our heads and responded in approximately the same way. It had nothing to do with God for us; it had to do with incorporated values—you are supposed to leave this world a little better than you found it, we both said almost in unison. It was several years later before I learned just how very Jewish that value was and how much my moral and ethical sense had been shaped by Jewish values without my even realizing it. At a later time, I realized that my interest in historical scholarship was probably also tied to my Jewish cultural connection.

For a long time after I first began doing psychotherapy, I was uncomfortable whenever a client—any client—mentioned his or her religious faith, regardless of the particular religion involved, but especially if the client mentioned Christ. I do not recall this having arisen during my internship or while I was being supervised, and I don't think I have ever discussed this issue with either a supervisor or another therapist. For a long time, I mostly stayed silent whenever a client spoke of his or her faith. I do not recall exactly how or when my feelings about this changed. I am now more comfortable in talking with individuals of any religious persuasion about their faith. I do not usually bring up the issue but I will, when appropriate, translate some therapeutic point into their religious terms. I do not know precisely when I arrived at this point but I think that it has occurred as I have become more comfortable with my own relationship to religion. Most often, when it comes up, I will tell a client that I am Jewish, although, on occasion, with more severely disturbed persons, I will let them continue to assume that I am not Jewish. Some of these individuals have religious delusions and irrational beliefs. I have sometimes omitted telling them about my Jewish identity when I felt that it would interfere with the therapeutic relationship and my ability to continue to help them.

I have learned through my contact with clients that each religion gives its own particular twist to people's psychological makeup. I am most familiar with Jewish guilt, Catholic shame, and the varying effects of different kinds of Protestant prohibitions. Not everyone in these religions carries these general themes in the personality but a number of people do. I have not seen enough non-Christian or non-Jewish religious people to get a feel for how other religions affect people's psychological development.

During the 1960s and 1970s known as the humanistic era in psychology, I was chided from time to time for my lack of spirituality. At one time, I owned that as a personal defect. My best answer came during a workshop with Ira Progoff. His work is based on Jungian ideas and involves a structured form of journal writing. In this workshop, I wrote a dialogue with my inner wisdom figure who turned out to be an old New York Jewish woman, accent and all! "Don't worry," she replied in answer to my question, "It'll come when you're ready." My father was defiantly nonspiritual and pragmatic in his approach to life and I know that, in part, my approach comes from him. I have from time to time been attracted to, although I have never fully accepted, the Goddess ideas of new age feminists. Since 1981, I have worn, as a sort of amulet, a small gold reproduction of the Primordial Goddess plate from Judy Chicago's "The Dinner Party."

In fall 1995, I visited Ellis Island, now a museum in which the original immigration station has been reconstructed. Although this is not a religious setting, my experience there was indeed spiritual. I was glad that I was alone. I wandered around with tears in my eyes for four hours, letting the awareness of the painful experiences of my parents, grandparents, and so many others, seep into me.

During the same months, I accidentally heard a talk Ram Dass had given at the University of Judaism. After waking one night at 3:30 a.m., I turned my radio on to use as background noise to help me get back to sleep. I had heard Ram Dass before and viewed him as one of the more sensible new age religious personages. This time, I was enthralled as he talked about his middle-class Jewish upbringing in Boston as Richard Alpert, the absence of spirituality in that setting and his subsequent search. I listened for two and a half hours, and I did not sleep again that night.

Shortly afterward, I attended the 1995 Feminist Therapy Institute meeting in Albuquerque. Our evening "entertainment" was a performance piece by Rabbi Lynn Gottlieb incorporating modern dance, Jewish tradition, and feminist ideas. In one part, she dealt with the relationship of rebellious Lilith to Adam, and in another, she portrayed Sephardic Jews from Spain who did not even know they were Jewish. If I lived in Albuquerque, I would have no qualms about attending her services.

Rabin's assassination occurred during our FTI weekend. Sunday morning, Rachel Siegel, always able to touch an important emotional core, said "Thank God it was a Jew," meaning, of course, that chaos and war would likely have occurred if the assassin had been an Arab. I then expressed my feeling: "Oh my God, it was a Jew," reflecting the remains of my feeling that Jewish people were ethically superior to others.

So, where am I now? Open, I think, more open than I have ever been to the values of my tradition where once I tended to ignore my background. I probably won't join any temple or ever ascribe to traditional views, but I will continue to listen and learn and broaden my view of what spirituality can offer me in my life. I know now that Jewish history and tradition are a large part of what has formed me and allowed me to do what I do, and I have become comfortable with this. In the future, I hope to learn even more about Jewish history and literature. I am recognized and fully accepted as a Jew in all the circles I care about despite my lack of religious affiliation. I also have accepted myself as a secular Jew, but a Jew nevertheless.

Chapter 18

The Politics of Coming Home: Gender and Jewish Identities in the 1990s

Rachel N. Weber

INTRODUCTION

We are witnessing a retreat from the melting pot ideal; the stew is evaporating, leaving chunks of undissolved difference and unassimilated identities. Liberal pluralism, the basis for our system of democratic governance, is in disarray. For example, forty years ago *Brown v. Board of Education* sought to desegregate the schools, decrying a system that separated children solely on the basis of their race. Today, school districts in Baltimore and Detroit are attempting to develop single-sex public schools for African-American boys in order to remedy the same feelings of inferiority that the *Brown* decision in 1953 sought to eradicate. Segregation, cultural immersion and acknowledging difference, many now claim, are the only means of achieving substantive quality (Smith, 1996).

This dramatic course reversal represents a choice that many Jewish women face, whether consciously or not. In both choosing a Jewish identity and pursuing equality, one confronts a variety of options: between a Jewish identity limited to cultural affiliation or one more rooted in theology, faith, or politics, or between balancing one's own difference with others' claims for more radical kinds of difference. At their heart, these decisions force us to confront our often conflicted and ambivalent desires to identify as Jewish women in contemporary American society, a society struggling to come to terms with cultural and religious pluralism. How can we be both equal and different? How should we value and express our Jewishness? Do we even have a choice? What is distinctive and worthy in the Jewish tradition that we wish to perpetuate? What tragic flaws do we wish to transcend?

The following essay is an attempt to explore these questions, questions which comprise what political philosopher Iris Marion Young (1990) calls "the politics of difference." Oscillating between personal anecdotes and academically mediated reflection, this chapter is a frank meditation on my own ambivalence about Jewish community and Jewish identities. In a time when the alienation of young Jews from organized Judaism is a tremendous cause for concern, it is especially significant to recognize that some of the reasons for this alienation lie within the cracks of our own communal identities.

COMMUNITY AND DIFFERENCE

For many Jews, the ideal of community is shrouded in a soft, warm glow. We talk about "the Jewish community" as if it were one big congregation pursuing a common, but unstated, goal. We pity others who do not possess such communal resources—the after-school programs, the summer camps, the social networks, the well-documented histories—that many Jews around the world are able to draw upon. Those who gravitate toward a more secular Judaism claim that it is the community, and not so much the theology, that sustains their identity, their sense of belonging.

But there are also critics of the community ideal. Some question the possibility of such forms of social organization in contemporary America. Community, they claim, is a nostalgic concept whose heyday has come and gone with the advent of suburbanization and its accompanying spatial fragmentation. Trading in the *shtetl* for the suburb, many American Jews have found it difficult to retain a sense of belonging and community when it is not imposed on them, by residential segregation and poverty, for example.

And for those who do not feel accepted by the mainstream, community is synonymous with exclusivity. Iris Marion Young (1990) points out how too often community has connoted sameness and homogeneity to the detriment of those who are perceived to be different from the representative majority. A multiplicity of oppositional voices are stifled in an attempt to craft a cohesive American-Jewish community, a singular and monolithic Jewishness. Growing up in a suburban Conservative synagogue, I do not remember hearing these voices: gay and lesbian Jews, Jews critical of Israel's treatment of Palestinians, Jews challenging the status and wealth that so many in the congregation seemed to enjoy. I remember hearing how Jews should not air such multiplicity in public because "it's a *shondah* for the *goyim*."

Although I too strive for a particular ideal of community, part of what has turned me away from organized Judaism is a kind of smug exclusivity, what I see as an exaggerated dichotomy between assimilation and retaining a sense of cultural distinctiveness. Community has been reinvented and deployed by those who advocate for a symbolic *shtetl* of difference, removed from an American mainstream. Many with a stake in organized Judaism seek to reify the boundary between an "us" and a "them." In order to preserve this sense of difference, representatives of organized Judaism frequently have opted for two strategies: (1) accentuating the negative aspects, such as the persistent antisemitism, of mainstream America; and (2) accentuating the benefits that accrue exclusively to Jews because they are members of a special community. I am uncomfortable with both strategies.

As an example of the first strategy, I revisit a rabbi's recent Yom Kippur sermon. In the fall of 1995, I went to synagogue in need of spiritual guidance for turbulent times. The Republicans had raided Congress and were beginning to dismantle the welfare state, the Israeli-Palestinian peace accord had been signed, and the religious right seemed to be gaining ground in all parts of the world. How could we, a congregation of Jews in upstate New York, make sense of such events? The rabbi indeed picked up on the topic of religious fundamentalism, but his message was not meant to help us interpret events or even to take a stand and condemn the blending of politics and religion. Instead he warned, with hellfire and brimstone rhetoric, that evangelical Christians were singling out Jews for conversion and that, once again, we were the targets of zealots. He said nothing about what this meant for the United States generally, only that we, *as Jews*, needed to be on our lookout yet one more time. Stick together and stay inside where it is warm, he seemed to urge;

retreat from the cold and soulless world of the gentiles because they still despise you. Such is our lot.

The second strategy is something that I have internalized, and for which it is harder to identify a culprit. All my life, I have heard that Jews have a monopoly on achievement. A high political office, an Oscar, a great thought—all Jews, knowing shrugs—what else would you expect? And a litany of reasons follow: Jews have had to be better than their (whose?) best, because we've been excluded for so long. We needed to prove ourselves on their (whose?) terms. We have always emphasized family and education and success.

I realize that these success stories are complex survival strategies. These stories are not all bad; after all, they have served to legitimate my own goals and ambitions. As I toil on my dissertation, I like to think that I am traveling on the well-worn footpath of all the brilliant Jews who came before. In my moments of doubt about my own position as a woman in academia, I am comforted by the fact that I have inherited a legacy of Jewish excellence. I look to the picture of Hannah Arendt pasted on the wall in front of my desk. However, these feelings also stand in the way of me attributing my success to my own personal investment and merit. Legacies are not as self-empowering as the feeling of individual accomplishment.

The rabbi was urging his congregants to adopt a particular kind of Jewish identity—an identity based solely on years of domination, an outgrowth of historical inequity and discrimination. He was reminding us that Jews are different because they are perceived to be so by the outside world. On the other hand, however, we are told that we are entitled to success in this world simply because we are Jews. In a sense, these two strategies are perfectly compatible with each other; prejudice and chauvinism have bred an often exaggerated sense of collective specialness. Regeneration has required some mental line-drawing.

But neither option convinces me that I should be part of a Jewish community. I do not want my Jewish identity to be based on fears of antisemitism nor do I want to assume the smug sense of entitlement that I have observed in the halls of privilege. In trying to salvage my own Jewish identity, I hope to challenge the assumption that Jews are different simply because we have received unequal treatment. I am certainly not denying the importance of the historical injustices that have been directed at Jews. Identities based only on years of suffering or on exclusivity, I believe, prevent the formation of an identity that is not premised on inequality; we should, I believe, be focusing on what is good and unique and joyous about Judaism while continuing to keep the memories of suffering alive in order to support our own struggles and the struggles of others.

GENDER DIFFERENCE

In his book *Jewish Renewal,* Michael Lerner (1994) rightly points out that many Jews have left Judaism not because assimilation offers such enticing prospects for personal advancement or because it is so difficult to retain a sense of Jewish identity. Rather they have left because organized Judaism has imbibed some of the worse traits of wider American society: its materialism, its slavish pursuit of the market, its conservatism. For me, perhaps the most disconcerting aspect of this mimicry is what I perceive as organized Judaism's treatment of gender. Is there a place in contemporary Judaism for single women—feminists like myself? For women who work outside of the home and may not have time/money/status to join the sisterhood? For lesbians and gays?

At a recent family event, my aunt asked, "When will we be able to call you 'Doctor Rachel'?" Before I could open my mouth to answer, my uncle burst in, "More important, when can we call you 'Mrs. Doctor Rachel'?" This is not such an out of the ordinary exchange; when I return to the congregation in which I was raised, I feel that my professional achievements are regarded as secondary to my social life. I am confident that my generation has it easier than the previous *Sheila Levine Is Dead and Living in New York* (Parent, 1972) generation. Nonetheless I feel that I am judged by different standards. I must be able to entertain and make a chicken like my mother and raise bright, beautiful children in addition to pursuing my career goals. I must wear outfits and groom myself in a manner that meets community standards. While my brother is able to define himself through a broad spectrum of activities, I am judged on those terms that relate to my ability to marry and create a home.

The more I delve into tradition and texts, the more I find how deeply embedded sexism is. From the laws of ritual purity to the denial of women's *aliyot*, so as not to ruin the concentration of praying men, patriarchy pervades some of Judaism's most basic customs. Jewish traditions have excluded women from entire spheres of experience and deprived us of many opportunities for positive religious identification.

I have tried on a variety of Jewish denominations and communities for size and have encountered sexism in each. I thought that I had at last found a home in the Jewish world when I joined a small Orthodox congregation in Berkeley, California. Here were other academics and progressives actively engaged in seeking knowledge and breathing new life into ancient texts. Men and women were separated by a thin rail, but there were announcements about a women's Talmud study group and women's Torah reading lessons. One Friday night, I came to pray and found nine men engaged in a huddle with frowns on their faces. "Rachel, please help us out," one asked. "We need one more man for the *minyon,* and Dr. Greenbaum is stuck home with his kids. Could you go and baby-sit for him so that he can come and pray with us?"

Judith Plaskow (1973) writes "Every time I let myself be lulled into thinking that I as a whole person am a member of this community, some event lets me know in no uncertain terms that I am wrong." She argues that to be inclusive of women, Judaism must be transformed at its core. This involves new interpretations and reevaluations of existing traditions—continuing the work that many Jewish feminists began, as a more clearly defined movement, in the early 1970s. Judaism must be able to offer a retreat, an alternative paradigm if it is to attract and sustain independent women.

CHOOSING JUDAISM

In the 1990s, we are told that free will and agency are the name of the game, allowing us the freedom to "choose" any form of religious practice that our heart and soul crave. In an interesting article about conversion titled "Choosing My Religion," Stephen Dubner emphasizes this fact noting that "We have *chosen* our religion, rejecting what we inherited for what we felt we *needed*." Dubner (1996) states that this new freedom contrasts sharply with the experience of our parents and especially our grandparents; they had little or no say about whether or not to identify as Jews, and their spiritual practice was more or less circumscribed by the heavy hand of tradition, prejudice, and family. Although he ignores the experiences of Jews from previous generations who challenged the mainstream and chose alternative routes, such as, socialists, and ethical culturists, he raises many important issues regarding our attitudes toward our faiths.

Dubner believes that such unencumbered freedom is a distinctively American phenomenon. America is a rare nation, he states, where religious identities are optional and available. Countless numbers of people, estimated by some to be about 30 percent of the population, are taking advantage of this freedom to switch denominations. Choosing a religion means more than choosing a new perspective on God—"it informs how we talk, eat and vote, how we think about justice and history, money and sex. We choose a new religion to choose a new self, to set ourselves apart from where we have come." For some, choosing means hopping from one denomination to another, and for others, like myself, it means renewing and, in the process, reevaluating the religion one inherited at birth.

But "choice" is a funny word, a word that although venerated by free market principles and the political doctrine of free will, does not adequately describe behavior. Our decisions are never so unencumbered; they involve weighing obligations with notions of what we judge to be feasible and acceptable. Shopping for a spiritual practice that will fit one's needs reminds me of how much consumerism has come to mark every aspect of our lives. Although it is just a metaphor, the notion of exercising choice and individual preferences in the marketplace of religions obscures the complexities of lineage, obligation, and prejudice.

Sometimes you don't have a choice. I was in a bar in Dallas, Texas, so you could say I was asking for it. But then again, I wanted to prove to myself, and indirectly to the world at large, that a Jew could be in Texas, that a single woman could be in a bar. The idea of "knowing one's place" seemed like an anachronism in the 1990s; I felt that my street smarts and world weariness provided me with a passport for infinite mobility. Out of the corner of my eye, I saw the guy with the crew cut approach. He stuck his face in my field of vision and asked casually, "You a Jew?"

"Why do you want to know?" I stammered, my passport for infinite mobility dissolving.

"See my friend over there?" he said, pointing to a similarly puffy, crew-cutted fellow. "He likes Jewish girls."

I couldn't think of a retort. "I'm not going to answer that question. It's rude."

"Guess that means you're a Jew." He started to walk away just as the magnitude of the situation hit me. I reached for his shoulder and cursed him as a small group of onlookers congregated. He ran for the door, his friend following on his heels. I went to the bathroom and stared at my face for what seemed to be hours. What gave me away? Is it written on my face, on my nose, in my hair, in my posture, my voice? It doesn't matter whether or not I choose, voluntarily, to identify as a Jew; I will always be identified, involuntarily, as one. There are moments when I relish this identification and others when I want to run from it.

A DIFFERENT JUDAISM?

I have always known that I learn the most lasting lessons about difference by closely attending to the ways in which the differences inside me lie down together. (Audre Lorde, 1988, pp. 117-118)

Identifying as a Jew is fraught with complexity because there is no such thing as a typical Jew. We must challenge the notion that there is one singular Jewish identity, despite the fact that many of us carry around stereotypes of what ideal Jewish women are. We are all constituted of multiple identities and roles which come together in some instances and clash in others. Although it may feel confusing and conflicted, this mutual recognition should be celebrated because it gives us a wellspring of experiences to draw upon in order to understand the world. Both bell hooks (1984) and Susan Moller Okin (1989) say that our moral understandings grow as we move through a series of roles and positions. Moller Okin states that it is both possible for moral agents to deliberate from the perspective of different people, and that it is a desirable model for reasoning and decision-making in a pluralistic society.

Judaism emphasizes these transcendent and empathetic qualities. Through table conversations framed by the *Hagaddah*, my family, friends, and guests shared accounts of Jewish life and spirit at our Passover *seder*. As we told the story of the exodus, narrative accounts of our own experiences bubbled over. My grandmother, who fled Germany in 1939, told of her exodus, and the younger people at the table, many of whom had never spoken with an actual survivor, were transfixed. She ended her story with outrage about the genocide in Bosnia and an angry question: "Why do we give our money to memorials to the Holocaust when there are so many living the Holocaust today?" The command to remember the stranger and the oppressed is unconditional but the memories and stories should also be models for understanding and guides to action.

As an heir to these rich stories, I often wonder what chapter I'm in now. I'm nostalgic for the ethnic enclaves and communal identities of my parents and grandparents, but I also see where this has led them in the later years of their lives: to senior communities and malls in Boca Raton, Florida, models of exclusive homogeneity with racist undertones. Is there a community that I would feel at home in?

I would be at home with a spiritual and political practice built on hope and idealism, concern for economic and social justice, new moral convictions, intellectual dynamism. This is not just my laundry list of what I "need" from a religion; it is a revelation of what Judaism is at its core, what I could find there if I chose to dig a little deeper. I am inspired by the recent movement for Jewish Renewal and the magazines *Tikkun* and *Lilith*. It is the transformative power of Judaism—the ability to see the world as flawed and in need of fixing—that has always encouraged me to think in terms of alternatives. When I observe the increasing polarization and spatial segregation of our society, when I observe the job loss and the pain, the violence and the degradation, I know that things can change. Where did this liberatory political vision come from? Not from evidence or historical proof of what is politically feasible but from my own, Judaism instilled, convictions about the possibility of God's presence. Despite my frustrations about finding a place in organized Judaism, I see that it too can change.

REFERENCES

Dubner, Stephen (1996). Choosing my religion. *The New York Times,* March 31.

hooks, bell (1984). *Feminist theory: From margin to center.* Boston, MA: South End Press.

Lerner, Michael (1994). *Jewish renewal.* New York: Grosset/Putnam.

Lorde, Audre (1988). *A burst of light.* Ithaca, NY: Firebrand Books.

Moller Okin, Susan (1989). *Justice, gender and the family.* New York: Basic Books.

Parent, Gail (1972). *Sheila Levine is dead and living in New York.* New York: Putnam.

Plaskow, Judith (1973, Summer). The Jewish feminist: Conflict in identities. *Response, 18*, p. 12.

Smith, Stacy (1996, March). *Voluntary segregation: Gender and race as legitimate grounds for differential treatment and freedom of association.* Paper presented at the Annual Meeting of the Philosophy of Education Society, Houston, Texas.

Young, Iris Marion (1990). *Justice and the politics difference.* Princeton, NJ: Princeton University Press.

Chapter 19

"Why Kafka?" A Jewish Lesbian Feminist Asks Herself

Evelyn Torton Beck

To my knowledge, I was neither a lesbian nor a feminist when I began my Kafka research in 1966, but that doesn't explain my continuing interest in his life and works long after I began to use a feminist lens and even after I came out as a lesbian in the mid-1970s. It only explains why gender issues are not part of the discussion in my 1971 book, *Kafka and the Yiddish Theater: Its Impact on His Works.* This essay is an attempt to chart my journey with Kafka and to explore the meanings of my absorption in his work which continued long after I had lost interest in working with texts by virtually all other male writers of fiction, including those I had been teaching in my "Yiddish Literature in Translation" courses.

Perhaps it will help if I explain how I came to Kafka in the first place. In ten years of graduate education in literature (at Yale and at Wisconsin), I had never been assigned a single Kafka text, and given his reputation for incomprehensibility, I was not especially eager to try one. But in those days, I had a theory that often proved true. If one did not "fill one's gaps" of essential knowledge oneself, one would eventually be forced to fill them under severe pressure (I called it "the revenge of ignorance"). And so it came to pass that I had to read *The Trial* in a single sitting for a class I had unexpectedly been assigned as a Teaching Assistant at the very last minute.

With Kafka and me it was not love at first or even second sight. I taught *The Trial* (Kafka, 1956) in a frantic and groping fashion that was matched only by Josef K.'s blind and ultimately futile struggle. You may remember that K. succumbed in the end, while I ostensibly succeeded, thankful to have gotten through the semester, but still singularly unimpressed with this "master of modern literature" who was said to speak for "modern Man." Kafka's work did not come to life for me until much later, when I read his *Diaries* (1949) and *Letters* in which his life-long struggle to make sense of the universe is linked to his experiences as a Jew. Suddenly, his fictive world seemed connected to something that felt familiar, though I could not yet articulate what in my life he tapped. Although I was not a young graduate student, but a returning faculty wife and mother of two, my awareness of just how deeply my experiences of being a Jewish child survivor of the Holocaust had marked me was still dim and not speakable. Had I allowed myself to think about it, I would have had much evidence in hand.

I would never have come to do my Kafka research at all had I not been pressed by my father to study Yiddish at an after-school Jewish center of learning. These studies began a few years after my family and I landed in Brooklyn, having narrowly escaped the Nazis in Vienna (where I had been born) and Italy (to which we had fled). Had I not learned Yiddish, I would never have thought of trying to unearth the Yiddish plays that had influenced Kafka in Prague. And I would never have discovered that the overall themes of these plays and many of their individual scenes had found their way into Kafka's fictions in transmuted form without the historically specific details.

And of course, it is the details that give it away. Take, as only one example among many, the opening scene of *The Trial* in which Josef K. is arrested for no apparent reason by two bumbling warders dressed in identical costumes who seem to have no idea of what he stands accused. The transparence of the language disorients by the incomprehensibility of the events it so easily describes. How differently we read this scene once we know its origins in an obscure Yiddish tragi-comedy set at the time of the Inquisition, in which the hero is arrested by two clowning henchmen because he has indeed been denounced to the authorities by someone who knows his true identity as a hidden Jew.

Because Kafka was born into a Jewish family in the last decades of the nineteenth century, the "Jewish question" was part of his frame of reference from his earliest years on. But it was not easy for

Kafka to come to terms with Jewish identity, something he had not chosen and did not know how to embrace, though it never ceased exerting a powerful pull. In the openly antisemitic climate of Prague (and the even more virulent Jew-hating of nearby Russia and Poland), Kafka could not easily ignore this fact of his life. He had, already in his adolescent years, rejected both religious observance and membership in the Zionist youth movements, the two paths chosen by many of his Jewish contemporaries. Instead, he created a sharp division between the personal and the public.

He kept the specificity of his confusion over the meaning of Jewish identity out of his fiction and instead, recorded it in his private writings. There he could allow himself to speak of painful episodes of childhood taunts, as well as the more open antisemitic attacks which he witnessed and experienced as an adult. Throughout his life, Jewish identity remained a source of ambivalence for Kafka—one that he met with a mixture of pride and pain, comfort and shame, which he found difficult to voice directly. As French critic Marthe Robert has insisted, because the word "Jew" is continually repressed in Kafka's fiction, it becomes charged with a powerful dynamic that presses upon his texts and begs to be named (Robert, 1982).

Pain has many ways of hiding and even more ways of revealing itself. In reflecting back on what sustained my interest in the Jewish base of Kafka's symbolic vocabulary, it seems clear that my own ambivalence about my Jewish experiences must have fueled that project. Was I perhaps drawn to this work because it allowed me to focus on, while at the same time keeping from my consciousness, an identical scene of arrest to which I had been witness as a young child in Nazi occupied Vienna when one evening, two men dressed in brown coats knocked on our apartment door and came to arrest my father "without his having done anything wrong?" (Kafka, 1956). This arrest and the chaos that ensued completely shattered my world, and only narrowly missed leading to my murder. With hindsight, it seems to me that Kafka's fiction allowed me to distance myself from my own experience by providing an avenue of dealing with it indirectly, parallel to the use Kafka himself made not only of the Yiddish theater plays, but his own writings.

I feel certain now that Kafka continued to appeal to me because I, like Kafka, was in search of an authentic Jewishness. Like Kafka, I could not get very far with religious belief, but "being Jewish" was something I could not and did not wish to give up. Like Kafka, I felt myself divided, and like him, struggled with what it might mean for a "modern Jew" to be part of the Jewish people, because we both are and are not one. Ironically, I was able to put my Kafka work to good use in my own process, so aptly phrased by the (formerly East) German writer, Christa Wolf as, "this coming-to-oneself" (Wolf, 1974). While I do not remain as torn as Kafka, neither have I found a firm answer, nor do I expect to.

But this is jumping ahead, for I did not make these discoveries until I had been immersed in the Yiddish material for at least a year, and did not see the parallel to my own life story for another two decades. At the time, simply undertaking to read these plays, painstakingly, slowly, one word at a time with an open Yiddish/English dictionary by my side, was itself a journey. This journey took me back into my Jewish/Yiddish immigrant child's world in which we cringed when our beloved teacher, *Chaverte* Novak from the Shalom Aleichem Folk-shule, otherwise so considerate, humiliated us by talking loudly in Yiddish on the subway when we traveled together as a class to that other world, Manhattan. Reading Kafka's journals in which he records his family's blatant disapproval of the Yiddish theater, I remembered the subway and grasped at once the disrepute in which the Yiddish language was held among the assimilated German-speaking Jews of Prague. I also grasped Kafka's longing to feel at home in something Jewish, and beneath that, his hidden fear and shame.

I understood his ambivalence, because I could easily recall my own Jewish Austrian-born German-speaking mother's contempt for the Yiddish that my father insisted I learn, although she fully supported that effort and would have balked at my quitting the school. For you see, my mother, like Kafka's parents, believed in being Jewish—but only up to a point. To open yourself fully to Yiddish, as Kafka did late in life, and as I had been taught to do as a child, was to go beyond the zone of safety for a modern Jew. Working my way through those Yiddish plays brought back the intimacy and the comfort of a Jewish way of life that was self-enclosed and comforting for a child survivor, safe but shameful, a treacherous terrain even within the family, even among Jews.

Kafka learned in his family that to embrace Yiddish was to respond to the Eastern European Jew within, a despised, unassimilable kernel. "Lie down with dogs and get up with fleas," Kafka's father said of the Yiddish actor, Yitzkhok Levi, with whom Kafka had struck up an intense friendship and from whom he was learning about a "more authentic" Judaism than his father had offered him. This insult must somehow have struck a personal chord in me, and perhaps found its way into my determination to legitimate Yiddish and the culture that gave rise to it. Had I not discovered the connections between Kafka and the Yiddish theater (which leapt out at me once I revived my Yiddish and could easily read the plays), the entire shape of my professional life would have been different.

I believe in the Freudian premise that there are no accidents. Yet, how else can I account for the sudden arrival on my campus of the Yiddish writer, Isaac Bashevis Singer, as a visiting professor just as I was nearing completion of my Kafka project? Whatever it was that the person who introduced us thought we would have in common (besides Yiddish), he could not possibly have known that Singer had just finished writing a short story entitled, "A Friend of Kafka" (Singer, 1970). The main character, Jacques Levi, was based on the obscure Yiddish actor, Yitzkhok (stage name Jacques) Levi—the very one Kafka's father had damned and who was a major focus of my then on-going Kafka research. It seemed that Singer had become acquainted with this Levi in Warsaw, years after Levi's Prague performances, but well before he was deported to Auschwitz during the Nazi occupation of Poland. How can I, at this remove, convey the impact of such a convergence on a mind completely immersed in a long-forgotten, obscure world in which Levi existed as a quasi-fictional character whose written legacy I was in the process of translating? While I had truly believed that I was the only living person who knew (or cared) that Levi had ever existed, here sat an established writer who not only claimed to have known the man, but had written him into a story. Upon hearing of my Kafka work, Singer immediately offered to read me "A Friend of Kafka" in the original, the very next day. And because I could by then easily follow the Yiddish, and because I laughed in all the right places, Singer asked me instantly to be his translator.

Now anyone who knows anything about Singer's life knows that if one accepted working with him, one inevitably became one of an army of translators with whom he worked closely. In recent years, the translator and he always rewrote the story in English as the work progressed, without making the corresponding changes in the original Yiddish. This Singer viewed as a grand joke on future scholars who would now never be able to identify any texts as the "true original." Perhaps because Singer responded to Kafka with awe, admiration, and a sense that "one Kafka in a century was more than enough," he did not interpret his own behavior as a symbolic act worthy of a Kafka parable—neither that, nor the army of translators. But it is difficult to keep from reading Singer's feigned innocence as a way of thumbing his nose at the literary establishment which had not taken him seriously enough (perhaps because he wrote in Yiddish within an explicitly Eastern European Jewish fictive world?). Years later, after he had won the Nobel prize for literature and I had developed a feminist perspective that made me read both Singer's and Kafka's texts from an entirely different stance, I was able to see the similarities in Kafka's and Singer's objectified, instrumental representations of women, in spite of great differences in their worldviews.

While these layered meshings took time to surface, the impact of the Kafka/Singer/Levi convergence was immediate. I did become one of Singer's translators and worked closely with him on several short stories that appeared in *The New Yorker, Southern Review,* and *Commentary,* and were reprinted in volumes of his collected stories (Singer, 1974; 1982). Although the Singer translations held up my Kafka research for many months, by then I was solidly hooked to I knew not exactly what, except that it was Jewish and was taking me somewhere I hoped I really wanted to go.

Looking back, it is easy to see that the Jewish Kafka work compelled me far more than I knew at any step along the way. The Kafka work that led to Singer that led back to Kafka ultimately resulted in my first professional activism on behalf of Yiddish, a protest against its exclusion from the literally dozens of languages and literatures represented at the Modern Language Association.

Though the process could have resulted in a scenario worthy of *The Trial,* in fact, all that was needed to create a place for Yiddish was a petition signed by ten members of the Association, and I was easily able to get several times that many. What began as a small ad hoc seminar in 1972 has in the intervening years become a well-established, securely institutionalized section with a large following. The Kafka/Singer/Kafka connection led to my researching other Jewish influences on Kafka (including Yiddish prose) and resulted in my working within Jewish professional groups. This feeling of comfort as a Jew working with other Jews in a professional context came to an abrupt halt after I had the proverbial feminist "click" described in the first issue of *Ms.* magazine. This made me realize that neither women, gender nor sexuality had been part of the critical tradition in which I had been trained. Because it was not very rewarding to do feminist critiques in those circles, and because I felt the urgency of a more activist stance, I began to focus on the works of Yiddish women writers, only a few of whose texts had been translated at the time. In recent years, considerably more material has become available (Forman et al., 1995).

Once started, the process of "coming-to-myself" did not end with professional activism, but included the recognition of my own lesbian identity which began to occupy me over the next several years, both personally and professionally. Part of this process included lesbian activism in professional organizations which in those years were still quite homophobic and resistant to the inclusion of lesbian themes as legitimate scholarly pursuits. Surprisingly, in the early years of feminist organizing, even the National Women's Studies Association, a substantial percentage of whose members were lesbian, was not as open to lesbian scholarship as one might imagine. While it was difficult to accept the homophobic limitations of feminist organizations, I was totally unprepared when I discovered a similar resistance to the inclusion of Jewish themes not only among feminists, but lesbian feminists as well. I was especially disturbed at the deliberate exclusion of antisemitism as part of the agenda at a time when questions of "difference" were becoming increasingly central to feminist theorizing. This acute awareness of betrayal by all of the worlds in which I believed I could claim a legitimate place led me to try to put my worlds together by editing *Nice Jewish Girls: A Lesbian Anthology* (1982). This book and its reception set into motion a process that influenced the shape of my work in the decade to follow to the same extent that the Kafka work had been formative in the decade that preceded it. What I did not anticipate was that this Jewish lesbian work would create a deep longing for Jewish community, nor how difficult it would be to fulfill, even in the newly gay/lesbian congregations being formed across the United States, Europe, and eventually Australia.

The intersection of my Kafka work with a feminist perspective came about in stages. In the process of showing students the sexist biases of the male writers who comprised the curriculum I had been teaching, anger soon gave way to boredom, and I spent the next years educating myself in a wide spectrum of women's contributions to literature, art, and culture. But when colleagues began to ask me whether I was developing a feminist critique of Kafka's work (which was not surprising given that I was known to be both a Kafka scholar and a feminist literary critic), my first response was a simple, "No." At the time I genuinely did not believe I had much to say on the subject, beyond challenging the assumed "universality" of Kafka's texts. I eventually did spell out the implications of such a perspective in essays that demonstrated the androcentrism of Kafka's worldview which made women instrumentally necessary to the system he was describing, but entirely marginal to the central focus of his texts—the power struggles among the male characters (Beck, 1983).

I finally presented this material at a professional meeting and began (in the self-reflective manner common to feminist approaches) by owning that I myself had ignored gender in my previous Kafka work. My point was misunderstood in Kafka circles, which to this day are male clubs most of whose members resist or ignore the implications of feminist theorizing. The upshot was a rumor overheard in the elevator shortly after my presentation, "Have you heard? Evelyn Beck has become a lesbian and recanted her Kafka work!" a juxtaposition that suggests causation. But far from recanting, this new sensitivity to issues of gender was leading me to see the homosociality of Kafka's fictional worlds and to link this dimension of his work to the homoerotic tensions that emerge from the texts and are made particularly explicit in the deleted sections of *The Trial*. I was only able to make these connections once I allowed myself to set aside the heterosexual imperative embedded in virtually all Kafka criticism (including my own earlier work). Entering "an old text from a new direction" (Rich, 1979) allowed me to see gender patterns that were not only homosocial, but strongly suggestive of the homoerotic. This was not named, but acted out in symbolic actions which were not difficult to read once you allowed the possibility of their existence (or should I say, did not categorically shut them out?) I now paired my understanding of the unspeakableness of the word "Jew," which, as Robert had observed, already pressed upon his texts, with the unspeakableness of a "homosexual" sensibility, which would have been unthinkable in the context of the Jewish worldview embodied by Kafka's family (Beck, 1986). Kafka's psyche and his texts would thus be doubly pressed by the shame of two unspeakables—*Jew* and *homosexual*—that were central to his life. That I had made these the cornerstones of my own work did not entirely escape my notice.

But the story does not end with these insights. Parallel to my involvement with Kafka, I had also been immersed in teaching and researching the work of the Mexican (German-Jewish-Hungarian) painter, Frida Kahlo. Her images would not let me go once I was introduced to them in the mid-1970s when they were brought together in a rare one-woman exhibit in Chicago. One day, I was showing my class a slide of Kahlo's "The Broken Column." In this painting Kahlo depicts her wounded body split open yet girdled together in a bleak landscape, arrows piercing her skin, tears frozen on her face; I involuntarily said aloud, "Franz Kafka!" At the time I thought I had moved away from Kafka's writings, but Kahlo's visual images had precisely the effect on me that Kafka had called for. Her focus on wounds brought Kafka's work even more forcefully to mind. He had written, "A book should be like an axe to chop the frozen sea within us." The violence of this image is surprisingly apt for Kahlo, since it accurately describes the effects of those of her paintings in which blood and wounds assault the viewer. Fortunately, the Women's Studies students knew of my previous Kafka work and were thus only a bit mystified, but to me the connection was crystal clear and has remained so over two decades. Incongruously, and without any conscious volition, my next project had been born.

Wounds of Gender is the title of my current work in progress—a book-length study focusing on the intersection of the writings of Kafka and the paintings of Kahlo. It is not a study of influence, as my early Kafka work had been, but of confluence—the unexpected, pervasive, and insistent coming together of parallel themes and images across multiple lines of difference, where issues of gender, ethnicity, religion, physical disability and sexuality play central roles in the production and signification of the art. While many commentators have noted Kahlo's sense of duality as a biracial Mexican-European, no one has paid much attention to the possible workings of the Jewish elements of her heritage which she gleaned from her photographer father. Nor has enough been made of her abiding passion for the many women with whom she was lovingly intimate, sometimes amorously, throughout her life. As must be obvious, this new work brings together all of my long-time interests within a newly developing psychological frame. Because the membrane separating life from art was extremely permeable for each of these "wounded" artists, understanding their lives helps to make their frequently baffling and bizarre images more comprehensible. In a parallel process, interrogating the connections between those literary texts, visual images, and clinical cases that capture our imagination allows us to make visible the links between our professional work and our own histories. In a paraphrase of Virginia Woolf's eloquent insistence that art is not separable from life, I offer her words which might well serve as a guide not only for the study of the arts, but for the construction of all knowledge, "imaginative work . . . is not dropped like a pebble upon the ground . . [it] is like a spider's web, attached ever so lightly perhaps, but still attached to life at all four corners." (Woolf, 1928).

REFERENCES

Beck, Evelyn Torton (1971). *Kafka and the Yiddish theater: Its impact on his work.* Madison, WI: The University of Wisconsin Press.

Beck, Evelyn Torton (1982). *Nice Jewish girls: A lesbian anthology.* Watertown, MA: Persephone Press. Revised and expanded edition, Boston, MA: Beacon Press, 1987.

Beck, Evelyn Torton (1983). Kafka's traffic in women: Power, gender and sexuality. The *Literary Review. 26*(4), 565 – 576.

Beck, Evelyn Torton (1986). Kafka's triple bind: Women, Jews and sexuality. In Alan Udoff (Ed.), *Kafka's contextuality* (pp. 343 – 388). Baltimore, MD: The Gordian Press.

Forman, Frida, Raicus, Ethel, Swartz, Sarah Silberstein, and Wolfe, Margie (1995). *Found treasures: Stories by Yiddish women writers.* Toronto, Ontario: Second Story Press.

Kafka, Franz (1945). *The trial.* New York: New Directions.

Kafka, Franz (1949). *The diaries of Franz Kafka: 1910-1923.* (2 volumes). New York: Schocken Books.

Kafka, Franz (1956). *The trial.* The definitive edition. New York: Schocken Books.

Rich, Adrienne (1979). When we dead awaken: Writing as revision. *Lies, secrets, and silences: Selected prose. 1966-1979.* New York: W. W. Norton & Co.

Robert, Marthe (1982). *As lonely as Franz Kafka.* New York: Harcourt Brace Jovanovich.

Singer, Isaac Bashevis (1970). "A friend of Kafka." New York: Farrar, Straus & Giroux.

Singer, Isaac Bashevis (1974). *A crown of feathers.* New York: Farrar, Straus & Giroux.

Singer, Isaac Bashevis (1982). *The collected stories of Isaac Bashevis Singer.* New York: Farrar, Straus & Giroux.

Wolf, Christa (1974). *The quest for Christa T.* New York: Dell Publishers.

Woolf, Virginia (1928). *A room of one's own.* New York: Harcourt, Brace & World.

SECTION IV:
EVE AND THE TREE
OF KNOWLEDGE:
WOMAN'S PLACE AMONG
THE PEOPLE OF THE BOOK

Chapter 20

"I Don't Know Enough": Jewish Women's Learned Ignorance

Rachel Josefowitz Siegel

My dear and beloved sons, I do not need to urge you to give proper education to your sons, for I know that of your own accord you will educate them in Torah and piety. Yet I command you that you should command your sons, and they theirs, that they should be careful not to teach their daughters Torah . . . . (p. 176)

Thus said the Ridwas, a famous and highly respected rabbi, in his last will and testament, published in 1908 (quoted in Karp, 1987). Such is the cultural and religious heritage that still prevails in ultra-Orthodox circles and that still has an impact on the feelings and behaviors of many Jewish women, even when they are far removed from the direct influence of such patriarchal dictums.

I have heard "I really don't know enough," or some variant of that phrase, at every conference of Jewish women, almost every time a Jewish woman gets up to speak of Jewish matters. At the 1992 First International Conference on Judaism, Feminism, and Psychology in Seattle, it was an opening remark that punctuated

This chapter is a condensed version of my invited address at the Association for Women in Psychology 1995 meeting, on the occasion of receiving the Jewish Caucus Prize for Distinguished Scholarship in the Field of Psychology of Jewish Women.

Many thanks to Jeanne Adleman, Paula Caplan, Joan Fisch, Elizabeth Reed, and Sharon Siegel, for their generous feedback.

informal conversations in the hallways, as well as formal presentations and workshop discussions. I realized that I, too, whether I voiced it or not, had a similar feeling of not being really entitled to my opinions or observations because I was not sufficiently steeped in Jewish texts. I have become aware of my own anxiety about speaking on the topic of Jewish women's issues, and I have realized that my sense of not knowing enough is not unique to me but is shared by other Jewish women. This may, in fact, be central to understanding certain elements in the lives of Jewish women today.

The male-centered North American culture is one of many cultures that teach women and girls, Jewish and non-Jewish, to feel insecure about speaking up. In addition, however, Jewish women are exposed to specifically Jewish pressures that increase our discomfort about learning, knowing, and speaking of Jewish matters. Jewish women's collective sense of not knowing enough has many roots and manifests itself in many forms. It could well be called Jewish women's "learned ignorance." We have learned to remain ignorant for several, sometimes opposite, reasons. Chief among these is a Jewish tradition of keeping women out of the male bastions of Jewish learning and synagogue ritual, a tradition that has only begun to be questioned and open to change within my lifetime, starting timidly in the 1950s, and more vigorously since the 1970s. Jewish studies have traditionally not been available to women, and references to Jewish women's topics within Jewish tradition and literature have been few. Those of us who have grown up within or close to Jewish observance or culture have received repeated messages about Jewish women's exclusion from Jewish learning and only a few of us have had access to the more recently available advanced levels of Jewish studies.

Our ignorance may also reflect a resistance to Jewish learning that reflects the sadness and anger of not having been allowed or expected to learn. Our childhood experiences with Jewish education are widely diverse. For many of us, the issue is not that we were excluded by Jewish men, but that we were never exposed to Jewish knowledge at all, for it was not part of our parent's way of life. Others have had sketchy or negative learning experiences, frequently ending abruptly after Bat Mitzvah.

There is much more to this learned ignorance than the question of access to Jewish education. Much as we would like to know more, we may have also shied away from Jewish learning for a variety of self-protective reasons. Our avoidance is grounded in part on two problematic issues. The first is that Jewish learning of necessity evokes all the painful and complicated feelings of belonging to an oppressed and persecuted people; the second is that Jewish history and tradition are so thoroughly male centered that many Jewish women find it distasteful to even begin the study of Jewish texts.

Our sense of not knowing enough is never absolute and depends somewhat on our own frame of reference. We may feel more ignorant than we actually are, especially when we make the common mistake of assuming that Orthodox Judaism is the only and true measure of Jewishness, when in fact only 10 percent of American Jews consider themselves Orthodox.

Furthermore, Jewish women's issues have far too often not been welcomed or included among non-Jewish or mixed audiences, even when the discourse is intended to be "multicultural," or in earlier days, when the well-meant use of the Christian term "ecumenical" often did not include Jewish. Our ingrained sense of learned ignorance embodies the multiple dimensions of "otherness" that so many of us experience as Jews in a world that is predominantly non-Jewish, and as Jewish women in a Jewish world that is defined and dominated by Jewish men.

Among non-Jews, I learned not to draw attention to my otherness, my Jewishness, out of fear of anti-Jewish responses that could shatter the illusion of temporary privilege or acceptance and even endanger my family or the Jewish community. I knew that it took only a minor incident to turn the non-Jewish population into a life-threatening mob, intent on blaming Jews for conditions such as plague, poverty, and general unrest, even in countries that tolerated a Jewish presence and where Jews had achieved a measure of acceptance or prominence.

Jewish women carry the double fear of anti-Jewish as well as antifemale reactions. Like Jews, women have always been the other. Like Jews, women have always been the targets of societal blame. Like Jews, women have been silenced by the fear of losing privilege, or of provoking ridicule, harassment, and violence. Nora Gold's chapter in this volume gives examples of the discounting and trivializing that Jewish women encounter when we try to bring up Jewish topics.

Whenever I speak of Jewish matters to a mixed audience, or of Jewish women's issues to a Jewish audience, I am somewhat on guard. Do I know enough to appear knowledgeable? Will my words be questioned, discounted, perceived as unsubstantiated generalizations or exaggerations, or attributed to my own wounds or pathologies? The attack may not even come from men or from non-Jews. It is just as likely to come from Jewish women who do not wish to apply a feminist lens to Jewish customs, who do not want to hear yet one more litany of Jewish pain, or who simply find it difficult to attribute legitimacy or authority to a woman's voice and therefore find it easy to criticize or to disagree. I also fear that I might embarrass my Jewish sisters by saying something that could trigger a subtle anti-Jewish response or be perceived as being too loud, too pushy, too whiny, too Jewish.

It seems to me that our learned ignorance is an important aspect of our day-to-day lives as Jewish women today, emerging under many circumstances and most forcefully when we participate in the rituals traditionally reserved for men. I suggest that it is such an integral part of our personality, that it may well inhibit other areas of knowledge and of discourse. This sense of not knowing and not being allowed to know, or to speak as if we know, is a key element in the Jewish ambivalence that plagues so many Jewish American and Jewish Canadian feminists today.

Collective and yet unique for each of us, the concept of learned ignorance bears some resemblance to the concept of learned helplessness (Seligman, 1975). As with learned helplessness, we get double messages. Since Adam and Eve, the Jewish messages against female learning have been consistent. In order to be good Jewish women, we are expected to remain ignorant and speechless in Jewish matters, and yet, we are also expected to know enough so that we can convey Jewish culture and traditions to future generations. If we don't know enough about our Jewish heritage, we may feel stupid and excluded, and if we know too much in the area of male-defined Jewish learning, we may feel that we are threatening the self-esteem and dignity of Jewish men. Like women in other oppressed groups, we have been taught to be protective of our men and not to undermine their domi-

nant position within our group (Cantor, 1995). I was taught that
only Jewish men have the right to study and to interpret the holy
texts, that only Jewish men have the right to be heard in religious or
judicial debates, that a woman's voice is lascivious and not worth
listening to.

The Jewish messages about knowledge and speaking that I learned
as a little girl, growing up in Switzerland in the 1920s and 1930s, differ
from those received by my daughter in the Conservative Jewish congregation of Ithaca, New York in the 1950s; what my granddaughters
learned during their preparation for Bat Mitzvah in their egalitarian
Vancouver *chavurah* differs again from what my Vermont granddaughter absorbed within her secular, divorced family of mixed
religious background. And so it is for each of us; our relationship to
Jewish knowledge or to its absence is a very personal matter. As a
Jewish girl and woman within the Jewish community, I learned that it
was okay to speak among women as long as I deferred to male
authorities. As a Jewish woman among non-Jews, I learned that it was
okay to speak of many things, as long as I did not bring Jewish topics
into the discourse or use Jewish mannerisms. How then can I speak at
all? And how can I dare to speak of Jewish issues in a non-Jewish
environment when the history of my people has taught me that it is
dangerous to become visible, it is dangerous to be heard, it is dangerous to make waves as a Jew.

And yet, and yet, in spite of all this and perhaps because of all this,
it is absolutely essential that I, an *alte Yiddene*, a Jewish American
woman in her seventies, gather the courage to overcome these hesita-
tions, to grapple with these taboos. It is essential that I speak out of my
own experience, that I write, that I encourage other Jewish women to
speak and to write of their own experience. While none of us can
assume to represent all Jewish women, our individual accounts can
begin to form a body of knowledge about Jewish women that conveys
the importance of who we are and what we know.

My story has to do with being the daughter of Lithuanian Jewish
parents, born in Berlin, educated in Switzerland, and then becoming
a Jewish immigrant among American-born Jews. It is about carrying the pain and insecurities of my particular Jewish childhood into
adult life and eventually transforming and integrating those early
experiences by means of feminist consciousness and feminist analy-

sis. To some extent, every Jewish woman has to deal with similar elements in her own Jewish story, though the particulars of her story may be very different.

I remember sitting next to my mother in the women's gallery in the balcony of our beautiful little synagogue in Lausanne, Switzerland. I could have been eight, or ten, or eleven, for it happened every year. I hardly knew enough Hebrew letters to follow the prayers in the prayer book. I did not know the order of the service and never knew what page we were on or what to say or do. I assumed that my mother knew, since she was a rabbi's daughter and competent in other areas, yet I was never sure that she really did. Only a few of the women in the women's gallery appeared to be immersed in prayer or to know when to stand up and when to sit down. I followed my mother's cues, embarrassed and ashamed at faking it.

I remember the mixture of feeling deeply connected to the assembled Jewish community, but feeling strangely excluded from what was really going on in the main sanctuary downstairs, where I saw my father and brothers participating in the Torah service. While I could not have named these feelings at the time, I wanted *in* most desperately, and I also wanted *out* and away from the unnamed tension of ignorance and exclusion.

Unlike my brothers, I was never instructed in these mysteries. I learned that girls are not supposed to know. To this day, some sixty years later, having learned something about the order of the service, having learned enough Hebrew as an adult to understand the gist of most prayers, I still feel that I have no right to know and that I will stumble or forget. Now that I am a widow in my seventies I still feel hesitant about leading our family *seder* (Siegel, in press). I was relieved to know that I was not the only woman who felt this way, when I read Nora Gold's account in "Ima's Not on the Bima" (Gold, 1995), and Michele Clark's chapter in this volume.

Jewish women today are permitted to say the blessings over the *Torah*, and to read from the Torah in most synagogues, with exception of the Orthodox. Yet I continue to get very anxious when I stand before the open Torah scroll, and I have to remind myself not only that I know the words but that I actually have the right to know the words.

This early image of not knowing, and not being allowed or expected to know, is a very powerful one and one that I believe holds the key to my relationship toward Jewish religion and Jewish community. I have vacillated over the years between wanting in and wanting out. I have expressed my ambivalence at times by compulsive overinvolvement and at other times by half-heartedness, but I have never withdrawn entirely as some Jewish women have. I see no contradiction in wanting access to the male privileges of Jewish ritual and wanting to feminize the very same ritual by bringing female wisdom and consciousness into it. I believe that much of my adult development as a Jewish woman can be traced back to the childhood experience of wanting to belong and to be Jewishly knowledgeable, not on male-defined terms but on my terms, while also wanting to be fully accepted as a Jewish woman outside of the Jewish community.

Much like women in other spheres of male dominance, having partly achieved some of those goals I then began to question the words that I had been excluded from saying all those years. As I learned more, I became aware of my aversion to the sexist, hierarchical, and vengeful messages that are embedded in Jewish texts. I began to ask myself whether this was what I really wanted to perpetuate. The question that emerged was whether it is possible to retain the positive elements of Jewish teachings, while reframing or rejecting the objectionable elements. In answer to that question, I have fought for the inclusion of women in Jewish prayer, in Jewish institutions, and in Jewish communal leadership; at the same time I have initiated changes in the text and challenged the status quo.

The ignorance that was imposed on generations of Jewish women has been partly overcome within my own lifetime. I am deeply moved when my daughter chants the story of Jonah in fluent Hebrew during the *Yom Kippur* service, I am delighted with the ease and familiarity with which two of my granddaughters approach religious services and traditions, while my third granddaughter confidently writes about her evolving Jewish identity. I am impressed with the scholarship of women rabbis of my daughter's generation. I am in awe and somewhat envious of the younger women of my congregation who lead the service and chant from the Torah with confidence and competence. I take great pleasure in the emergence of secular as well as religious publications by and about Jewish women.

However, much like other advances attributed to the women's movement, we've got a long way to go. The institutional changes are far from universal and often have the quality of crazymaking illusions, being only superficial, while the basic attitudes and behaviors have hardly changed at all. In Jerusalem a recent court order forbids women to pray together or to read from the Torah at the *Wailing Wall.* In Rachel Weber's chapter in this volume, she gives a poignant example of her encounter with a supposedly egalitarian *minyan,* when instead of being counted as the tenth Jew, she was asked to baby-sit for one of the men so that he could take her place. We are not so far removed as we would like to think from the attitude expressed by Rabbi Yosef Wolf (quoted in Kadish, 1994), founder of the ultra-orthodox Beit Yakov School for girls in Israel: "If we succeed in instilling in our girl students that the purpose of their studies is to aspire to emulate our matriarchs, *who did not study,* than we have succeeded in educating our daughters" (italics mine) (p. 29).

This shocking statement is of course not typical of the attitudes of Jewish educators in America today, and yet, vestiges of the taboo against female learning are still in our psyches and in the strongholds of Orthodox male authority. Our wonderful new Jewish role models—women rabbis, scholars, and activists—do not yet operate from a well-established power base; their voices, even at full strength, are isolated solos, easily drowned out by their male counterparts. Their work is likely not to be read or quoted by the men who still control Jewish learning.

Much like other oppressed groups, we have unfortunately internalized the negative attitudes of the dominant group toward Jews and toward women. In many cases, this causes us to feel ambivalent about acting, speaking, or being Jewish. How much more so when we feel insecure in knowing our Jewish heritage. The ambivalence and the wish to avoid being noticed can cause us to turn against each other and to feel threatened by the differences among us. I believe that this profound ambivalence, based partly on learned ignorance and female exclusion within Judaism, and partly on negative stereotyping and persecution from the non-Jewish majority, is a feeling that is probably shared by many Jewish women. It is an ambivalence not only toward religious expression but also toward our Jewish identity and toward our place in the non-Jewish world, often causing splits in our own identities or in our relationships with other Jews. We may reject or blame our own Jewish background, thus denying an important aspect of our own identity, or we may reject and blame other Jews as we struggle to maintain our own Jewish equilibrium.

In spite of the negative internal and external climate of discouragement, Jewish women are beginning to make our Jewish voices heard. Feminist Jewish study groups and *Rosh Chodesh* groups are flourishing. Jewish women are introducing new areas of Jewish study that focus on women. We are sharing our enthusiasm at international, national, and regional conferences, exploring and legitimizing our issues and concerns, appreciating the differences among us.

We have established vibrant Jewish Caucuses at the National Women's Studies Association and at the Association for Women in Psychology, bringing Jewish topics into feminist discourse. *LILITH* magazine and *Bridges*, the first independent Jewish women's publications not affiliated with any religious or philanthropic organization, are contributing to our fund of knowledge about Jewish women. Jewish women have become rabbis, Jewish scholars, and teachers, bringing respect and status to Jewish women's academic studies and acting as role models. Our Jewish women's voices are changing the very face and texture of contemporary Jewish life by claiming our rights to Jewish learning and leadership.

We have begun to speak out of our own and unique Jewish experiences and our own wisdom. Our truths may not conform to a male-determined body of Jewish knowledge, and we may not agree on a unified body of female Jewish knowledge. But we have begun to understand ourselves as Jewish women and to know each other. We have begun to show that Jewish knowledge can and should legitimately include the essential topics of women's lives. Our studies and conversations can be focused on our own experiences as Jewish women and need not be limited to the traditional and male dominated areas of Jewish learning.

Our present task is to help each other overcome the learned ignorance and the learned silencing of our past. We are bringing our Jewishness into the foreground and, as Evelyn Torton Beck says in her chapter in this volume, each of us is "searching for our authentic Jewishness." The silence is no longer necessary, the taboos are no longer effective. We might find that we are not as ignorant as we think. We are never too old to learn.

It is time to sing *Shehehyanu*. Let us rejoice together, for we have given birth to a new field of Jewish study that places Jewish women at the center. Let us celebrate the beauty of women's voices affirming the varied ways of Jewish knowing.

REFERENCES

Cantor, Aviva (1995). *Jewish women Jewish men: The legacy of patriarchy in Jewish life*. San Francisco, CA: Harper.

Gold, Nora (1995). Ima's not on the bima: Psychological barriers to women taking leadership in religious practice. In Kayla Weiner and Arinna Moon (Eds.), *Jewish women speak out: Expanding the boundaries of psychology*, (pp. 55 – 74). Seattle, WA: Canopy Press.

Kadish, Rachel (1994). The paradox of female knowledge. *LILITH, 19*(4), p. 29.

Karp, Abraham J. (1987). Ridwas: Rabbi Jacob David Wilowsky, 1845 – 1913. In Leo Jung (Ed.), *Sages and Saints*. (p. 176). Hoboken, NJ: Ktav Publishing.

Seligman, Martin P. (1975). *Helplessness: On depression, development, and death*. San Francisco, CA: Freeman.

Siegel, Rachel J. (in press). Who will lead the Seder, now that I stand alone? In Susan Berrin (Ed.), *Wisdom from the heart: Growing older as a Jew.* Woodstock, VT: Jewish Light.

Chapter 21

Learning to Leyn

Michele Clark

On the day of my daughter's *Bat Mitzvah*, I tried, in a small way, to redress a large injustice. My Aunt Harriet, although a synagogue-goer all her life, had never had an *aliyah*, the honor of being called up to the *Torah*. In her Conservative congregation on Long Island, after twenty years of discussion, women had still only arrived at the opportunity to open the doors of the *Ark*. But, in my egalitarian congregation in Vermont, where the Bat Mitzvah was taking place, women have the same opportunities as men. And so, I offered my favorite aunt her first, and given her seventy-something age and how slow her synagogue was moving, probably her only, moment of being called up for honor before a congregation.

In doing this I was fulfilling what Cynthia Ozick (1983) calls "the missing Commandment," the one which reads, "Thou shalt not lessen the humanity of women" (pp. 142 – 149), and which Ozick wants the Jewish people to repair "for the sake of Torah; to preserve and strengthen Torah itself" (p. 151).

Being called up to the Torah involves standing by the scroll in the center of attention and saying three brief blessings, after which a passage from the scroll is *leyned*, read in a swift, melodic chant, by another person who is experienced with the handwritten text which has no vowels and no punctuation. After the leyning of the passage is completed, the person being honored recites a last short prayer. This is followed by handshakes and well wishes all around.

But when I told Aunt Harriet about the aliyah, she looked at me with black fear in her eyes and whispered that she didn't know Hebrew. I tried to reassure her. I told her that there was a transliteration of the prayers on a piece of paper which lay on the *bimah*, the ritual podium. I told her that many people read from that paper. But it was no use. She would not do it unless her husband, my Uncle Julius, went along and even then she stood behind him while he said the blessings and her eyes were dark with anxiety.

Later, when I thought about this attempt of mine to repair a piece of the imperfect and unjust world, I had to admit that I know something about the fear of standing in front of a congregation. For myself, even though in my professional life I have led workshops for twenty, thirty, even fifty people, taking ritual space in Jewish life did not come easily. Despite being in an egalitarian congregation, for many years I avoided offers of an aliyah. The first time I had one, it was on an unassuming Saturday in the middle of summer, when someone who was supposed to have the honor had not arrived. And the truth is, on that day, I trembled. I trembled and was embarrassed about trembling and tried to hide it, but someone in that small *minyan* noticed and asked me if this was my first aliyah, and, of course, I had to tell the truth, and the minyan burst into a song of luck and praise "*Siman tov and Mazel tov and Siman tov and Mazel tov. . .*" which made me feel both exposed and touched.

The feminist psychologist in me would explain the trembling and the reluctance by saying that I was moving into male territory, and I was afraid because women have, sometimes, been punished for this. And I think this is a part of the explanation for myself and my aunt. But there was something else going on as well. Because I am not usually a trembler, nor is Aunt Harriet.

The something-else going-on has to do with concepts which, as a modern person, I can't say without an apologetic twist to my lips— words like awe, holy or sacred. Concepts which seem pretentious to aspire to; concepts associated with either phoney gurus from India, or at best, people in other lands a long time ago. Nevertheless, it was because I consider the Torah scroll a sacred object that I wanted to stand before it. It was because the sacredness and the standing in male space was fused that I, and my aunt, were afraid.

Susannah Heschel (1996), Judith Plaskow (1990), and many other women have written about how, as young people, they protested the injustices of Judaism in relation to girls and women. But this was not true for me. As a child, injustice in Judaism was not apparent to me, although it should have been obvious. I would have been insulted and defensive if anyone had intimated that I was not treated the same as my brother and male cousins. My concept of gender inequity was that women were treated unfairly in the bad old days, but these were the good new days and that did not happen anymore.

If I had understood the problem as institutional injustice, perhaps I would have stayed and fought for my rights. But, instead, my interpretation was personal: I don't fit in, I'm too loud, I'm too wild. And so, I went away. One day I was there, a top Hebrew student, active in the local chapter of United Synagogue Youth (USY), the next day I had transformed into a teenage beatnik who attended different rituals—poetry readings and folksings. Here, although I did not know it, I was implicitly joining another tradition, the secular humanist one. In this one, which begins say, in the late nineteenth century, with the early anthropologists and ethnographers, all the world's myths and rituals are studied and admired but no one observes any and none are believed. In this tradition it is other people who have awe and reverence and we, the observers and recorders, respect and retell their ways. I spent quite a long time there, twenty-five years. And this is still the place in which, in many ways, I feel most comfortable and where my husband and all my closest friends live. In cultural politics this is still the place I defend because of its emphasis on the brother-and-sisterhood of all people.

But, as personal nourishment, this tradition had become thin gruel to me by the time I returned to being actively Jewish, about six years ago, and I was hungry to be the subject of my own ethnic and religious activities. Specifically, this meant I was hungry to hear and speak Hebrew, engage in some observance, be part of an articulated Jewish community. I could not bear, for one more minute, watching the ceremonies and celebrations of others.

And so, in my mid-forties, I took up the task I had avoided at age fourteen, the struggle to find and keep a place in Judaism. Thousands of women had already been at this task for over a decade. Probably I would not have done it at all if they had not, as a beacon, gone before me.

Fortunately for me, the Jewish institution which was, and is, available to me is the Beth Jacob synagogue in Montpelier, Vermont, which is small, unaffiliated, and that functions because of member participation. There is no rabbi; men and women act in leadership roles in both ritual and in administration. At Beth Jacob, women's participation is both welcomed and necessary.

Nevertheless, for a long time I did not take advantage of any of the ritual options that were available. I participated in activities at which I was already comfortable. I attended services, took my daughter to the religious school; I helped organize cultural events, and led some adult education classes on Jewish women in literature. Once I was asked, and I agreed, to lead a Friday night service, but it did not suit me and I did not do it very well, either.

Then on a late summer day, a few weeks before the High Holidays, Sarah, a woman I admire, who makes her living as a freelance teacher of Judaism (no small feat in Central Vermont) asked me if I would leyn one passage—just one little passage—for Rosh Hashannah, the New Year.

"We need people," she said, "There are a lot of readings on the Holidays."

"I don't think I'm ready for that," I said, remembering my trembling on that unassuming Saturday, and Aunt Harriet's dark, anxious eyes. "Let me think about it."

Once I did think about it, I realized that I would never, actually, feel ready. And so, following the precept articulated in Exodus when the people are gathered at the base of Sinai, and also, a sound principle of behavioral psychology, I decided I would do first and expect understanding to come later.

Sarah taught me the *trop*, the notes, and also made me a tape of the story of Hagar in the desert. I practiced for three weeks and leyned three sentences, perfectly.

I have now been leyning for about two years. I no longer use a tape, but I still need to prepare quite carefully in advance.

Leyning suits me, personally and specifically, in a number of ways, none of which I would have understood in the absence of actual practice. First, there is my love of Hebrew, though I am not in any way fluent. When I am leyning I have a focused reason for speaking and hearing Hebrew. My knowledge of the language is a patchwork of prayer book and modern, along with some basic grammatical structures. I know how to look for the root of a word, and I know something about the way prefixes and suffixes change the root. But I don't know that much, and so, when reading Torah, it is a continual surprise and excitement to me when I can follow or generally understand. In this way, my limitations actually keep my pleasure fresh.

Then, too, I love to sing, though I can barely carry a tune; a raspy alto does very well in leyning, and besides music is not exactly what is expected. Yet it is a kind of music.

Third, there is my love of storytelling, something I have not had an opportunity to indulge since my children were school age. So far, most of the passages I have leyned have been from the great stories of Torah which are family sagas of abandonment and reclamation, envy and aggression, regret and restitution. Many of these stories are old friends and yet we have not met for many years. Some of them I hear as I heard when I was a child, others I hear with a new perspective. Many I know, many others I am listening to for the first time.

When I am leyning, at home as I practice, or during the service, I am both inside and outside the text. I am simultaneously listening to and telling the story. In this I am participating in Torah literacy which "stands at the center of the meaning of Jewishness" (Sered, 1995, p. 209) and which has been, in the past, reserved for men. Torah literacy is an active process. As Samuel Heilman (1983) points out in his account of modern study circles in Jerusalem, "For the Jews, the Torah can transform its people only insofar as they repeat its words, chant in its cadences, think along its syntactic lines, and thus make them their own" (p. 161).

Sometimes the stories I leyn speak to me of my own personal history. When Jacob is reunited with his beloved son Joseph and says "Now I can die, now that I have seen your face," I remember with a flood of feeling all my own family struggles, which were also struggles over the place of Jewishness in my life. I am reminded of the guilt I felt at fifteen, the pain at twenty-five, the resolution I now feel.

Other stories make me acutely uncomfortable and dismayed, as when a younger Jacob lines up his wives and children in order of preference, so that if Esau attacks, the least loved will be the first harmed. For a while I didn't know what to do about this type of story. I considered refusing to read these, since there are often many choices within the weekly portion. But an individual rejection seemed ridiculous, because the story is still there, in the sacred text; there is nothing I can do to change that.

Then, in reading for this chapter I found a concept in Judith Plaskow's *Standing Again at Sinai* (1990) which explains what, in fact, I experience as I leyn. Plaskow, following the Christian theologian, Elisabeth Schussler Fiorenza, describes an engagement of "suspicion and remembrance," in which it is accepted that male domination is inextricably interwoven with religious meaning. The text is explored as a precious fragment of "the source we have . . . to reconstruct Jewish women's history . . ." (p. 14–15). Dismay, itself, becomes an engagement because it rescues and explores the stories of the women and children who were calibrated by the father's approval. In reading with suspicion and remembrance, I am allowing the patriarchal consequences in the stories to be attended to, rather than merely mentioned. Or, at least, I begin this process.

In every part of the act of telling I am claiming space in Judaism, the space that Plaskow says is implied at Sinai but never actually articulated. It is the space that many women in recent years have claimed, but which is not the norm in much of the Jewish communal world, and whose enduring character is, at best, uncertain.

I still rely on Sarah, my original instructor and tape maker, who has continually nurtured and encouraged me in this process. If a passage is puzzling me in terms of cadence or if I'm confused about what trop, or note, is indicated, I call her or stop by her house and review the problem. She praises me, as do other members of the congregation. Occasionally I have the pleasure of surprising her with how well I am doing. "The student has outstripped the teacher," she says, though perhaps that's just "good job" teacher talk. In addition, I feel the satisfaction that comes from being needed, being necessary for the services to proceed correctly.

Sarah admires those who can glance over a passage at the last minute and be ready to leyn. Her anecdotes on this subject have all featured men. She tells me of once hearing the progressive *Chasid* Zalman Schacter-Shalomi leyn first in Hebrew and then retell the passage in a leyning cadence in English.

In private, at my desk, I have been practicing versions of an English leyn. I would like to be able to do this in front of the congregation, so that the stories will be heard by those, like my

Aunt Harriet, who do not read Hebrew, and perhaps therefore, have never engaged. But this would mean, for me, really being a pioneer, since no one has done this with Torah in our synagogue. And, as far as I know, this is not commonly done anywhere.

I don't know when or if I will be able to do this. Perhaps, as Rabbi Tarfon says in Pirkei Avot (2:21), The Sayings of Our Fathers, it is not required that I complete the task, but only that I have started, and that I persevere. Probably, if this possibility has occurred to me, somewhere someone else is also thinking about it or already doing it. Perhaps, as with other things, I will have to wait for other women, perhaps many other women, to do it first.

REFERENCES

Heilman, Samuel (1983). *The people of the book.* Chicago, IL: University of Chicago Press.

Heschel, Susannah (1996). Bringing heaven down to earth. *Tikkun, II* (2), 48 – 56.

Ozick, Cynthia (1983). Notes toward finding the right question. In Susannah Heschel (Ed.), *On being a Jewish feminist* (pp. 120 – 151). New York: Schocken.

Plaskow, Judith (1990). *Standing again at Sinai.* San Francisco, CA: Harper and Row.

Sered, Susan (1995). Toward an anthropology of Jewish women: Sacred texts and the religious world of elderly, Middle-Eastern women in Jerusalem. In Maurie Sacks (Ed.), *Active voices* (pp. 203 – 218). Urbana: University of Illinois Press.

Chapter 22

Better Late Than Early:
A Forty-Eight-Year-Old's
Bat Mitzvah Saga

Nina Perlmutter

All this Jewish stuff is pretty new to me, but don't get me wrong. I have always known I was a Jew—just not a very observant or religious one. Most of my life I called myself a "secular" or "cultural" Jew, a modern distinction non-Jews often don't understand, but which, say, Navajos and others still familiar with their peoples' ancient lifeways and perspectives, do.

I was never a *knowledgeable* Jew; I was hardly a conscious Jew. Maybe because I am a second-generation-American-born Jewish kid from Miami Beach. There the whole world seemed Jewish.

Perhaps most critical was the fact that I am the daughter of Nate and Ruth Ann Perlmutter. Dad spent his entire adult life with the Anti-Defamation League of B'nai Brith, starting as office boy, dying while National Director. My parents were known worldwide, respected or despised, as important Jews, "professional Jews" who defended civil and human rights for everyone They took on anti-semites and bigots of all kinds—loudly and effectively.

My folks truly embodied Hillel's great dictum: "If I am not for myself, who am I? If I am only for myself, what am I? And if not now, when?"

They tried to pass this wisdom on to us kids. I mostly heard the "being for others" part. The first insight seemed less pressing in my secure little world. There, for example, I once reported to my folks that some of my new Cuban refugee friends had "American" names. They were Hellersteins; only the Gonzalez' or Martinezes sounded alien to me.

Besides, I was a 1960s liberal-lefty sort: a devout internationalist, a professional activist on behalf of immigrants, Vietnamese peasants, victims of war and nuclear madness, a defender of human rights for minorities anywhere. It felt more virtuous to work on behalf of others than on behalf of a group to which I belonged. Working for my own might be, or appear to be, for only selfish motives, rather than purer universal ones. Now I admit my blind spots. In thinking "Hellerstein" was pure American, I had missed both Jewish and American history. I hadn't appreciated how long my people were ostracized. That there was a uniquely Jewish culture, and that it deserved a place in my ideal, multicultural universe had never occurred to me. Looking back, I grew up sensing that being Jewish meant having an eye and fervor for actively improving the world—and having grandparents with thick Yiddish accents.

So how did I get from there to Bat Mitzvah at forty-eight? One manageable way of explaining is to share my responses to the questions most frequently posed to my face, and behind my back. What is it that I have been doing these past two years? What happened for such a switch to occur? What nagged at me the most? And, how does all this feel?

The answer to the first question is easy—well, almost easy. For the past two years I have been learning Hebrew and Jewish history, studying *Torah*, memorizing *trope*, observing Sabbath and *Havdalah*, chanting *Shema* twice a day with *kavannah*, intention. I have been voicing *Baruchas*, exploring *kabbalah*, attending services, gobbling up as much about myriad kinds of Jewish ideas and experiences as I can find.

I have spent countless hours trying to discover, remember, hear from my heart, open to, face, love, and wrestle with my new and old understandings of Judaism as religion and culture, as *my* religion and culture, and with the many, often contradictory ways that I somehow "feel Jewish." I have been exploring how it is to live in the world as a conscious Jew, to look out at that world through committedly Jewish eyes. I have stepped into a Jewish space to feel out what fits and what doesn't from the vast pool of my ancestors' rituals, thoughts, and reflexes.

In short, I have been trying to live more of Hillel's wise words, so I too can stand with the people and culture from which I spring. I have added new adjectives to my notion of myself as a Jew, words I never dreamed of years ago—could barely say without blushing. I admit now to being more than "culturally" or "secularly" Jewish. I am "spiritually," "religiously," "observantly" Jewish, even as I muddle through what each of these inadequate terms really mean.

To the second question, "What happened, Nina, for such momentous changes to occur?" I say, "Lots." Leave Miami Beach, grow older, move to very WASPy central Arizona, survive a mid-life crisis and therapy, face questions too persistent to be ignored: personal identity questions, cultural identity questions, meaning-of-my-life questions.

What happened was a litany of intense, transforming, close encounters—some with people. There were many, but a few stand out more than others. Like the three women who became my first true Jewish sisters: Carolyn Silver, Toni Kaus, and Ellen Strauss Cole. We dubbed ourselves "The Oy Luck Club." For whatever reasons, we were each ready and anxious to start exploring more closely what being Jewish meant to us in our times, what being feminist Jewish women in central Arizona meant to us. We are four very different women with different backgrounds and life struggles. Once a month for a year we made time and place for open, genuine support and terrific dinners. We taught ourselves Hebrew blessings, and how to drink tequila. There were no holds barred, no litmus tests applied to each other's experiences, joys, or pains with Judaism or Jewishness. We shared, we challenged, we agreed and disagreed. Mostly, we discovered. The Oy Luck Club's chemistry and solidarity changed my Jewish life.

Carolyn and I were the religious contingent. Her holding to the soul-heart was always grounding. Her joyful, unhesitating love for her own Jewishness was contagious.

And there were endless conversations with my beloved husband, Tom. Without his encouragement, I know I never would have gone through with this. Although he's not Jewish, Tom has been my closest Torah study partner, my most enthusiastic booster, shoulder, and *noodje* at every step of my Jewish journey. He learned as much about Judaism as I; he certainly read more. We talked so much about so much, that Jewish images invaded his dreams!

With Tom's commitment, *Shabbas* became a welcome, important new habit—even away from home. He insisted we pack candles and *challah* for camping trips. He'd start Havdalah on the back of the pick-up, where we'd belt out *"Eliyahu Hanovi"* while watching blazing sunsets—sacred moments indeed. In Tom I encounter my true soul mate, my best friend, the greatest blessing of my life.

Probably the single most influential person in my return to Judaism is Julius Lester. Reading his autobiography *Lovesong: Becoming a Jew* (1988) turned me homeward. In it, Julius shared the arduous, yet joyful, journey of his soul. Long defining himself as a militant black radical, he became a Jew. Discovering his Jewish ancestors helped explain his lifelong emotional resonance with Judaism. Julius' total commitment to his spiritual core's truths and needs, even at the expense of long-internalized political and group-contrived definitions of his life, grabbed me where it both hurt and helped more than I could stand. His changes cost him on more fronts than I could imagine, but that never stopped him from what he had to do: live as a Jew.

After reading the book, I wrote him a four-page, single-spaced letter of thanks and self-revelation—for my sake more than for his. I wouldn't have been surprised if this busy and well-known author had chosen not to respond, but he did. An honest, exhilarating, sometimes painfully challenging correspondence followed. Slowly, naturally, he was becoming my spiritual mentor.

Julius lives more from his spiritual core than anyone I know. A true teacher, he cut firmly yet gently through my endless ego-games and intellectual distractions. He opened me to Judaism's diverse worlds within worlds, and to assorted Jewish understandings of the divine force that regrettably gets lost in English translation or less informed interpretations. He opened me to Judaism's deep and ever-present ties to the earth—in our calendar, holiday cycle, rituals, and *mitzvot*. Julius never pushed me to be more Jewish, but what he shared pulled me home. Mostly he showed me ways in which I had never really left.

He revealed how Judaism was vast enough to embrace my unique way of being a Jew. I had a long list of beliefs and impulses that I somehow thought were "not allowed" in Judaism: about nature, about God and god-language, about evil in the world, and more. Julius shared a far larger sense of Judaism than Sunday school or parents or rabbis or synagogues combined had ever provided. In this more spacious Jewish universe, much to my surprise, virtually everything I thought and felt was acceptable. Nor was I the first Jew to think as I do! There are ancient rivers of Jewish thought that parallel mine, though often as minority voices. I no longer felt I had to choose between being my authentic self and standing in the world as a "real" Jew. I no longer equated Judaism with my incredibly limited, youthful experience of it.

Julius never suggested a Bat Mitzvah. His philosophy and style are too gentle and noninvasive to push another human being's soul around. But I know that if I had not found Julius Lester, the saga leading to this article would likely not have happened. Julius led services for my Bat Mitzvah, although we had never met face to face until three days before The Event—at least not in this life!

There were others who added momentum to my *teshuvah*, my return. Rabbis like Zalman Schacter-Shalomi and the late Aryeh Kaplan, about whom I first learned in Rodger Kamenetz' *The Jew in the Lotus* (1994). They shared and practiced the contemplative, meditative, and mystical paths within Judaism—as unfamiliar to most Jews as to others. Julius had always said Judaism was more an "Eastern" tradition than a "Western" one. How exciting to find further confirmation. Discovering Jewish meditation techniques was certainly another clincher in my return.

Prior to Kamenetz' book, I had no sense of the historical forces that had denied me such knowledge. What I longed for, and "went East" to get, were complements to the Jewish traditions of social justice and intellectual curiosity. I sought inner-looking disciplines, meditation and visualization techniques, spiritual work that entailed silence, chanting, stories. In Kamenetz' book, the Dalai Lama, whom I have long admired and many of whose teachings I also embrace, urged all seekers to "go home" to their own spiritual roots. He said all we needed awaited us there; he was right. He voiced tremendous respect for the Jews' "secret of endurance as a people," arousing my own interest in our against-the-odds survival.

I still subscribe to Jewish-Buddhist and Jewish-Quaker newsletters, but no longer call myself a "Jew-Bu." I am a Jew especially indebted to Eastern traditions. Buddhist meditation and psychology, for example, helped me realize my Jewishness. Learning from and about other traditions has enriched my own spiritual experience, and given valuable insights into the nature of the divine and soulwork.

Judaism teaches us to acknowledge distinctions, yet not get carried away with them. This approach has changed the way I teach Comparative Religions, where students regularly claim that all traditions are really one. They do share much, but the differences are also rich and delicious! A Buddhist saying expresses our view so well that Tom and I have inscribed it in our wedding rings: "We're really one, not two and we're really two, not one."

Finally, I encountered incredible Jewish feminists who simultaneously love and honor Judaism *and* work to expand the role of women and the feminine within it. I have met women in their seventies who still cry because they were denied the chance to study Torah, or prepare for Bat Mitzvah as young girls, or become rabbis though it was clearly their calling. My Bat Mitzvah was not only for me, but for generations of females denied permission or encouragement to do this. Maybe my doing it will help other Jewish women feel more comfortable and welcome. The new prayer books with diverse or gender neutral language may help. It will certainly help to have more women in the rabbinate. There are strong Jewish women within all denominations who are integrating the best of feminism and Judaism. They are improving both and inspiring many.

In my studies, I happily found that neither Judaism nor Jewish life are simply "patriarchal." There is some evidence for considering the tradition as a whole more "androgynous" than many traditions. If that's going too far, a good case can be made that the Jewish view of women is at least mixed, and often downright positive, especially considering the alternatives in surrounding cultures in its 3,500-year history. Yes, there is work to be done—but now with love, more patience, and knowledge. The women who inspired me most on this front include: Marge Piercy; women rabbis in the Renewal and Reform movements; Blu Greenberg and others who meld Orthodoxy and feminism; the women behind *LILITH* and *Bridges* magazines; and Judith Antonelli, a feminist Torah commentator who calls Jewish apologists on their sexism, and calls uninformed or narrow-minded feminists on their mistaken readings of Judaism.

Not all of my pivotal encounters were with people. One was with the movie *Schindler's List*. Tom thinks he saw my family's name, Perlmutter, flash across the screen. I'm not sure. I know I left the theater understanding more viscerally than ever before that I am in the first generation of Jews truly *free to be* Jewish. And I realized how my ignorance—my ignoring of—my Jewishness would only aid and abet the perennial antisemites' agenda to destroy us. The tragedy, the irony of Jews voluntarily opting out at the very moment in history when we could continue with comparative freedom, was just too overwhelming. Understanding this history now, I cannot continue to contribute to the demise of my people. Yes, Hillel haunts. Nor could I continue to deny my feelings when in nature. Surrounded by the nonhuman world, I quickly enter what I now call my "Sabbath-mindspace." There I feel enveloped by and permeated with some dynamic, mysterious, wonderous, interconnected process: life's Oneness. I call this "The Infinite Nearness" or the "Life-Force/Life-Source," my own translations of *Adonai Elohenu*. Sometimes it seems as if I hear or see this presence, though it is not audible or visible in any ordinary way. I feel indescribably humbled, grateful, awed.

I usually consider the Life-Force/Life-Source to be nonpersonal, much like the Tao. So I was most surprised to find myself at times envisioning it, even addressing it in personal terms. Now when I say words like "Divine," or "God," what I am addressing is this Mystery, this ineffable ground of being. Having long known what these words did not mean to me, I am getting glimpses of what they do mean.

Julius taught me that god-language tells us more about humans than about God. I cannot count the times I railed on and on about how I wasn't sure I could be a Jew because I don't usually think of God in personal terms, except when I am really angry and want to yell and express anger at some*body*. Julius' take on the matter has become mine. He wrote, "I don't know if God is personal, but I sometimes want to relate to God personally. I don't know if God is impersonal, but I sometimes want to relate to God impersonally." I admit to sometimes loving this presence/force, sometimes being mad at it. I never fully grasp it.

At my Bat Mitzvah, the role of nature in my personal spirituality became part of my *d'var Torah*, a talk based on the prescribed weekly Torah reading. In my week's section, both Sabbath and the *Shema* are given to the Jewish people. I shared how being in nature opens and enhances my experience of both. It is outdoors where I most easily, regularly discover deeper layers of Sabbath-consciousness, Shema-consciousness, and a mutually reinforcing connection between them.

It works something like this: the Shema calls upon us to deeply listen and connect with the Divine Force. To do this, we must enter a mindspace of openness, centeredness, presence. Ever since I was fourteen years old in Girl Scout Camp, I've known that nature moves me into such a space. Quiet time in nature helps me tune into the everpresent call of the Divine—to "hear" it! Conversely, the more clearly I hear, the deeper my Sabbath-consciousness becomes.

Prior to Jewish practice/studies I couldn't explain why or how entering natural spaces moved me so. Nor could I explain why the observance of Sabbath felt like meditation time, or how it brought me to another level of experiencing that-of-which-I-am-a-part and which is larger than my usual sense of self. In nature, the wisdom of Judaism and other meditative traditions came together: to *hear*, we must be *here*, that is, fully present. I have since taken the Hebrew name "Tivona." It means "Lover of Nature."

There were compelling, transforming encounters that I will never understand, but which I had to acknowledge, and act on. I could no longer ignore powerful dreams with vivid, beckoning Jewish themes. Nor a growing impulse to express out loud my wonder at, and appreciation for life—dozens of times a day! Once while driving, I abruptly had to pull off the road. I simply couldn't squelch an urge to give my fullest attention to voicing a Barucha for the great beauty before me. Who can explain why I have gotten goose bumps since childhood every time I hear a certain Hebrew line in the Torah service? I learned last year that it means "return"! Sometimes clear pointers are worth heeding, even without rational explanations.

Friend Sheila DeWoskin, who had a Bat Mitzvah in her early fifties, gently drove this point home. I recall telling her that I was inching toward having a Bat Mitzvah, but was waiting until I knew why, and could be sure my reasons were good ones. She smiled, then suggested that sometimes we just need to know *that* a decision is right for us—even if we don't know why.

But it wasn't only these encounters that pushed me toward Bat Mitzvah. There were nagging questions like the following:

"Aren't I embarrassed to teach Comparative Religions all these years, knowing so much more about other traditions than about my own? Isn't it time to admit that my interest in the religious experi-ence has become personal, not just academic?" and "Really, isn't it time to explore words I reflexively avoid: 'God,' 'religion,' 'spiri-tuality' to find words and images that *do* speak to me, albeit poorly? Eastern traditions taught me the limits of words. Meditation shows that sometimes *beyond* words are truths and states of being worth noticing. Am I so hung up on words that I will deny my most compelling experiences?"

"And I, who teach Mythology and Joseph Campbell, can I deny how many stories, themes, values, with which I have defined my life are Jewish?" My compulsion to improve the world is clearly my internalization of *tikkun olam*. My deeply embraced story that good people take on important, hard issues expresses the very word for the Jewish people, *Israel*. It means "one who contends with the Divine," a god-wrestler. There's virtually no issue or idea Jews are forbidden to scrutinize, wrestle with, including God and Torah. Centuries of *Talmudic* dialectic and disputation in search of under-standing, and in service of justice and the Great Mystery flow through me—in my personal approach to life and my professional life as a philosophy teacher.

There's more. I've always resonated unconsciously with the Jew-ish story that we exist fundamentally *in relationship*, not as isolated individuals. My activist impulse always stemmed from a sense of deep community: with other humans, other beings, and with earth.

I've always had an instinctive sense that people are *cocreators with the Great Life Source*—a preeminent Jewish story. We are not passive subjects, lacking power or responsibility. As Jews, there is no limit to our *response*-ability.

These have long permeated my being. In discovering their source, I unearthed my Jewish self. Yes, similar values are available elsewhere. But I know that I got them from Judaism.

Some ask, "How does your journey back to Jewishness feel?" I feel that I'm coming out of my head and into my deeper core—and starting to trust being there. In Hebrew, as in Chinese and Japanese, the notion of "mind" is tied to "heart," not to brain. My heart-mind is expanding.

I feel that I've "come home," and "come out" and "come to terms with" a Jewish core I barely knew I had, and never realized was so important to me.

I feel that I am resonating with centuries of a committed community, and with a profound civilization. It is a happy resonance, a comforting resonance—with many Jewish rituals, with some of the liturgy. It is a poignant, sometimes sorrowful, resonance with Jewish hardships and losses.

I feel some sadness. So many American Jews of my generation, like me, took our Judaism for granted. We had no clue to its depth, variations, nuances. Our Judaism was dormant, limited, aborted. Maybe we knew secular and rational Judaism, but little else. When our hearts and souls longed for more, we went elsewhere. Although forever indebted to those other traditions, I grieve at the depth of my ignorance. I grieve, too, for the unspeakable loss of 80 percent of Jewish spiritual teachers in the Holocaust. Had they lived, perhaps the chain would not have come so close to breaking. That unconscionable crime nearly sent spiritual Judaism into oblivion; it understandably sent many of us into religious shell shock.

Still, I feel optimistic. There is a bona fide Jewish renewal happening. Many of us are coming home in our mature years. With others who never left, we are revitalizing wonderful ancient and new images for God. We are revitalizing prayer services, starting more inclusive *chavurahs*. We are taking our place in the Jewish tradition of on-going, respectful evolution.

I still feel confusion, frustration, disappointment, even anger with some aspects of Judaism, Torah, synagogue life, Israel, Jews, God. Some of these feelings have softened, or dissolved since I've learned more. Even where they remain, they no longer turn me away from my Jewish family, my community.

For I have decided that the good of Judaism and Jewishness far outweighs the bad. And that being committed to my relationship with Judaism is like being in any other mature, long-term relationship. In a true friendship or successful marriage, there comes a time when we stop demanding perfection, of ourselves or the other, and instead accept that there will be hard times and fights as well as fun and agreements. This is more realistic and thus makes for more fulfilling, enduring relationships.

Jewish teachings constantly ask us to be whole, rather than perfect, in our relationships with self, others, religion, and God. This insight has made an enormous difference in my appreciation and expectations.

So for the rest of my life I expect to be a God-wrestling, Torah-wrestling, Judaism-wrestling, Jewish woman. But I do this now from a loving place, a knowledgeable place. Being a good Jew involves being true to both the embrace and the struggle.

Through all this I feel humbled . . . before the wisdom and spiritual devotion of three millenia of Jewish men and women. There is no end to what I can learn from them.

Mostly my journey home feels right. It is time for me to stand in the world as a newly self-aware leaf on the ancient tree of the Jewish people. I am happy and proud to be a Bat Mitzvah, an adult Jewish woman in search of what this means about myself and about what is so much bigger than I.

May I continue to both love and challenge. May I continue the process of becoming a Nina-kind-of-Jew: a nonaligned, post-denominational, honest-with-myself Jewish woman.

When friends ask, "Why now?" I used to say, "Better late than never."

Now I say, "Better late than early." It means so much more.

REFERENCES

Kamenetz, Rodger (1994). *The Jew in the lotus: A poet's rediscovery of Jewish identity in Buddhist India*. San Francisco, CA: Harper Collins.

Lester, Julius (1988). *Lovesong: Becoming a Jew*. New York: Henry Holt and Company.

Chapter 23

Exploring Adolescent Jewish Female Identity: Reflections About Voice and Relation

Carol Philips

Like all the Jewish women I know, my own history has a heavy hand in the articulation of what both being Jewish and female have meant for me. Let me begin the story with my girlhood as a Jewish New Yorker. My mother's extended family was made up of both immigrant and native-born Americans, all Orthodox Jews, except her renegade mother, a Labor Zionist, who emigrated to Palestine before I was born. My father's parents were Polish/Russian immigrants; his father, a Socialist intellectual by choice and house painter by trade; his mother a *balebusteh*, and when economic necessity demanded, a highly capable shopkeeper. My own parents brought me and my sisters up so secularly that until adulthood, I had never heard of, much less heard, a Haggadah. Nonetheless, my parents identified themselves emphatically as Jewish, which seemed to me to be more or less synonymous with progressive. When they, as they frequently did, asked the classic question, "Is it, whatever *it* might be, good or bad for the Jews?", this query seemed to be meant both in earnest and with an ironic twist, and yet a third mysterious dialectical incarnation as encompassing these two apparently opposing poles.

Thus, I grew up in Jewish neighborhoods, went to Israel on a teen tour after my junior year in high school, and subsequently left for college at Brandeis University, the epitome of secular Jewish intellectualism. Although I was aware that, theoretically, not everyone was Jewish, this concept had little reality for me. Several years after graduating from college, I became involved with the man who became my husband, a Jewish man with whom I have lived for almost twenty years. Generally, we keep the faith in my family tradition, through dedication to lox and latkes, gatherings with friends at Jewish holidays, sometimes punctuated by the singing of such classics as *Joe Hill* or *Down by the Riverside,* and regularly visiting New York. While I have learned the Haggadah through seders at my in-laws and with other friends, the several times when I went to temple, even one with a very eclectic progressive congregation, I was uncomfortable hearing about a God whom I didn't know if I believed in, in a language I couldn't understand, connected with unfamiliar rituals that held neither fond memories nor meaning for me. These forays into Judaism qua religion were made because we have two daughters, one almost adolescent, and because we live in Vermont, where I have learned more viscerally about the minority status of Jews.

That is, while the family lives in Vermont, I have been commuting to Cambridge, as a doctoral student in Human Development and Psychology at the Harvard Graduate School of Education, home of "different voice" (Gilligan, 1982), or what I will call "voice/relational" psychology. It is at this juncture that the plot thickens. A committed feminist, daughter of a feminist, mother of presumable feminists-to-be, when given options among course requirements for my degree, I chose the Psychology of Adolescence taught by Annie Rogers, feminist voice/relational psychologist. I figured that in taking the course, I would not only recognize myself as an adolescent, but that it would help prepare me to raise my daughters through what recently has been loudly and widely decried as a period in which girls' self-esteem plummets. What follows, then, is the story of my venture into this material: a summary of the voice/relational interpretation of the experiences of adolescent girls, followed by my own speculations about identity issues peculiar to Jewish girls within those interpretations.

VOICE/RELATIONAL PSYCHOLOGY
AND THE ADOLESCENT GIRL

From the advent of developmental psychology, identity formation as synonymous with achieving autonomy has been the avowed goal of adolescent development. Since this construction of identity more accurately describes the trajectory of boys raised by mothers in nuclear families than a universal developmental norm, theorists who propounded it as normal, not surprisingly, have found girls' development and women's psyches to be wanting (Chodorow, 1980). Through the ground-breaking research and theorizing of such women as Betty Friedan (1963), Phyllis Chesler (1972), Jean Baker Miller (1976), Dorothy Dinnerstein (1977) and Carol Gilligan (1982), a feminist psychology began to flower. In rejecting the typical male pattern as both normal and superior, it alleged that "the strength or wholeness of the self . . . does not depend only or even centrally on its degree of separation" (Chodorow, 1980). Eventually, feminist psychology came to offer a new lens not only for viewing women, but to account for the development of girls as they become women. This alternative construction of female development suggests that an adolescent girl's identity is optimally achieved not through separation, but through maintaining relationship.

In their profound exploration of girls' development, Carol Gilligan, and her colleagues (e.g., Brown and Gilligan, 1992; Gilligan, Lyons and Hanmer, 1990; Gilligan, Rogers, and Tolman, 1991; Rogers, 1993), explicate a crisis they perceive as central to female adolescence. To summarize, they conceptualize two paths available to girls in our culture. One path is that of the good girl whom the culture rewards. To follow that path a girl eliminates from public view all emotions and behavior that do not conform to the perfect girl stereotype; this puts her at significant psychological risk since she denies essential parts of her being, particularly strong emotions, especially anger. While that which she represses returns to erode her psychological and physical self, through such conditions as depression and eating disorders, the relationships which she has taken such care to guard by denying her own voice, are, of necessity, false ones since she has denied her voice/self to remain in them. The loss she suffers is a multiple one.

An alternative path for a female adolescent is to retain her self and voice, thereby risking the culture's retribution. Girls who take this second path are considered political resisters by voice/relational psychologists and are likely to find themselves in conflict, if not trouble, with those in authority. Good and *selfless* or bad and *selfish*, such is the inevitable dilemma every adolescent girl faces. Although voice/relational research is qualitative, indicating no percentages of which girls take what routes, its message seems to be that the greater portion of girls take what appears to be the path of least resistance, sacrificing their own selves for societal approval. The picture presented of nice repressed, depressed, and somatizing girls is certainly not a pretty one.

WHERE ARE THE JEWS?

But this picture did not seem entirely familiar to me. I noticed that while reading the voice/relational material, I began to ask myself a mutation of the classic question I had heard so often: "Is it good or bad for the Jews?" In its place, I wondered: Where *are* the Jews? Although I had grown up in an America where being Jewish was unquestionably to be a member of an ethnic and minority group, I had noticed that during the 1970s and 1980s, Jews seemed to have been subsumed under the larger heading of Caucasian. In the literature of voice/relational psychology, Jewish girls and women seemed to have entered this larger, and in my experience not satisfactorily representative, category as well. While in a single article, Annie Rogers (1993) explicates country of origin, sexual orientation, "class, race, ethnicity, and socioeconomic status" of researchers and researched alike, there is no reference to whether these girls and women are Jewish.

Since I knew that at least one of these women was Jewish, what was I to infer about other participants?[1] For instance, when I read the story of Anna, an adolescent described as a "political resister" who says "I don't see how anyone cannot have a viewpoint and not want to say anything about it" (Brown and Gilligan, 1992, p. 193), I wondered "Is Anna Jewish?" As I continued to read about researchers and girls who were identified as European-American and European-Canadian, African American, Asian American, girls of Indian and Arab descent, those of varying class backgrounds, and those who were lesbian identified (see, for instance, Brown and Gilligan, 1992; Kim, 1991; Robinson and Ward, 1991; Rogers, 1993; Smith, 1991; Ward, 1990; Zemsky, 1991), I found myself increasingly ill at ease. More to the point, I failed to find myself at all.

"Within the biography of each individual African American, the convergence of race, gender and class has its unique configuration" write Tracy Robinson and Janie Ward in their study of African-American female adolescents, thus stressing the range of personal variations on general themes associated with "the subordinate status of our race and gender." Furthermore, they assert that "many of the challenges and concerns we have confronted in the passage from childhood to adult status have been largely ignored in social science literature" (1991, p. 87). I wish to make an analagous claim for Jewish girls. My concern that this claim be made derives in part from the arguments made about female adolescents in other subordinate groups in the recent work of voice/relational theorists that I have noted. They have established differences among the situations of female adolescents in particular subordinate groups. Sometimes, as is the case for African-American girls, differences from white norms seem to encourage girls toward political rather than psychological resistance (Robinson and Ward, 1991). Furthermore, it is recognized to be imperative that adolescents whose identity is not Caucasian/middle class/heterosexual address these aspects of their identity during adolescence (Robinson and Ward, 1991; Savin-Williams and Rodriguez, 1993; Spencer and Dornbusch, 1990; Uribe and Harbeck, 1992; Ward, 1990; Zemsky, 1991). How might Jewish girls address the Jewish aspect of their identities, I wondered, if even feminist voice/relation psychologists seemed to have left them to that most ignominious fate of silence?

IN DIFFERENT DIFFERENT VOICES

In considering this problem, it occurred to me that Jewish girls had much in common with two other subordinate groups, lesbians and African Americans. Reading about both these groups inspired me to think further about Jewish female identity in a way which draws from its similarities with them. Like Caucasian lesbians and gays, Jews have had the dubious luxury of "passing." If a girl doesn't have a Jewish name, either does not look, or has changed her looks so as not to look, stereotypically Jewish, and does not act stereotypically Jewish (i.e., loud, pushy, demanding), she can virtually disappear into white Christian culture. Interestingly this disappearance is characterized by a similar paradox to the one that occurs when girls give up their voices to be in relationship: if you remove yourself to remain in relationship, your relationship is by definition a false one. If, as a Jew, you repudiate your

Jewish self in an attempt to remain in relationship, not only is that relationship necessarily a false one, but in repudiating your Jewish self, you have repudiated a significant part of your self. As is attested to by gays and lesbians, to relinquish such an aspect of your identity in order to "pass" in the larger culture is a psychological move with gravely self-destructive consequences (Savin-Williams and Rodriguez, 1993; Uribe and Harbeck, 1992; Zemsky, 1991).

Like African Americans, Jewish girls enjoy a heritage of strong women on whose shoulders we may stand. When I read Beverly Jean Smith's description of being "raised as a resister" (1991, p. 137 by her African-American mother and "Aunties" and hear the message she receives from these women in her family and community to "Speak your mind . . . You betta learn to open up your mouth and speak for yourself" (p. 147), I *know* whereof she speaks. While I don't remember any such injunctions from my own mother's lips, I heard her speak her mind unfailingly. In a similar vein, Smith describes a conversation with her female friends that could as well be a conversation at one of my family gatherings, with my numerous female cousins: "all of us are speaking at the same time and on the same subject that has been raised by someone" (1991, p. 141). On a more somber note, both Jewish and African-American girls regularly experience that their ways of being and looking are unacceptable in the larger culture. Who they are (not Christian for the one, not white for the other) how they behave (such as speaking their minds) and what they are likely to look like (not blonde, not thin, not blue-eyed) continues to be devalued.

As I reflected, my sense was that a stronger strain of what Annie Rogers calls healthy courage (1993) may appear in the lives of Jewish girls more frequently than in those of other female Caucasians, resulting in part from our experiences as outsiders. This belief, grounded in reflections on my own life and casual observation, was confirmed in an interview in which I arranged to explore these issues with Hannah, a fifteen-year-old Jewish girl,who, like me, is the daughter of a progressive feminist mother. I find it difficult to square voice/relational psychologists' description of typical adolescent girls with my experience of Hannah who openly shared her feelings, thoughts, opinions, and theories with me. Unlike the female adolescent described in voice/relational theory, she had no cover story, exhibited no self who is nice and kind without bad thoughts and feelings. On the contrary, Hannah seemed closer to Rogers' description of the desirable "'true I' . . . the self who describes her experience courageously, rendering a story in detailed transparency, voicing a full range of feelings" (1993, p. 273).

"I DON'T KNOW"

Although there are certainly aspects of being Jewish, and the way society and history impinge upon the lives of Jews, that cause Hannah, and have caused me, distress and confusion, the Hannah whom I heard seems to differ significantly from the nice, selfless, voiceless European-American girls to whom others I have discussed have reported listening. To continue my exploration of how Jewishness and voice might be related in adolescent girls, I decided to trace the phrase "I don't know," reputed to be a telltale sign of lost confidence among female adolescents (Brown and Gilligan, 1992), as it appeared in the transcript of my conversation with Hannah. To illustrate the difference in the use of this phrase between Liza, one of the girls about whom they write and Hannah, I include excerpts from transcripts of their voices. Liza, in talking about her relationships with friends says:

> . . . *I don't know.* Like if you are, *I don't know,* if you're sort of like thrown together with someone you try to adapt to like them, so *I don't know.* You just sort of have to, *I don't know. . .* (Brown and Gilligan, 1992, p. 208, italics mine)

A typical excerpt from Hannah is this:

> I guess there are times when it [being Jewish], when I felt like it, affected my life more and times when it didn't. Like, you know, every year around Chanukah and Christmas, I felt really like this is so ridiculous. I would feel so overwhelmed with all the like Santa Claus and like especially when I was younger because I really kind of wanted to be getting (pause), I felt like kids who celebrated Christmas would get more presents and it was like more fun and it's a bigger deal. Like Chanukah isn't really a big deal and this is made into a big deal around Christmastime and like, and you know family holidays are kind of a bigger deal when you're younger. I never felt like "Oh, I wish

that we celebrated Christmas," but I guess I would sometimes feel like so "I'm glad we don't celebrate Christmas cause it's stupid" y'know. So fake and commercialized. Not like my sister who said she wanted to *be* Christmas. *I don't know.*

Given the emphasis "I don't know" is accorded as a marker in data analysis by researchers using the voice method, I carefully considered Hannah's use of the phrase when it did appear. The first time she said "I don't know" was at the end of the passage above, having discussed a range of feelings about Chanukah and Christmas. Her "I don't know" in this case seemed to signal that she had said all that she had to say on the topic, that she literally did not know anything further.

Another use she made of "I don't know" was as a preliminary response to a question which she hadn't previously thought about, meaning "I don't know yet, but I'll tell you as soon as I figure it out." This usage appeared when I asked how she felt about two experiences she described: her school's treating Christmas, Chanukah, and Kwanza as equivalents and reading books about the Holocaust. When she later said "I don't know" in considering her response to an overtly antisemitic experience, I think she was describing her confusion at the time. Given the "scary" situation in which she found herself, she did not know what to do about it. While these instances could alternatively be interpreted as Hannah's response to her discomfort with her own feelings, particularly those she finds threatening, I think it would be difficult to see her use of "I don't know" as a sign of loss of self.

MARKERS OF DIFFERENCE: CHRISTMAS AND THE HOLOCAUST

My interview with Hannah, in addition to suggesting a different voice qua different sense of self than generally reported in Caucasian adolescent girls by voice/relational psychology, points toward two major sources of awareness of difference which Jews encounter well before reaching adolescence. While different subordinate groups receive different subtle, and less than subtle, messages communicating their difference and inferiority, for contemporary American Jews such knowledge often comes, I believe, from the experience of Christmas and knowledge of the Holocaust. At Christmas, it is inescapably evident that one's experience is incongruent with that of the vast majority of the population. This message is relentlessly reinforced from Thanksgiving Day onward by radio and television programming, commercials, newspapers, trips to a festooned downtown, walks around the block, in anything but a Jewish neighborhood, and in conversations which, for children, often begin "What do you want for Christmas?" and invariably end "Have a Merry Christmas." In mid-December, my then four-year-old daughter dreamt that while "everyone was going to a big parade downtown" she was the "only one" who could not go. At that time, parades were her most beloved activity.

I began my interview with Hannah by saying "I'd like to hear what growing up Jewish had meant" for her. Her first and immediate response was to describe herself in elementary school, recalling her feelings about being Jewish at Christmas. Many of her vivid recollections of that time appear in the paragraph that records her voice. I found Hannah's ability, at fifteen, to articulate these various qualities—overwhelmedness, jealousy, envy, resentment, flavored perhaps by some defensiveness, grappling with personal morality—not only to be impressive but to stand in direct contradiction to the stereotypical nice girl's lack of awareness of her true feelings. Furthermore, she was comfortable expressing her anger, that most prohibited of female emotions. When she said "Well, I guess I just really felt like Christmastime everything in the media was just saturated with the idea that everyone celebrates Christmas which is just so *not true,*" her voice was filled with righteous indignation. She was angry about the disparity between the "everybody's different" philosophy of her school, which she caricatured in a high pitched "nicey-nice" voice, and the genuine isolation that she felt when "you'd go home and watch TV and it would just be like now that Christmas is coming you could go buy your stockings which isn't *true for everybody.*" As Hannah realized, when looking back at her childhood from the vantage point of her adolescence, what she described "wasn't being Jewish as much as like not being Christian, like not being part of the larger culture." That is to say, she was experiencing a part of the oftentimes painful recognition of difference that belongs to the process of identity formation for a member of a subordinate group.

As for the Holocaust, it seems self-evident that if six million people were exterminated merely for having been like you, who you are is potentially undesirable, if not blatantly unsafe. At least, it was entirely self-evident to me, over thirty years ago, even in the largest remaining Jewish community in the world, when I fearfully and obsessively read and reread graphic excerpts of the Eichmann trials in the daily newspaper. As she had done with Christmas, Hannah broached the Holocaust—and its treatment in her school— of her own volition. Once again she was able to discern many feelings, including angry ones: "reading [about] that would make me cry and it would make me very angry"; "it was astonishing to me that there were like people who didn't know about what the Holocaust was in my class"; "I guess I was proud that I was more informed than the rest of my classmates." Among them is a certain degree of wariness and defensiveness—"I think I was sort of waiting for somebody to say something that I would find offensive so that l could get all fiery at them."

FOR FEMALES ONLY: MOTHERS AND PRINCESSES

While Christmas and the Holocaust are phenomena with which I believe all American Jews must come to terms, two robust stereotypes attach themselves to Jewish females only: the Jewish Mother and the Jewish American Princess. Before exploring their import for girls, I want to flesh out their definitions. The Jewish Mother, as evoked in comedy and literature, appears to be overbearingly involved with her children. As well as interfering in her children's lives, she tends to be anxious, compulsive about housekeeping, and generally demanding. Viewed differently, she is unassimilated. She fails to conform to white Anglo-Saxon Protestant norms for women/ mothers. Her daughter, the perhaps even more maligned Jewish American Princess, is an assimilated version of her mother as her middle name, "American," suggests. As an assimilated person, she has transferred her mother's old world obsession with children and house to an American obsession with material acquisition.

What is it about women that is despised in the personae of the Mother and the Princess? Interestingly enough, in light of feminist voice/relational psychology, I suggest that its essence is relation and voice. What is the single most terrible crime of the Jewish Mother? She wants to remain *in relation* with her children. She *voices* her anxieties, which come from an historically real experience of persecution. And the Princess? She, too, *voices* her feelings and thoughts—she says what she wants and is determined to get it. What, after all, might those stereotypical descriptions—pushy, loud and demanding—allude to other than the exercise of an unacceptably full vocal range for a female? Such "voiceful" attributes are unacceptable in the American female, she who is allgiving, whose attributes seem to bear a resemblance to the Virgin Mary.

The effect of these stereotypes on the lives of Jewish girls is to reinforce that they are in the wrong as humans not only by virtue of being females, but by virtue of being Jewish, thereby potentially belonging to the despised group Jewish American Princesses and growing up to become reviled Jewish Mothers. While the presence of these stereotypes may provoke shame in Jewish girls, the desire to escape them can lead a girl to self-hatred and the possible denial of an integral part of her self, her Jewishness, including self-mutilation (e.g., the infamous "nose job"). If Jewish women, who are so despised and ridiculed, are loud, pushy, and look wrong, then I, concludes the Jewish girl, will be quiet and self-effacing and change my appearance (Beck, 1991). Conversely, if the characteristics of voice and true relation are associated with Jewish girls, they become that much more unacceptable to the Christian majority.

As suggested by this discussion, I believe that this disavowal of body, voice, and relation have different complexities and consequences for a Jewish girl than for her white Anglo-Saxon Protestant sister. A middle- to upper-class white Christian girl's mother may be somewhat like the ideal American woman. In losing her voice, that girl joins her mother, albeit to the detriment of both. A Jewish girl, in contrast, when adopting the perfect girl persona, parts company from her Jewish mother. Thus the Jewish girl's dilemma: to be like my mother and be despised or to be like the Christian girl and despise my mother. And so another paradoxical lose-lose situation presents itself, given that the loss of relationship with her mother is a profound one for any girl.

The plight of the theoretical Jewish girl I've described above strikes me as similar to that of Nawal, an Arabic girl described by Lyn Mikel Brown and Carol Gilligan (1992). Like a Jewish mother, Nawal's mother is wrong, if in other ways. She "has black, curly, really wild hair, she wears a huge silver earring" and she seems oblivious to a perception that is all too evident to her daughter: she "does not fit the Laurel [elite private school] mother stereotype, does not." Recalling how she felt as a younger girl, Nawal says "I hated being different, and I hated having an Arabic name. And I was really almost embarrassed by my Mom" (p. 225). Having taken part in a feminist study of girls in relationship, Nawal came to change her feelings through direct discussion with her mother, realizing that she did not want her mother to be like everyone else's. Accepting and being like her mother encouraged Nawal to speak out publicly herself. For Nawal, being like her mother meant retaining as opposed to losing voice, a momentous distinction. I suggest that her story may be a more likely one for many Jewish girls as well.

HEARING A RESONANCE

This suggestion is supported through using the methodology of "turning to a text written by an older woman" whose life has common features with an adolescent girl and in whose words I would expect to "hear a resonance" (Rogers, 1993, p. 276). I turn to the writings of Grace Paley (1985), a woman who like Hannah, and like me, sees Jewish lives as defined by culture rather than religion, and sees Jewishness as intertwined with a leftist political orientation. Paley's Jewish women are anything but subdued and trying to conform to an ideal of feminine goodness. Deciding among the strong, loud, pushy, loving protagonists created by Paley is not easy, but I choose the words of one who, as she speaks, recalls the voices of generations who created her tradition of speech:

> I lean far out the window. Stop! Stop! I cry.
> The young father turns, shading his eyes, but sees. What? he says.

His friend says, Hey? Who's that? He probably thinks I'm a family friend. A teacher maybe.

Who're you? he says.

I move the pot of marigold aside . . . Once not too long ago, the tenements were speckled with women like me in every third window up to the fifth story . . . This memory enables me to say strictly, Young man, I am an older person who feels free because of that to ask questions and give advice . . . First, I want to say you're about a generation ahead of your father in your attitude and behavior toward your child.

Really? Well? Anything else, ma'am?

Son, I said, leaning another two, three dangerous inches toward him. Son, I must tell you that madmen intend to destroy this beautifully made planet. That the murder of our children by these men has got to become a terror and a sorrow to you, and starting now, it had better interfere with your daily life. (pp. 100–101)

Although this ocular protagonist suggests that her propensity to involve herself in strangers' lives, make judgments, and demand political activity is due to her advanced age, Jewish women characters abound in Paley's (1985) fiction who behave in these same ways while still young. They talk a lot, analyze a lot, feel a lot, analyze their feelings a lot. Paley's Jewish women are political, pushy, and proud.

I hope to have shown that the voices of these proud Jewish women—my own, my mother's, those of my sisters and friends, the voices of Hannah and her mother, of Grace Paley and her characters, and, I anticipate, the voices of my own daughters—resonate on a different note from the one generally described in the voice/relational literature about Caucasian adolescent girls. To the extent that my speculations about the lives of Jewish girls and women hold some truths, I believe they are important in several respects. First, they open the door to an additional model of cultural possibility which militates against girls' being silenced. Second, they suggest a natural alliance between Jewish girls and girls of color from having experienced these similarities in our cultures: a model of strong womanhood—voice and relation—in our foremothers, and the hatred and ridicule of the dominant culture based on our appearance and behavior. Similarly, Jewish and lesbian girls may be natural allies for both having experienced the hatred of our groups and having dealt with the ambiguity of passing.

Finally, my dearest hope is that the voice of the Jewish adolescent girl and woman will henceforth be recognized in the voice/relational conversation. My hope is that in the future Jewish girls and women will not experience the confusion and loss of identity concomitant with not hearing one's own voice acknowledged, nor reading one's own name. Rather, as they turn to texts about girls and women, may they be inspired by their own, particularly Jewish, likeness to this girl who bravely speaks her feelings and her thoughts, that woman who has raised her voice in anger, love, and truth.

NOTE

1. I have discussed this issue with her. She not only acknowledged the problem I describe here, but encouraged me to continue with this work.

REFERENCES

Beck, Evelyn Tort (1991). Therapy's double dilemma: Anti-Semitism and misogyny. In Rachel Josefowitz Siegel and Ellen Cole (Eds.), *Jewish women in therapy: Seen but not heard.* Binghamton, NY: The Harrington Park Press.

Brown, Lynn Mikel and Gilligan, Carol. (1992). *Meeting at the crossroads: Women's psychology and girls' development.* Cambridge, MA: Harvard University Press.

Chesler, Phyllis (1972). *Women and madness.* New York: Avon Books.

Chodorow, Nancy (1980). Gender, relation, and difference in psychoanalytic perspective. In C. Zanardi (Ed.), *Essential papers on the psychology of women* (pp. 420 – 436). New York: New York University Press.

Dinnerstein, Dorothy (1977). *The mermaid and the minotaur: Sexual arrangements and human malaise.* New York: Harper Colophon Books.

Friedan, Betty (1963). *The feminine mystique:* New York: Dell.

Gilligan, Carol (1982). *In a different voice.* Cambridge, MA: Harvard University Press.

Gilligan, Carol, Lyons, Nona, and Hanmer, Trudy (Eds.) (1990). *Making connections: The relational worlds of girls at the Emma Willard School.* Cambridge, MA: Harvard University Press.

Gilligan, Carol, Rogers, Annie, and Tolman, Deborah (Eds.) (1991). *Women, girls, and psychotherapy: Reframing resistance.* New York: The Haworth Press.

Kim, Hyo-Jung (1991). "'Do you have eyelashes?'" In Carol Gilligan, Annie Rogers, and Deborah Tolman (Eds.), *Women, girls, and psychotherapy: Reframing resistance* (pp. 87 – 105). New York: The Haworth Press.

Miller, Jean Baker (1976). *Toward a new psychology of women.* Boston: Beacon Press.

Paley, Grace (1985). *Later the same day.* New York: Penguin Books.

Robinson, Tracy and Ward, Janie (1991). "A belief in self far greater than anyone's disbelief: Cultivating resistance among African-American female adolescents. In Carol Gilligan, Annie Rogers, and Deborah Tolman (Eds.), *Women, girls, and psychotherapy: Reframing resistance* (pp. 87 – 1105). New York: The Haworth Press.

Rogers, Annie (1993). Ordinary Courage. *Harvard Educational Review. 63*(3), 265 – 294.

Savin-Williams, Ritch and Rodriguez, Richard (1993). A developmental, clinical perspective on lesbian, gay male, and bisexual youths. In Thomas Gulotta, G. Adams, and R. Montemayer (Eds.), *Adolescent Sexuality* (pp. 77 – 101). London: Sage Publications.

Smith, Beverly (1991). Raising a resister. In Carol Gilligan, Annie Rogers, and Deborah Tolman, (Eds.), *Women, girls, and psychotherapy: Reframing resistance* (pp. 137 – 148). New York: The Haworth Press.

Spencer, Margaret Beale and Dornbusch, Sanford (1990). Challenges in studying minority youth. In Shirley Feldman and Glen Elliott (Eds.), *At the threshold: The developing adolescent.* (pp. 123 – 147). Cambridge, MA: Harvard University Press.

Uribe, Virginia and Harbeck, Karen (1992). "Addressing the needs of lesbian, gay, and bisexual youth: The origins of PROJECT 10 and school-based intervention." In Karen Harbeck (Ed.), *Coming out of the classroom closet: Gay and lesbian students, teachers, and curricula.* New York: The Haworth Press.

Ward, Janie (1990). Racial identity formation and transformation. In Carol Gilligan, Nona Lyons, and Trudy Hanmer (Eds.), *Making connections: The relational worlds of adolescent girls at Emma Willard School.* (pp. 6 – 30). Cambridge, MA: Harvard University Press.

Zemsky, Beth (1991). Coming out against all odds: Resistance in the life of a young lesbian. In Carol Gilligan, Annie Rogers, and Deborah Tolman, (Eds.), *Women, girls, and psychotherapy: Reframing resistance* (pp. 185 – 201). New York: The Haworth Press.

Chapter 24

First There Are the Questions

Ellyn Kaschak

The three traditions of Judaism, feminism, and psychology have, in differing and dynamic combination, taught many of us how to question and what to question. As Jews and as women, we are accustomed to not being considered in other people's questions or to being considered in questions whose answers compromise, criticize, or minimize us. We are all wounded in various ways by other people's questions and other people's answers. The movement toward reclaiming ourselves and our own experiences begins in the questions, the questions that we have already asked and have yet to ask. It lies in the courage of each of us in being able to face the difficult questions and not resolve them prematurely with easy answers.

Feminist philosophy and its academic stepchildren, psychology, sociology, and athropology are leading us to the eptistemological foundations of daily life. They have taught us that we can and must ask the right questions and ask them ourselves because therein lie the answers. There are no neutral questions; rather they are asked from particular perspectives, and if we take a white, Christian, male perspective as the norm and the normal, then we are, by definition, abnormal. We are different. We are the other. We are invisible, not just to them, but, even more dangerously, to ourselves as well. If we learn to see ourselves through other people's eyes, to judge ourselves against their standards, then we are always found, and find

This essay is based on my opening keynote address delivered at The First International Conference on Judaism, Feminism, and Psychology: Creating a Shelter in the Wilderness, held in Seattle, Washington, in 1992.

ourselves, wanting. Unless we can ferret out the hidden perspective in every question and in every answer, we are doomed to live our lives in the margins, at best hidden or minor characters in other people's stories, at worst, endangered. It is no accident, no twist of the tongue that my book, *Engendered Lives* (Kaschak, 1992) is often referred to as *Endangered Lives*. Engendered lives are endangered lives, as are any lives controlled by another's vision.

Why should we be held to their standard and they not to ours? In the right to ask the questions, and to have one's questions matter, lies the first moment of real power. Our theories and our practice depend entirely upon who asks the questions, for our questions come from ourselves and lead right back there. Our lives are determined first by epistemology and, only after that, by the answers, the political and psychological justifications for the laws, the wars, and the acts that control our societies and individuals.

As women and as Jews, we have often been in response to other people's questions—the Jewish Question of non-Jews and antisemites, and the Woman Question asked by nonwomen and misogynists. What do women want and who can understand them anyway? Held to a masculine standard of psychological development, we are undeveloped. To a masculine standard of normal, we are abnormal. To a Christian definition of a family and of family values, our families are often considered matriarchal—dangerously abnormal, just as are African-American families in one well-known racist formulation (Moynihan, 1965). Again, we must look carefully at who defines the terms of the argument and how. Let us consider the question, "Is the Jewish or the African-American family matriarchal?"

As a feminist and a psychologist, I would answer that in a matriarchal family, women would be respected and girl children cherished. There would be no abuse, incest, and rape. Any such acts of hatred would shame the perpetrator, not the victim, and these acts would not be the norm, but severely abnormal. We would not have Jewish princess jokes or Jewish mother jokes. Where are the Jewish father jokes? The strengths of African-American mothers would not be suspect. We would not be tempted to feed our sons and starve our daughters, for a daughter with a healthy appetite is not the unambivalently happy thing for a mother that a son is. No woman would ever try to starve herself into a diminutive size that brings women self-esteem. Perhaps a more relevant question is whether any man is man enough to live the life of a woman.

For many Jewish women and men, and other members of identifiable and identified groups, who we are, and are not, is persistently defined by others. In this way, we come to know ourselves through others' eyes or in opposition to the presumptuousness of others. This results in an experience of fragmentation rather than an appreciation of the complexity and the richness of all our varied experiences. We must all say "No" to being defined in opposition either by a Christian or Jewish audience, a black or a white audience, a female or a male audience. We must Take Back the Questions.

Any fully engaged feminist project has to start with the act of reclamation and insistence on the fullness of our own experience. So we must begin this excavation, this reclamation project, as carefully as if a tangible structure were going to stand upon the foundation we are helping to create. In reality, something of much greater consequence is in the making, the reclaiming of ourselves.

There is a story told about a traveler in the wilderness coming upon three construction workers. As she was also a Jew and a psychotherapist, she felt compelled to ask them some questions and began by inquiring about what they were doing. The first explained to her that they were laying bricks. The second replied that they were building a wall, but the third reported that they were building a temple. This may be a lesson in standpoint, but it also speaks of the importance of having and maintaining a vision through the most ugly ordinary daily work, whether it is laying bricks or doing psychotherapy.

In asking our own questions, we may not be constructing a temple or even a permanent structure for ourselves or each other, but a shelter in the various wildernesses we inhabit as individuals and as a community. A shelter is more temporary and more ordinary than a temple. And the ordinary, the world of dailiness, is where women reside. Our shelter may be only a straw hut, as is the *Sukkah*. The Sukkah conveys a paradoxical notion of protection in that true shelter does not exist in physical permanence, but in exposure and in living in community.

How do we develop an authentic vision of our own that allows for the common ground that we share, as well as for our many differences? It will not be exactly the same vision for each of us, as we see with our own eyes, but to build anything, even a temporary shelter, we need to share some common ground upon which to build.

What are the important questions for a traveler in the wilderness to ask? We must certainly ask who we are? What unique combination of Jew and feminist is each of us separately, and who are all of us collectively? We must find a way to ask the hard questions and not settle into the easy answers. We must insist upon not seeing ourselves through others' eyes as Jews or as women, but instead reclaim our own vision, place ourselves centrally in our own stories, come in out of the wilderness, out of exile and out of the margins of men's stories, no matter what their religion or ethnicity.

In my own work, *Engendered Lives* (Kaschak, 1992), I have reconsidered a well-known psychological family story, that of Oedipus the King, the tragic son of Laius and Jocasta, and the four children of the marriage of Oedipus and Jocasta. In Freud's reading, this family drama centers almost exclusively on the perspectives and dilemmas of the men involved, particularly those of Oedipus. The women are only sub-versions in a tale of a man. In my own reading, they take center stage, where they and their lives matter. The tragedy of Oedipus' life centers not on sexuality, but on vision and blindness, on seeing and not seeing, and particularly on his kingly sense of entitlement. I consider, from the perspective of his daughter/sister, Antigone, how it might be possible for her and her mother, Jocasta, as well as for all of us women, not to be extensions of someone else's vision/blindness, but to see for ourselves, to maintain our own vision.

Our Jewish tradition also offers us many parables of complete families that somehow focus almost exclusively on the struggles of the fathers and sons, with women absent or hidden in the margins. The tale of the first Jewish father, Abraham, and his son, Isaac, can certainly be taken as a parable about fathers and sons in a patriarchal system, about the willingness of fathers to sacrifice their sons in war or even about the castrating father, a concept I have never heard used by psychologists, although it is clearly the fathers who endanger their sons in both stories.

Even in the margins, in the sub-versions, among Greeks or psychologists or Jews, women are not safe and are never blameless, even when powerless. Wasn't Sara really to blame for not stopping Abraham? Certainly our current nonfeminist theories would consider her part of a dysfunctional system or perhaps the Bible's first codependent, as much as they would fault Jocasta for the sins of both her husbands. The vision that predominates is that of the king, even the blind king.

Women and our own perspectives are lost in men's stories. If we matter at all, it is as the embodiment of men's sins and men's temptations. A man holds a knife above his son, ready to murder him or cast him out to die, and psychology, for generations, invokes the name of the "castrating" mother. The women in both stories, Antigone and Jocasta, Sara and Hagar, exist only in the service of the men and their vision. They ask no questions of their own.

As psychotherapists and as women, merely shifting our understanding of female psychology to the pre-Oedipal phase is tantamount to understanding ourselves as Jews as pre-Isaac or as pre-male. We can no longer see ourselves as pre or post or Oedipal anything, but must instead develop our own psychologies, our own metaphors, our own stories, our own questions and our own answers.

The themes of exile and wilderness recur throughout history for Jews, as they do for women. The Passover Seder is a bittersweet time; a time to remember the release from slavery and from exile. Yet the traditional family ritual involves only the youngest and oldest males. Only they seem to have something to remember. In my own family, my grandfather read what seemed, in child's time, interminable words in Hebrew that only he understood. As always, there were the questions, but only the youngest boy present was permitted to ask them. I had many questions of my own, but I was silent. "Why is this night the same as all other nights? Why are only male voices heard? Why are all the women in the kitchen cooking and cleaning? Why don't I belong in either room? Why don't I get to ask any questions?"

As I developed into adulthood, my questions developed and matured also into the questions of a feminist, a psychotherapist, a Jew. As a woman and a feminist, do I have or want a place as a Jew? Do I have to accept Jewishness and being a Jewish woman as defined by men? By other women?

Some years ago, I joined two feminist organizations already several years in existence. Soon after joining, and on two separate occasions, I was taken aside by Jewish women members, who firmly cautioned me with almost identical words. "We are working on diversity in this group and we don't mean issues of Jewish women.

There are already too many of us." This was said conspiratorially to me with an assurance that I would know exactly what they meant. And what amazed me is that I did. As insiders, we were outsiders. By virtue of being too visible, we—or at least an important aspect of each of us—must be kept invisible. Somehow to remain invisible is to be respectful of others and to be safe from harm. Where had I heard this before?

What was this unchallenged and almost invisible antisemitism in feminist psychology organizations? Was it a reflection of a more general influence in other women's organizations and in the feminist movement itself? If so, how was it being internalized or, at least, not questioned by Jewish women?

In other words, what seemed to be shelter could turn into wilderness. As Jews given temporary shelter in other people's lands, we have certainly known this. For many women, what appears to be shelter, the home, is often the least safe place. As Jewish women, we have expected our homes, marriages, and relationships to provide shelter, and have been shocked and shamed when they turn out to be the most dangerous places of all.

At least viscerally I understood that Jews were too visible and were somehow in danger and to blame, but, upon reflection, I realized that I didn't understand at all. Exactly what were we to blame for? Was the danger invisibility or visibility? Exactly what and from whom were we hiding and why? Who were "we" anyway? None of the stories that I had heard told by other Jewish women were mine. Was I even united with other Jewish feminists and in what ways? Jewish was not the first or even the second or third adjective that I would have used to describe myself.

That I am able to consider these questions at all is largely attributable to both the successes and the failures of the American Dream. Women are, in a sense, the newest immigrants of the American Dream. Yet the American Dream of the melting pot stopped a generation ago, with the generation of the 1960s and 1970s, the Civil Rights Movement. African Americans could not melt. They remained black. Many Jews tried to melt with differing degrees of success and with different prices to pay for that bittersweet success. Large numbers of a whole generation changed their names and lost themselves in other people's names, as women of every generation do. When the second wave of the Women's Liberation Movement arrived, it soon became clear that women could not melt either. They remained female even in the most man-tailored dress-for-success suits. For the various ethnic pride movements that have followed, melting has meant stirring in a very diverse recipe, all of whom were to exit uniformly, but the uniform was white and it was Anglo-Saxon and, if not Protestant, it was certainly Christian.

Are there ways in which the Women's Movement has also demanded that we melt? For many of us, feminism, in combination with psychology and Judaism, has given us a sense of self and self-respect that has allowed us to come in out of the wilderness. Not to be just outsiders, visitors in a Christian world, in a masculinist patriarchy, or even in a Women's Movement in which Jewish women have fully participated, often not as Jewish women per se, but instead as some generic form of white women. Or claiming a Jewish identity and then being viewed as not entitled to other aspects of our identities. My many friends and colleagues who are Latin American Jews are considered not to be Latin American or citizens, but instead Jews and outsiders, in the antisemitic climates of their homelands. Once in the United States, they have been dismayed to discover that many feminists unwittingly concur in defining them as Jews and their non-Jewish counterparts as Third World women.

As feminists, as women, and as Jews, we can no longer choose between erasure and exclusion. We must join those who have not and are not about to melt and instead demand of ourselves and others respect for our richness and differences, along with our commonalities.

I now attend feminist seders unlike those of my childhood, ones that could not even have been imagined in the years of my childhood. Women cook and clean, but also pray and read and sing and testify. I do not understand most of the Hebrew and do not feel the connection to Judaism that most of them do. I miss the sound of the Spanish language which has become my second language as an adult. Yet the language of the seder is the language of liberation and release from exile, and that aspect matters to me. That it is all said in women's voices matters most of all, for women's voices are my own.

How did Spanish become my second language? How did I, as an adult, begin to make a second home in Latin America, and begin to discover Latin American Jews who had escaped from the Holocaust to a life of further exile and antisemitism? What drew me to this complex shelter in a different wilderness, to an exile within someone else's exile? Until recently I would not have said that I was in the wilderness, but traveling, sightseeing in other people's lives. As a psychologist and psychotherapist, a guide on other people's journeys, a visitor from another psyche, from inner space. Yet I have been traveling in the wilderness of other people's exile.

Certainly I cannot think about Latin America or Latin Jews without consideration of the events of 1492, the beginning of another form of exile, another wilderness, another diaspora, that is, the Inquisition and Expulsion or forced conversion of the Spanish Jews, declared more than 500 years ago in 1492 by the same monarchs who sent Columbus on his voyage. In fact, Columbus himself noted in his logs that ships filled with departing Jews were lined up next to his. This decree was signed by King Ferdinand and Queen Isabella of Spain, whose names are familiar to most of us from early lessons in school, along with that of Christopher Columbus, the "discoverer" of America. At least 150,000 Jews were forced to leave Spain by July of that same year. These Jews fled into exile, as the indigenous peoples of the Americas were about to be "discovered" and to be subjected to 500 years of systematic genocide.

More questions. How is it possible to "discover" a land that was fully inhabited by approximately 75 million people and to claim it for oneself and one's king and queen? Imagine going about the daily routine of your life and suddenly being discovered one day. The "Indians" discovered in the West by Columbus were not even accepted as human by Europeans until they were decreed to be so by a papal bull in 1537. At the same time, even those Jews who converted to Catholicism became known as *Marranos* or "swine." What is a human being according to this perspective? Most of us know the answer all too well and the actions that can be justified if their victims are not viewed as human. In many important ways, we share 500 years of genocide with the native peoples of the Americas.

As a result, many communities have existed in profound grief for all these years. For Jews, the Expulsion from Spain was followed by the pogroms in Russia and the horrors of the Holocaust. This is a collective form of trauma and loss, even for those of us for whom the atrocities are largely vicarious. There is a biblical, as well as a psychological, tradition for dealing with loss. Jeremiah (9:16–17) refers to professional wailers and lamenters for mourning and, of course, they are women, who even then were in charge of having and expressing the feelings for everyone else: "Thus said the lord of hosts: Consider and call for the mourning women that they may come . . . and let them make haste, and take up a wailing for us that our eyes may run down with tears, and our eyelids gush out with waters." This is perhaps the earliest biblical reference to feminist therapy. Yet as women, as feminist psychotherapists and often as Jews, we often grieve for others and not for ourselves or our collective history.

Grieving for a person continues their life in subjective time. Yet continued victimization, loss, and grief lead inevitably to depression and despair. Lowered expectations can then become a strategy that functions as an antidepressant. That is, one is never disappointed, but correct if things turns out badly. Not just the individual, but the entire group is weakened by this paradoxical attempt at protection.

Psychologists and psychotherapists are often taught to ask narrow, decontexualized, and depolitized questions about grief, loss, and victimization, taught to look for the cure in separation, individuation, and the taking of individual responsibility that is so implicit in white, middle-class, American masculine values. As women and Jews, not all middle class and not all white, we have all had our vision clouded by the power of this predominant perspective. It is time that we redefine the causes of and cures for depression, grief, and so-called psychopathology in keeping with our own experiences.

From our own perspectives, many Jews and many women suffer from cultural, rather than individual, depression. We must stop diagnosing, labeling, and pathologizing the effects of tremendous loss and grief, of genocide. Instead we must insist that psychopathology comes from an outraged sense of unfairness, of violation that is unbearable to experience or to see. As psychologists, we can learn here from the Jewish principle of *Tikkun Olam*, that is, we must work on the reordering of all that is "disordered" and not on "disorders."

We must come together as a community to mourn, to remember, and to create new forms, new memories, and a deepened and more committed sense of community in order to restore us and our mothers, sisters, and daughters to ourselves, to our own history. To come out of the wilderness of whatever exile each of us lives in as a woman, a feminist, a Jew.

Returning to my own experience in childhood and adulthood with the Seder both as a remembrance and an experience of exile, I can begin to formulate a feminist version of the four questions. I begin by asking, "Why is this day the same as all other days?"

Because on this day in North America, a woman will be raped every five minutes. A woman will be beaten every fifteen seconds. One out of three will be sexually abused before she reaches the age of eighteen. One out of two will be raped and two-thirds will be victims of battery. Nine out of ten will be sexually harassed at school or at work. Two-thirds of the world's illiterates are still female. Women and children constitute 90 percent of all refugee populations and 80 percent of all poverty populations.

On this day, fewer than one-third of all women have access to contraceptive information or devices. More than half have no trained assistance during pregnancy or childbirth. Although one-third of all families on earth are headed by women and women are one-third of the world's formal or visible workforce, we receive one-tenth of the income. Women own less than 1 percent of the world's property. Whether our exiles are in Egypt or Spain, Latin America or Russia, Canada or the United States, we are eternally searching for shelter in lands that are declared to belong to other people.

And why is this day different? Because we have begun to ask the questions and formulate the answers. Because we have named and identified these abuses and are working to change them through psychology, law, and political activism. And because our radical vision has, in many ways, become part of mainstream psychological treatment and temporary shelter for women and children. It is different because together we are creating temporary shelter in the wilderness, space in all our various forms of exile.

Women are the exiles among exiles. Whether in the story of Cristobal Colon, Oedipus, or Abraham and Isaac, women reside between the lines, in the margins, are home making dinner or committing suicide. Our perspective is from the subversion, so we are natural subversives. And the most subversive of our activities is to begin to question—not the questions of the male Talmudic scholars or of the analysts of the Oedipal complex and pre-Oedipal stages.

Our questions subvert their very perspective. As we see for ourselves, they must see that there is not just one correct perspective. Feminists and other subversives ushered in the post-Modernist age. We are no longer being discovered, but are discovering ourselves for ourselves.

Jews, women, and psychologists must define for ourselves who we are and what family, community, and shelter are and can be. To do so, we bring to bear all the skills of our traditions—Judaism, feminism, and psychology—and begin by bearing witness to ourselves and to each other. We can use, this time in our own service, the dual perspectives of exiles and outsiders, of those who exist in the subtext and at the margins. We must weep and wail, and argue, and support, and question, and question. And we must subvert the traditions that exclude women's perspectives with our subversions.

Although some of us have already experienced coming out of our various and shared exiles, it is long overdue that we begin coming in. Not separately one at a time, but together, in connection and in community. As feminists, we reject the individual struggle, the isolation and erasure of the American Dream and reach back to the tradition of our Jewish and feminist roots instead—to come in to ourselves and to each other. And to bring those who matter with us, those whom we have lost or who are lost to themselves, who have fallen in the undeclared wars against women or the declared wars against Jews, those who have gone into the darkness alone.

I would like to offer to them and to us an in vocation, a calling in, into the shelter that we are making.

A Coming In Prayer (In Vocation)

Restore us to our own history and to ourselves,
For no one will be whole until we know the whole story.
Help us to formulate new questions,
To live mindfully in the wilderness
And to make shelter and community when and where we can.
To protect our daughters and our sons
And to teach them both to respect women and themselves.
To resist the temptation to define ourselves as normal or
    normal as us.

To ask the difficult questions and not seek the easy answers.
To live life fully and consciously and bravely.
And to make shelter when and where we can.
We are grateful
That we have all
Come to this moment together.
For we are our own and each other's shelter.
Welcome.

REFERENCES

Kaschak, Ellyn (1992). *Engendered lives: A new psychology of women's experience.* New York: Basic Books.

Moynihan, Daniel Patrick (1965). U.S. Department of Labor, Office of Policy Planning and Research, *The Negro family: The case for national action.* Washington, DC: U.S. Government Printing Office.

SECTION V:
PAIN AND HEALING,
SORROW AND HOPE

Chapter 25

Jewish Battered Women:
Shalom Bayit or a Shonde?

Lenore E. A. Walker

The favorite Jewish expression uttered when exposing a shameful secret, "it's a *shonde*," is frequently used whenever anyone attempts to discuss Jewish battered women. The meaning of the message is clear to Jews: keep quiet! But, if we only honor the myth of *shalom bayit*, the peaceful Jewish home, we will never be able to learn how to prevent family violence nor provide the assistance they too need. After two decades of work with battered women and their families, it is clear to me that without exposing the violence in their homes, it is difficult to help them find safety and peace for themselves and their children.

When I began to explore the world of the battered woman and child during the 1970s, it felt like unveiling the darkest side of family life, destroying some of my most cherished beliefs. Although I knew it was necessary to open the doors of these families and document what was seen inside, in many ways it was like opening Pandora's box; once exposed, the horrors could never go back inside again. Today we call the effects on therapists exposed to these horrors "vicarious traumatization," but then, I only knew that I was changed forever by what I had witnessed! How could someone who loved a person also commit the most heinous abuse upon that person's body and soul? Families were sacred, my Jewish upbringing taught me; the people in them loved and nurtured each other; they did not use torture!

As I began to learn more about violence in the family, it became clear that neither the victims nor the perpetrators committed or experienced abuse because they suffered from what we knew as a mental disorder. Nor was the abuse comparable to the typical family dysfunctions that psychologists are used to treating in our offices. Why then did such horrors occur? My search for my Jewish roots helped me find meaning and comfort in my work as I explored the violence inside families who also loved each other. What goes wrong that creates the seemingly dual personality of the abuser, both loving and mean toward his or her[1] family? How does he justify his behavior to himself? Does he really believe the excuses and distortions he told the rest of the world, placing the blame on the woman who to him, "deserved it"? How could otherwise bright and capable women continue to believe that the perpetrator would change, even after experiencing many years of his violence and promises to stop it? How could fathers and mothers be so out of touch with their own needs, and the needs of their children, that they didn't realize how they were damaging them with their cruel words and actions? And, where was G-d in permitting this evil underside of life to continue, so that the lessons of violence learned in the family spilled over into the streets and communities, touching everyone's lives?

Shortly before he died in 1978, my gentle and nonabusive husband began to share with me his own memories that were surfacing about his abusive Jewish family. It shattered my beliefs that violence never happened in Jewish homes. Jewish women and men simply did not talk about this; it was truly considered a shonde. As I learned more about his own childhood and then, of others in the Jewish community, the Jewish moral code that had guided me as I grew up began to unravel faster and faster, first from the challenges put to it by feminist analysis of its lack of equality and therefore, real respect for women, and then from the untimely death of my beloved husband. We were working together with violent families; work that I had chosen without any knowledge of his past experiences, partially in hopes of fulfilling my obligation as a Jew to help make the world a better place.

Although I did not practice my religion in a traditional way, I had taken these moral obligations quite seriously. I did not know where to turn for answers to these moral questions, including understanding "evil," that swirled around in my head, even as I was gathering the necessary data to scientifically explain men's violence against women. Traditional rabbis simply didn't talk about such things, and liberal rabbis were more likely to espouse the psychological views that I myself was learning and writing about but that still had so many unanswered questions. Judaism had become less relevant in my own life until the death of my husband and my father, both within three months of each other. Issues of life and death have a way of reconnecting people to their religion, and I was no exception.

Of all the rituals in Judaism that help people get through what often appears to be insurmountable pain, those surrounding the death of a beloved soothe the most. Considering death a part of life, the rituals that help the bereaved to mourn their loss during the *shiva* period help avoid the denial that psychologists know can prevent a person from completing the necessary mourning. These rituals also provide a structure for acceptance of loss and appreciation for the continuance of life by expression of grief and acknowledgment of their loved ones through the *Yahrzeit* and *Yiskor* prayers. Despite my own shaken faith, arising out of the feminist critique of this patriarchal religion, and particularly my anger in the sexist exclusion of women from many of these rituals, including their community recitation, I desperately needed to find a place for my own pain. Although tempted, I did not turn away from Judaism, but rather, with encouragement from several rabbis, tried to follow all the mourning rituals, including saying the daily *Kaddish* prayers together with the men who came to make a *minyan*. I was angry that I could not be counted in the minyan at that time, but I personally felt connected to a higher power that also helped me make connections with the life and death nature in some of the more serious high-risk battering relationships.

EXPERT WITNESS TESTIMONY ON BATTERED WOMAN SYNDROME IN SELF-DEFENSE HOMICIDE CASES

At the same time that I was experiencing this upheaval in my personal life, I also had begun the long process to introduce expert witness testimony on the "battered woman syndrome" in the courts, to help explain the mental state—not necessarily mental illness—of abused women who killed their partners in what they believed was self-defense. These cases often bore no resemblance to the traditional "eye-for-an-eye" concept of self-defense because the women frequently acted before the impending violence became apparent to others, or after the beating appeared to be over, because the man was at rest or even sleeping. Thus, the cyclical nature of the abuse, including the intermittent pattern of violence, was not easily seen in many of these relationships, although even a sleeping man could be perceived as dangerous by the battered woman.

Even more difficult to explain were the behaviors and statements made by the women that at first glance seemed to negate some of the legal elements of self-defense. For example, it was common for the woman to admit to killing the man because she was terrified that he was going to kill her; however, in what was seemingly a direct contradiction, that same battered woman might also describe how she "knew" he would beat her again and so she went out and bought herself a gun to defend herself because she wasn't going to let him hurt her again! The woman's intention was to stop the beatings from reoccurring, not to kill the man, unless the violence was at such a high level of lethality that she believed she had no alternative if she wanted to stay alive.

Legally, to meet the burden of proving "self-defense," it was necessary to prove that the woman acted after a "reasonable perception of imminent danger" which of course was defined differently in the laws that are legislated in each state. After testifying in a few of these cases, it became clear to me that despite our best intentions, both the defense lawyers and I were in uncharted waters. For me, the use of violence against other violence was an anathema. My idea of a good battle was a verbal debate using logic and reason on even the smallest point. This comes from the Talmudic tradition of *pilpul* or arguments over each tiny detail. Defending murder as a way to stop violence was the last thing I ever thought I would find myself doing. Psychologists are healers; we believe that human beings can change their behavior, even when they don't appear initially motivated. Judges, too, were unclear about how to handle this new spin on an old justification defense . . . self-defense. And yet a battered woman who has had previous experience with the futility of attempting certain actions, such as trying to escape from the batterer, would be expected to reasonably perceive the need to use deadly force in situations that might not seem as dangerous to a nonabused woman or man. Thus, battered woman syndrome testimony was needed to help jurors understand the "state of mind" of that woman at that moment when she shot the man, that justified her use of deadly force . . . which is what we call "self-defense."

A battered woman usually takes on the batterer's mood. It is common for a victim of trauma to lose the ability to predict "neutrality." Anyone who does not stand loud and clear for her and in her corner, may be seen as the enemy, as being against her or at least able to cause her further harm whether or not intentional! Some women come into the abusive relationship having been abused in other relationships as well as in their childhood families. Each new abusive relationship causes the woman to lose more of her resiliency—she is able to bend less and less before coming to a "breaking-point"! Each time a new abusive incident occurs, in her minds' eye, she may be replaying other similar incidents that get stirred up and reawakened by this new incident. Thus, the emotional impact of new incidents gets more severe with each one. There are as many ways to physically, sexually, and psychologically abuse a person as long as there are those who let others "get away with it!"

Many batterers abuse women because "no one stops them!" Other batterers use violence against their families as well as committing other criminal acts. Still others have problems with regulating their use of alcohol, other drugs, and mental illnesses in addition to their propensity toward violence. Batterers and their victims often need other people's help to try to create a healthier atmosphere for their family. As the woman begins to feel stronger psychologically, she will begin to break the three-phase cycle of violence, reversing the learned helplessness that has developed, and may even be able to help the family to survive and stop the psychological abuse from continuing!

After interviewing and studying battered women for several years, I did not have personal difficulty in understanding the few battered women who were so terrified and desperate that they did kill their abusers, and so I began presenting their cases to judges and juries. I believed then as I still do today, that the community's intervention in preventing or stopping abuse at an early stage is a far better outcome than leaving the battered woman no other choice but to use deadly force to defend herself and perhaps her children too, if she wants to live a normal life in the future. Divorce, the most often recommended solution, does not stop the violence; batterers continue to harass, stalk, and abuse the women and their children often assisted by a legal system that colludes with the men and invalidates the reports of women. As I wrote in my second book for the general public, *Terrifying Love: Why Battered Women Kill and How Society Responds* (Walker, 1989), women and children who come from families where the man has been killed fare much better than those from families where divorce has occurred but the father remains in control of the family or in families who continue to stay together.

STUDYING TALMUD

But, how can murder be justified? Is it similar to the "eye-for-an-eye" concept discussed in the Talmud? Or the admonition to protect life and prevent disaster to another person? Is it about good and evil? Or are the fundamentalists who preach women's subservience and obedience to their husbands carrying G-d's true message for battered women? I could not begin to understand these moral and religious issues by myself. Neither could I turn to the *Torah* or *Talmud* to find the answers. A a girl I was not encouraged to study Hebrew or the Talmud, although I certainly was taught how to cook, clean, and perform the many rituals Jewish women do at home to celebrate the holidays. Perhaps it was not by accident that just at this time, I was invited to join a Talmud study group. The group was being formed by a new traditional rabbi who was willing to teach a class of men and women who wanted to study together in traditional but modern Orthodox ways. The class was to meet at an attorney's office in my building and we began by using the new Steinsaltz (1989) translation of the Talmud as the study guide. Rabbi Eli Braun, who was also a trained social worker who had worked in a child abuse agency, was quite supportive of Jewish feminist views. He encouraged me to join the group that ranged from six to twelve people who met during lunch hour once a week. He also understood my sometimes hectic travel schedule and made it possible for me and the others to drop in and out without feeling guilty about interrupting the class. Thus began my formal exploration of the Talmud!

During the first few weeks, it took every bit of self-control not to walk out of these sessions because of the strong emotions that the sexist ideas and language raised in me. I had to use self-talk to remind myself that my goal was to learn what the Talmud had to say from the original source, and that would require understanding the gender bias found in it and how that impacted the moral and religious beliefs of Orthodox Jews. Fortunately, Rabbi Braun had a great deal of empathy for feminism as well as antipathy for violence in the family. He was willing to let me raise feminist criticism whenever I felt the need to do so, and others in the class either joined in or were at least somewhat sensitive to the issues we discussed. This freedom made it easier for me to get beyond my initial need to constantly provide a running commentary and feminist critique. Soon I could really pay attention to the underlying moral principles that could be used to understand and guide people's behavior. When Rabbi Braun left Denver two years later, and Rabbi Howard Hoffman took over the class, I continued studying, after making sure that he too would permit the addition of feminist ideas in the debate over interpretation that Talmud scholars love to engage in. Most exciting was the ability of both of these rabbis to not only appreciate the richness that the feminist perspective added to our study, but also their willingness to help me in my efforts to apply what we were studying to find meaning in the work that I have been doing.

When I was struggling with my own fears of not being able to testify well enough to save a battered woman from being found guilty of first degree murder, the rabbi found a passage that discussed the process of doing good even if it was not successful. When I needed help to combat erroneous "biblical" information given to one of my battered women clients by her minister, I was able to go directly to the source.

I still will not enter a synagogue where the women are forced to sit behind the *mehitzah*—the curtain separating them from sitting with men while praying. I have, however, attended several Orthodox functions, including the wedding of two members of our study group, and even enjoyed the women's prayer groups and celebrations with those who choose to follow the *halakhic* or Jewish law. Recently, I attended the ground-breaking ceremony for a new *mikvah* that will be built by the Orthodox community in Denver. At the same time, I have steadfastly supported the women who have been demanding the right to pray at the Wailing Wall of the *Kotel Ha Ma'aravi* in Jerusalem. I have argued with the rabbis about their intransigent position on the *Aguna,* or a woman whose husband refuses to give her a Jewish divorce, called a *Get.* This is sexist and unfair as it keeps some women trapped longer in a battering relationship. Others who do leave, are unable to remarry and have recognized children. It has been important to me to spend time in Israel, training judges and those who work in battered women shelters and the state-sponsored treatment and prevention centers.

Just last year, when I was struggling with the criticism that I received for agreeing to testify in O. J. Simpson's defense, the rabbi chose a passage for my study group to read that dealt with the Jewish tradition of saving lives. We are required to protect someone who is about to be hurt by another but, if the harm has already been done, then we are required to make sure that the accused is judged fairly. The Talmud tells us that it is far better to let a guilty person go free, if we do not have sufficient evidence, than to possibly convict an innocent person because we used tainted or biased information. Whatever my personal opinion about O. J. Simpson, the Talmud supported my own belief that it is important to the future of the battered women's movement to make sure that the information disseminated to the public is honest and accurate. We do know that some battered women are at high risk to be killed by their batterers, but because we do not know which ones, we warn them all. However, in my professional opinion, we do not have the scientific ability to predict that one particular man who battered a woman would kill that woman. Therefore, my position in the Simpson case was simple; if I would have testified, I would have said that knowledge of prior abuse could not be used as evidence of motivation or prima facie evidence that he killed his former wife and her friend.

JEWISH RESPONSE TO FAMILY VIOLENCE

In addition to, or perhaps because of, the Talmud study group, I began to look more closely at Jewish battered women in the metro Denver community where I live. My own research in the Colorado region found that Jewish women came to the Battered Woman's

Research Center and its successor, The Domestic Violence Institute, in the same numbers as they were represented in the population— 4 percent of our respondents were Jewish and 4 percent of the population according to census data identified themselves as Jewish (Walker, 1984). As my work became better known in the community, rabbis began to refer battered women to me with the hope that I could help stop the violence. These Colorado rabbis held the same myths as did the general population: The problem was viewed as a "violent relationship" rather than a "violent man" who had to take responsibility for his abusive behavior. They believed that marital therapy would help resolve the violence by making the woman behave better and then, with the goal of shalom bayit, the man would no longer need to control her with abuse. They were frightened of my feminist philosophy, prejudging it as being "anti-male." The rabbis considered it a prelude to recommending divorce rather than trying to work on the problems. This meant that by the time I was referred a case, they had figured divorce was the only option. The problem, however, is that batterers use violence as an abuse of the power and control they demand—it does not matter what the woman does or doesn't do. If she wants to have some independent thoughts, some time alone from the man, some contact with people whom he cannot control, and some control over her finances, then the man who uses violence to gain his power over the woman cannot tolerate her attempt to be an independent woman.

Like many Jewish feminists, I believe that as prevention, the rabbis need to accept the responsibility of educating their congregations to the fact that it is reasonable for women to demand some independence. They must convey that it is morally reprehensible for a Jewish man to use intimidation, bullying tactics, and other forms of coercion to "make" a woman do what he thinks is best. This educational approach can help some of these men change their attitudes and behavior so that their families might survive! But rabbis, like many Jews, believe that it is a shonde to even talk about, much less look inside, the family. They simply do not want the responsibility of giving congregants permission to discuss the horrors that they must live with on a daily basis.

As Jewish women professionals became more active in the organized Jewish community, several of us became aware that our own community was not doing a good enough job in providing support to those who already were battered women and children. Nor was there a batterer's intervention program for Jewish men. Although the Jewish Family Services agency was willing to provide groups for Jewish battered women, very few used their services, even after a publicity campaign. It seemed that battered women were more likely to seek help from private psychotherapists, if the abuse was acknowledged at all. Teachers in the Jewish Day Schools were quite reluctant to report suspected child abuse to the authorities. Rabbis rarely reported abuse that occurred in the Hebrew or Sunday Schools. Jewish doctors at Rose Hospital, the medical center that was supported by the Jewish community, rarely identified child abuse or battered women. Jewish battered women, particularly those who were Orthodox, rarely called the battered women shelters in the community. And women who went to talk with their rabbi continuously reported that the rabbis in town rarely took them seriously, or referred them to helpful services, despite the fact that there were services for abused women available in the metro Denver area. The abuse had to be pretty severe before anything was acknowledged or done about it! As in Jewish communities elsewhere, the myth of the nonabusive Jewish man was persistent.

By the late 1980s then, it was time for me to turn my attention to Jewish responses to family violence. Like it or not, we had to acknowledge that shalom bayit was simply not always true. Publicity from Israel fundraising efforts for the battered women shelters and family violence treatment centers there helped point the spotlight on American Jewish families as well. Several highly respected Jewish women community leaders were able to persuade the Allied Jewish Federation (Federation) to form and support a task force that would examine violence in Colorado Jewish homes, and design ways to prevent and stop it. This task force began a five-year project whose activities eventually were transferred to a regular division under Colorado's Jewish Family Services.

The task force spent the first two years educating ourselves about how family violence was identified and treated in the community by gathering information from many sources. We began with the volunteer community representatives from the fund-raising arm of Federation, and then focused on the doctors at Rose Hospital, with a generous grant from their foundation. We invited representatives from the various agencies that provided services to identified violent families. These agencies include the district attorneys' offices, and the domestic violence community. Included were battered women shelters, Project Safeguard (an advocacy program to make sure that police make arrests and that the women receive helpful and accurate information about resources and their legal rights), and AMEND, the batterer's treatment program used in Colorado. We also talked to university-based researchers, child protective services, and other social service, psychotherapy, and legal agencies. We asked survivors of abuse to tell us about their experiences in getting help when needed. It soon became clear that there were a large number of Jews involved in most of the relevant community programs. However, the current information about abuse in the family, particularly the feminist perspective and the research findings, did not filter down to the Jewish family or their helpers in the community. Neither did their Jewish values knowingly impact their work.

I was an early member of the task force, and participated as it went through several identity crises until we coalesced as a group. Volunteer members included other therapists, lawyers, battered women advocates, doctors, rabbis, and other Jewish community leaders. We met monthly at the Federation building as did other official committees. Federation gave the task force a small grant to hire a part-time coordinator along with support staff that was located in the Federation building. This gave us legitimacy and resources from the mainstream Jewish community to accomplish our mission, which was to evaluate and educate the Jewish community about family violence. This was reflected in our name, the Jewish Response to Family Violence.

Initially, the task force identified several Jewish beliefs that kept women from exposing their abusive husbands. The myth of shalom bayit was so ingrained that battered women and children were very reluctant to expose the violence, fearing their own disgrace. This was not an empty threat; even today there are still many psychological pressures to sweep all problems in Jewish homes under the proverbial rug! This becomes a moral dilemma. Jewish women are easy to intimidate; like others in a silently oppressed class, we believe that no one will believe or protect us. After all, Jewish husbands are supposed to be a "good catch" since they support their families very well. Why aren't we more grateful, we wonder, in the self-blame common to most abuse victims! But, on the other hand, once Jewish women organize concerning an issue, they will leave no stone unturned! Although many of the Jewish volunteer women's organizations ignored even the possibility that abuse might exist in Jewish homes during the early 1980s, by the beginning of the 1990s, most of them had developed clear policies and programs to address the issue.

As the task force began to learn about the work of Jewish professionals in town, it became clear that although the professionals' knowledge about domestic violence was often superficial and outdated, they believed it adequate for their professional needs. The challenge was to find a way to help them understand that they personally could benefit from exposure to more information and motivate them to raise the priority of this issue in their already crowded list of professional responsibilities. The Rabbinical Council supported the task force and designated a member of its executive committee to represent the Council at its meetings. The rabbis, themselves, however, believed they had sufficient education on the topic for their needs and were resistant to any further training in the area. This was in direct contradiction to the task force's findings. Most Jewish abuse victims said that the first person they want to turn to is a rabbi, whether or not they were affiliated with a congregation. Those who did said they were disappointed in the response received.

Groups of Jewish lawyers and Jewish health and mental health professionals wanted the task force to develop a referral list that included their names; most of them, too, did not see the need for any further training in violence and the family. This was surprising because an informal survey conducted by the task force indicated that the average therapist who was being used as a referral source by a rabbi had almost no formal training in domestic violence. In fact, there were several high publicity cases including an attempted murder in a prominent Jewish family where several of these therapists were treating clients in "marital therapy." This is a modality that domestic violence trainers do not recommend as an initial treatment strategy, at least until the abuser takes responsibility for and stops his abusive behavior. It is popular, however, with the rabbis who believe that family therapy is better suited to create shalom bayit, obviously more important than creating a violence-free family. The teachers and the groups of volunteers said they were more interested in attending training sessions, probably because they were faced with making decisions about reporting questionable behaviors that indicate abuse, particularly child abuse in prominent Jewish families. The task force found an important but little discussed barrier; as in many small, closed communities, philanthropic giving by prominent wealthy members often buys them respectability. If these prominent individuals are exposed, it may cause them to stop their donations and threaten necessary community programs and services!

Eventually, the task force persuaded the rabbis to devote the theme of one sermon on the High Holy Days to information about violence in the Jewish family and supplied them with literature written specifically for rabbis. This was extremely successful, with most rabbis devoting at least some portion of a sermon to raising the issue of domestic violence and speaking out against it in the Jewish family. Not surprisingly, those rabbis who were attending task force meetings and several of the leaders of the large congregations gave passionate speeches incorporating much of the information from our resource materials. The positive response from this event made the Rabbinical Council more willing to work together with us. Several of them even attended a seminar when we brought in a national colleague to share more information specifically relevant to the needs of the rabbinate.

Soon afterward, the task force received a grant from the Rose Hospital Foundation that funded a one-day community training program to educate about Jewish family violence. The strategy used to get more of the Jewish private practitioners involved included inviting six different facilitators to lead each of six large discussion groups midway through the day's program. Publicity was well coordinated amongst the synagogues, the Jewish Community Center, the Jewish Day Schools, and Jewish volunteer organizations and the broader Jewish community outside of the metro Denver area. Over 350 people turned out for the Sunday workshop that we agreed to end before the Bronco football game started! Of course, thirty-six were the invited facilitators who had previously attended a training session to prepare for this event. They received copies of many of the materials the task force gathered, so they could both learn more information about the issue and the resources in the community for their own future use, as well as help lead the discussions in the groups. These invited participants represented medicine, psychotherapy, education, Jewish Scholarship and the rabbis, volunteerism and fund-raising, and the legal profession. To make sure that the ultra-Orthodox in our community were full participants, the task force requested the assistance from the few known Orthodox psychologists willing to work with the task force and the rabbis who had some prior interest in this area. One of the major supporters was Rabbi Braun, my Talmud teacher.

The sponsorship of the task force by Federation, and scheduling the meetings in the Federation building, which has been considered a neutral place, helped consolidate the often divided Jewish community. The task force contacted other groups in Chicago, Los Angeles, and New York, who had also tried to develop a systematic training and education program concerning family violence issues in the Jewish community, in order learn from their experiences. All members of the task force felt that it was a very successful day, well beyond expectations.

In effect, that community conference was used to launch an educational program in the community. A Jewish "helpline" was available to offer information and resources during the usual business hours. The plans were to staff the telephone in a manner similar to other successful "hotlines"—using trained volunteers to carry a beeper and respond to calls. However, a political turf battle soon followed with the Family Service agency announcing its own "helpline" first. The community never did use the services during the short time they were available. I personally was invited to spend several sessions providing training to the staff at the Jewish Family Services so that they would have internal resources as well as personal contacts with those who can provide additional community resources.

The task force then made the decision to keep the focus on education and prevention of family violence with the understanding that it may later choose to develop other programs. Such programs might include a referral list or even an ambitious volunteer "helper" program that would match families at high-risk for abuse with a trained community volunteer, in order to interrupt the cycle of violence and isolation that often provides the breeding ground for abuse to thrive. To date, we have developed a successful speaker's bureau using many of the trained Jewish professionals who have been associated with the task force. When the task force became an independent program administered by the Jewish Family Services, it lost some of its high public recognition since that agency is more low key, for obvious reasons of confidentiality. However, it gained the advantage of a solid funding base and a commitment from the agency to continue its growth and development with the members of the task force remaining as advisors.

INTEGRATING BEING A JEWISH, FEMINIST, PSYCHOLOGIST, ADVOCATE

The politics of using battered woman syndrome to describe and justify battered women's defensive actions has caused an uproar in both the feminist and the traditional communities. The first fears were voiced by men in power who were frightened that permitting a battered woman to get away with murder would declare open season on killing all men who abused women! My public response to that fear was a bit harsh: surely no man who learns to keep his hands to himself when angry with a woman would have anything to worry about. An angry woman would not kill him simply because she is angry and wants revenge. After all, women are the killers in less than 12 percent of the homicide cases in the United States and these figures seem somewhat comparable in other nations. Studies have shown that women are more likely to kill their current or former partners when they are terrified that they will be more seriously harmed or killed. In fact, studies now have shown that when battered women have more services available to them in the community, they are less likely to kill although they may be more likely to be killed by the abuser (Browne and Williams, 1989).

Feminist jurisprudence scholars have also begun to question the utility of using battered woman syndrome testimony as a way to bridge the gap between the traditional barroom fight standard of self-defense and the reasonable woman's standard. The reasonable battered woman's standard is established by her perception of danger. This is based on flashbacks to previous memories of abusive incidents and coping strategies that develop which make other actions, such as leaving the situation, too unpredictable for a battered woman who believes she could be seriously harmed or killed.

The feminist argument is based on the political issue of wanting battered women to be perceived as competent to accurately perceive danger rather than risk the confusion of battered woman syndrome being considered a mental disorder. The goal of these activists is social change in addition to providing testimony that might justify the actions of the individual woman. There are research data to support the existence of a category of symptoms, some of which are expected to develop in most battered women (APA, 1996; Walker, 1994). However, some feminist psychologists were also beginning to move away from the use of this testimony, leaving the woman on trial for her life without anything but feminist theoretical analysis to support her.

My work in Israel training judges in the courts and social workers in the special centers for the prevention and treatment of family violence and the battered women shelters is too complex to describe in this chapter. However, I believe that until there is a secure peace in the Middle East, women's concerns in Israel will continue to be trivialized, no matter what gains Jewish women make here in the United States even though attempts will continue to be made to try to stabilize the Jewish family. Hopefully, that will not mean a return to the secrecy, once again closing Pandora's Box and locking the abuse victims together with their perpetrators behind closed doors.

There is no question that the months during the O. J. Simpson trial when it was unknown whether or not I would be required to testify as an expert, took their toll on me, personally. I had spent twenty years building a reputation as an advocate and psychologist for battered women, and both the media and some battered women's groups were accusing me of abandoning them. But, my Jewish principles helped me get through those difficult times. Today, I am back doing the same things that I have been doing for the past twenty years, using my skills both as an advocate and a professional psychologist to help prevent and stop violence against women in the home, in the streets, in our communities, and in the world. Judaism insists on protecting life by standing up against injustice! I believe my work and my personal life are guided by those principles, and like the Talmud, with all its many interpretations, there is room for disagreement. It is the process as well as the end product that counts.

As with most things in life, the Jewish religion is neither all good nor all bad. Certainly the patriarchal and sexist attitudes have perpetuated inequality and facilitated abuse of women, but there are also clear mandates against the violence that men commit against women and children. There are Jewish laws to protect women and children from further harm. Judaism celebrates life and the laws that are set down are meant to be guidelines to behave in a moral way. I will not give up my Jewishness because of the sexism that is still quite present both in traditional Judaism and in its practice in the United States and Israel; rather, I shall continue to call on G-d for help while I stand up against the injustices that the feminist analysis exposes, and I shall continue to push the changes that are already in progress even further!

NOTE

1. I use the masculine gender in describing the perpetrator, batterer, or abuser and the feminine gender in describing the battered woman or child because most, although not all, batterers are male and most, although not all, victims are female. Of course, both boys and girls are emotionally abused as children with the data suggesting more boys are physically abused and more girls are sexually abused. Most of the serious child abuse, when removing the neglect cases, are committed by males. Statistical breakdowns that are applicable to Jewish families indicate that these numbers do not significantly vary in this population, either.

REFERENCES

American Psychological Association (1996). *Report of the presidential task force on violence and the family.* Washington, DC: American Psychological Association.

Browne, Angela and Williams, Kurt (1989). Resource availability for women at risk and partner homicide. *Law & Society Review, 23,* 75 – 94.

Steinsaltz, A. (1989). *The talmud: The Steinsaltz edition, Vol. I, Part I.* New York: Random House.

Walker, Lenore E. A. (1984). *The battered woman syndrome.* New York: Springer.

Walker, Lenore E. A. (1989). *Terrifying love: Why battered women kill and how society responds.* New York: Harper/Collins.

Walker, Lenore E. A. (1994). *Abused women and survivor therapy: A practical guide for the psychotherapist.* Washington, DC: American Psychological Association.

Chapter 26

Canadian Jewish Women and Their Experiences of Antisemitism and Sexism

Nora Gold

INTRODUCTION

The research presented here is part of a study of Canadian Jewish women and their experiences of antisemitism and sexism. Participants were located through advertisements in the English and Jewish newspapers in Toronto and Montreal, where the study was briefly described and interested Jewish women were invited to contact the researcher directly. The forty-seven women who responded were assigned to focus groups based on their place of residence and whether or not they saw themselves as feminists. In total, there were six groups of feminists (four from Toronto, two from Montreal), and two groups of nonfeminists (one from Toronto and one from Montreal). Each focus group met once for two hours with this researcher. The women in this study ranged in age from twenty-two to seventy-seven, and there was similarly wide variation in terms of their ethnicity (Sephardic/Ashkenazi), marital status, sexual orientation, income,

This project is dedicated to the women who took part in this study, sharing generously of their thoughts, feelings, and experiences, and to my Jewish sisters everywhere. It is hoped that this research will contribute to increasing understanding about Jewish women, especially among non-Jewish feminists and Jewish men, and that as we learn more about the insidious nature of oppression, in all its manifestations, we can work together more effectively to eradicate it from the world.

This research was generously funded by a grant from the Social Science and Humanities Research Council of Canada.

education (Jewish and secular), level of religious observance, and communal affiliations. There were no salient differences between the feminists and nonfeminists on any of the above.

The group discussions were structured around four main themes:

1. Experiences of Antisemitism

Under what circumstances do the women in the study feel comfortable, safe, understood, included, or appreciated as *Jews*? In what circumstances do they feel unsafe, uncomfortable, misunderstood, excluded, vulnerable, insulted, or degraded as *Jews*? How often do they feel the latter? In what contexts? How are they affected by these experiences?

2. Experiences of Sexism

These questions were parallel to those asked above, i.e., under what circumstances do they feel safe versus unsafe, etc., *as women*?

3. Similarities, Differences, and Points of Intersection Between the Experiences of Sexism and Antisemitism

What do they see as some of the similarities between the two sets of experiences? The differences? What comes to mind when they think about "a Jewish woman?" Where do their ideas about Jewish women come from? Because of the work by Siegel (1992, 1995), which suggests that Jewish women's feelings about their bodies can be negatively affected by sexism and antisemitism, women were also asked which parts of their bodies they thought of as "Jewish." Did they like these parts of their bodies? What about the "non-Jewish" parts? Where did those feelings about their bodies come from? (Jews/non-Jews? Males/females?)

4. Coping with Sexist and Antisemitic Experiences

How do they cope when they have experienced an incident that is antisemitic and/or sexist? Do they fight back? Do they withdraw? (From whom or what?) Do they talk to others? (If so, to whom? Jews/non-Jews? Women/men?)

ANTISEMITISM

The women who took part in this research have had some amazing things said and done to them. For example, one was asked, "Have you eaten a non-Jewish baby lately?" One worked in a store that had a 'jew-me-down" sale, others were called "dirty Jews," "Christ-killers," or chased home from school by boys throwing rocks at them. Women were picked on by antisemitic teachers, deprived of jobs they were qualified for, and told by non-Jewish children in their neighborhoods that they couldn't play because they were Jewish. One woman in charge of the antiracism initiative in a large agency was called "a Jewish princess" by a colleague, who received only the mildest of reprimands. Another woman had a noose hung from the tree in her backyard, and several women have had swastikas painted on their doors. A third woman purchased an old brooch for $5 at a garage sale. The next day she cleaned it, had it appraised, and discovered the pin was really worth $500. A few days later she was telling this story to people at work, boasting about her "find," and she was told, "Well, what do you expect? You're a cheap Jew."

The women in this study found these comments and incidents "shocking," "horrifying," and frightening. One woman said, "I felt terribly hurt; I got sick to my stomach; went away by myself and cried." Another woman said, "I got really angry—really angry. My blood was boiling. I couldn't believe what was coming out of this person's mouth." Another woman became hysterical.

Adding to the emotional intensity, even trauma, was the fact that when the women recounted these incidents later to non-Jewish friends and colleagues, their experiences were trivialized or dismissed. They were told that they were being too sensitive, that "jewing down," for example, was just an expression—it didn't really mean anything. This compounded the original pain by undermining the felt reality of the women, and constituted a kind of secondary victimization. One said:

> I think that we kind of tend to have a feeling that unless it's like somebody coming up putting a swastika on your door, it doesn't matter; it's not antisemitism. People have this attitude, which makes it very hard to talk about it. . . . People go,

"That's not antisemitism," and that makes me feel really uncomfortable, because people don't understand, so I often feel very uncomfortable talking about my experiences. They just dismiss it and go, "'Well, that doesn't sound so bad," or "Are you sure he was . . . "

Not surprisingly, when asked where they felt most comfortable, and safest, as Jews, the women in this study responded almost uniformly with "among Jews . . . [in Yiddish] *indzere* . . . among our own." A number of the feminists in this study, however, qualified this by saying that given the sexism in the Jewish community, they felt really safe only among Jewish women; and some were even more specific, saying only among Jewish feminists. Several commented sadly that a few years back, they would also have included as a safe place the feminist movement at large, and being among other feminists, Jewish or non-Jewish, but that this is no longer the case. One woman said:

I was in a women's studies class; it was feminist theory, and . . . I watched this black woman say, "Well, how could you compare a black, poor, single mother with a wealthy Jewish woman?" And it's a very bizarre thing to deal with, because on the one hand, I don't want to get up there and start saying, "Well, I'm Jewish, and you know, and I'm like, well, I'm white and Jewish, but I could be Sephardic and I could be having to deal with being both a woman of color and Jewish . . . " You know, it's ranking the oppressions which is a terrible thing, but it's difficult. It's difficult to come to terms with, "Oh, you're just a little white Jew—a middle-class Jew—who's opening your mouth." Antisemitism's there, in the feminist movement . . . it's in my safe little hold.

This reduction, this shrinking, of the "safe spaces" of the women in this study is directly related to Jewish women's dual oppression (Gold, 1993,1996), such that the non-Jewish world, including other women and even other feminists, is seen as hostile; but so is the male-dominated Jewish community, which was supposed to be their refuge.

SEXISM

The women in this study told many stories about the effects of living in a sexist world. One woman felt that sexism had deprived her of following her desired goal in life: she wanted to be a mathematician, but was streamed out of enriched math in high school because she was a girl. Another woman, a homemaker who got married in the 1950s, spent decades worrying about her adequacy as a woman, because she was "lousy at pouring tea, [had] no interest in mahjong, [was] a lousy interior decorator, and [was] not interested in fashion." She was attracted to chiropractic, but it never occurred to her to enter it; instead, she persuaded her husband to pursue this profession.

In terms of the sexism of everyday life, three women told similar and familiar-sounding stories about their interactions with male service providers: a car mechanic refusing to provide complete information about the bill for some car repairs; a contractor rejecting a woman's input about where to position a wall, and asking to speak to her husband; an accountant yelling at a woman on the phone, and at another time carrying on a conversation with her lawyer about her financial affairs in her presence, as though she wasn't in the room. When she insisted on being part of the discussion, the accountant actually said to her, "There there, dear."

Sexism at home focused on examples of unequal distribution of labor in family life: the exploitation of homemakers as wives, mothers, and caregivers, and women's "double duty" for those who work outside the home.

Sexism in the workplace was also common, and many examples were given, including discriminatory hiring practices, the underpaying and exploitation of women working in "female professions," and sexual harassment in both corporate and academic settings. One woman was actually fired from her first job for "not coming across." Women also spoke about sexism in the workplace in terms of the way they are treated on a day-to-day basis. For example,

> I find that most of the time I have to prove myself because . . . when I'm dealing with men they categorize women in a certain way, and once they see that, gee, she really has a brain, she can

think for herself, then their attitude changes. I always find that I have to prove myself.

Sexism in the Jewish community was also discussed. Many expressed eloquently the sense of exclusion, marginalization, and devaluation that they have experienced within the Jewish community and Jewish religious tradition. They described "watching the men dance with the Torah, and standing on the sidelines and not being allowed to take part." Many experienced Judaism as a "boys' club," and felt "unwanted" and alienated as a result. A number of women in this study gave up on Judaism in order to maintain their self-esteem as women, although two Orthodox women found Orthodox Judaism utterly compatible with their self-respect as women, and urged other women to learn more about Orthodox Judaism before rejecting it. Yet another subgroup of women found a meaningful relationship with Judaism through egalitarian forms of practice, such as the Reform, Reconstructionist, and *Chavurah* movements, and some of the rituals recently developed by and for women, such as women's prayer groups and *Rosh Hodesh* [New Month] celebrations. "[We're] creating something new and exciting," said one woman. "We're creating our own spiritual world."

SIMILARITIES, DIFFERENCES, AND INTERSECTIONS BETWEEN ANTISEMITISM AND SEXISM

There are certain obvious similarities shared by antisemitism and sexism. Conceptually, of course, they are both fundamentally about a power differential, and the exploitation of one group by another for social, political, and economic gain. In this study, women found their experiences with sexism and antisemitism alike in the sense that both were insulting, degrading, and painful, and that anyone who challenged sexist or antisemitic remarks was made to feel oversensitive. However, a very important difference between them was also identified. These women felt that sexism, unlike antisemitism, is recognized, and to some degree acknowledged, within the society at large (e.g., on talk shows and in magazines); with sexism, there was not the same silence. For example, during one focus group discussion, a woman was talking about being treated in a sexist manner by a car mechanic, and someone else piped up: "Oh, yeah, there was a program on about that, probing into how they treat a woman when she's going to buy or repair a car." Immediately the woman telling her story felt supported and validated, not just by one person, but by the society at large. This rarely, if ever, happens with antisemitism. In this sense, structural reality significantly shapes the emotional and psychological impact of an oppressive experience. One woman said,

> I put sexism and antisemitism quite a way apart. I can deal with sexism. Sexism we have a handle on—a little bit of a handle. It's being discussed in the media; it's out in the open. We don't like it; we're making a stink about it. But antisemitism—we're still cowering, we're still afraid. . . . How much progress have we really made with antisemitism?

The women in this study felt clearly that antisemitism was far more frightening and pernicious than sexism. This may reflect, first of all, these women's identities as "Jewish first, and women second," as one woman put it; but also, as previously mentioned, the social indifference to antisemitism, and, not unrelated to this, the historical awareness that within this last half-century, the Jewish people came closer than at any other point in history to being wiped off the face of the earth.

INTERSECTIONS

In light of the above two sets of experiences, what then does it mean to be Jewish and a woman? Is this merely additive, the sum of the above anecdotes about antisemitism and the sum of the anecdotes about sexism? I think not: the two oppressions feed on each other in some powerful and profound ways, and work together to create something new—a third thing—a dynamic which is at the core of Jewish women's experience. From the discussions of these focus groups, there seem to be three main places where such intersection occurs: one is in the stereotype of the JAP, the Jewish American Princess; the second is in regard to how Jewish women feel about their bodies, and in particular the "Jewish" parts of their bodies; and the third is in the relationships and psychosexual dynamics between Jewish women and Jewish men.

1. The JAP, or American Jewish Princess

Consistent with what has been written about the JAP phenomenon (Beck, 1988; Booker, 1991; Chayat, 1987; Marks, 1992; Siegel, 1986), the women in this study were very worried about being labeled JAPs, and went to great pains to differentiate themselves from "that kind of Jewish woman." In a variation of the "good Jew/bad Jew" game, we now have the "good Jewish woman versus the bad Jewish woman." Interestingly, the feminists and the nonfeminists in this study related in markedly different ways to the stereotype of the JAP; this was, in fact, the only notable difference between the two groups. The nonfeminists were significantly less critical of the JAP label than the feminists, less aware of the antisemitism and sexism contained in it, and more apt to accept the term and use it in conversation like any other word. In sharp contrast, none of the feminists in the focus groups expressed these sentiments, or casually used the word "JAP." Even if not liking "a certain kind of Jewish women," they without exception recognized the term JAP as both sexist and antisemitic and, in the words of one woman, "a put-down to all Jewish women," and refused to use it in their everyday speech.

2. Jewish Women's Bodies

Another point of intersection between sexism and antisemitism is in the Jewish woman's body (Siegel, 1992,1995). All women, not just Jewish women, have been taught to reject their bodies, because they do not measure up to an impossible ideal of beauty (Wolf, 1991). However, for Jewish women in this society, the issues of body image are further complicated, because the physical characteristics of Jewish women are in direct conflict with the non-Jewish images of beauty in the dominant culture (straight blond hair, small noses, and thin figures) (Siegel, 1995). Consequently, a fair number of Jewish women in North America have problems related to body image, focused on their dislike of specific parts of their bodies that seem to them to be "too Jewish" (e.g., frizzy hair, a big nose, or wide hips), because they have internalized the values of the dominant culture, including its antisemitism (Cantor, 1992; Siegel, 1995). According to Cantor (1992, 1995), Jewish women who are proud of being Jewish, and reject the lure of assimilationism, are relatively unlikely to suffer these kinds of problems with body image and self-esteem.

In order to explore this further, the women in this study were asked what parts of their bodies they thought of as Jewish, and how they felt about these parts of themselves. The answers were wide-ranging, and included almost every part of the body, but the most common answer was the nose. This is not surprising, since for Jewish women, the "nose job" is nowadays the most common way that they can express through their bodies the desire to "make themselves over" in a non-Jewish image. A parallel exists here, of course, to women of other ethnic groups, such as black women straightening their hair. In this study none of the women liked their noses. Several women explained that this was because it looked "so Jewish." Three women, when they were young girls, tried to force their noses into a more desirable, Aryan shape by holding them up or pressing objects against them. They were very aware of, and concerned with, the Anglo-Saxon beauty ideal and the undesirability of "looking Jewish." For example:

> I have a girlfriend, she said to me once, "You have a gentile body," and I said, "What's a gentile body?" "Well, Jewish women have the hips and the this and the that. You have beautiful long legs, and small hips." When people say to me, "You don't look Jewish," it's a compliment . . . I take it as a compliment.

3. Relations Between Jewish Men and Jewish Women

The comments of the women in this study were completely consistent with the dynamic described by Cantor (1995), in which many Jewish men project onto Jewish women their own internalized antisemitism, and then distance themselves from them. The women in these focus groups felt very put down and rejected by Jewish men because of their preference for non-Jewish women. This preference, of course, also had the effect of fostering competition between Jewish women and non-Jewish women. What could be more prototypically sexist than pitting women against each other in the fight over a man? However, as one woman put it, this is, for the Jewish woman, "a losing battle." She cannot possibly compete with the allure of the non-Jewish world, as so many Jewish men perceive it, or the "golden aura," as one woman put it, that surrounds non-Jewish women.

> Jewish men see these blondes, the ideal blonde goddess—who doesn't really exist, by the way—as upwardly-mobile, the way to upwardly . . . like the *Thirtysomething* couples . . . There's this thing: "Look at this, I got a blondie; I got a blonde one just for me . . ." It's a way of getting social approval from the non-Jewish world. And from themselves.

Understanding the reasons for this dynamic, however, did not necessarily ease the bitterness of it. Many of these women had been socialized to feel the burden of Jewish continuity and the importance of creating a Jewish home and raising a Jewish family. By definition, if they were heterosexual, they needed Jewish men to achieve these goals; yet Jewish men were intermarrying and therefore not available to them. As a result, many of them felt tricked, almost cheated, by their own community.

CONCLUSION

This research explored forty-seven Canadian Jewish women's experiences of antisemitism and sexism, some of the similarities and differences between these two forms of oppressions, and some of the ways in which they intersect in the lives of Jewish women. Interestingly, all three areas in which antisemitism and sexism converged—the JAP stereotype, the woman's body, and her relationships with Jewish men—all relate somehow to sexual identity and are extremely intimate. This, of course, is consistent with the feminist recognition that "the personal is political," and that structural inequalities and oppressions enter our lives at the deepest, most personal levels, where no aspect of our selves is immune.

REFERENCES

Beck, Evelyn Torton (1988). The politics of Jewish invisibility. *National Women's Studies Association Journal, 1*(1), 93 – 102.

Booker, Janice L. (1991). *The JAP and other myths.* New York: Shapolsky.

Cantor, Aviva (1992, October). Assimilation as the root of low self-esteem in nontraditional Jewish women. Presented at *The First International Conference on Judaism, Feminism, and Psychology,* Seattle, WA.

Cantor, Aviva (1995). *Jewish women/Jewish men: The legacy of patriarchy in Jewish life.* San Francisco, CA: Harper San Francisco.

Chayat, Sherry (1987). "JAP"-baiting on campus. *LILITH, 17,* 6 – 7.

Gold, Nora (Summer, 1993). Diversity, Jewish women, and social work. *Canadian Social Work Review* (Special Issue on Women and Social Work), *10*(2), 240 – 255.

Gold, Nora (1996). Putting antisemitism on the anti-racism agenda in North American schools of social work. *Journal of Social Work Education, 32*(1), 77 – 89.

Marks, Wendy (1992, October). A feminist/psychological reading of jokes about "JAPS" and Jewish mothers. Presented at *The First International Conference on Judaism, Feminism, and Psychology,* Seattle, WA.

Siegel, Rachel Josefowitz (1986). Antisemitism and sexism in stereotypes of Jewish women. *Women and Therapy, 5*(2/3), 249 – 257.

Siegel, Rachel Josefowitz (1992, October). The Jewish woman's body: Sexuality, body-image, and self-esteem. Presented at *The First International Conference on Judaism, Feminism,* and Psychology, Seattle, WA.

Siegel, Rachel Josefowitz (1995). Jewish women's bodies: Sexuality, body-image, and self-esteem. In K. Weiner and A. Moon (Eds.), *Jewish women speak out: Expanding the boundaries of psychology* (pp. 41 – 54). Seattle, WA: Canopy Press.

Wolf, Naomi (1991). *The beauty myth.* Toronto: Vintage.

Chapter 27

We Are Not As We Were:
Jewish Women After the Holocaust

Joan Fisch

Hear this, O elders,
Give ear, all inhabitants of the land.
Has the like of this happened in your days
Or even in the days of your ancestors?
Tell your children of it,
And let your children tell theirs,
And their children unto the next generation.

Joel 1: 2–3
(Translation by Shulamit Magnus)

For more than forty years I have struggled to understand how the Holocaust could have occurred and tried to find ways to understand the effect that these horrific events have had on survivors and their families. I thought of myself as not having been affected by the Holocaust because no members of my family had been subjected to the horrors of Nazi Germany. Then I attended a professional work-

This article is dedicated to the memory of my mother, Rose Laniado Junas, who encouraged and supported my educational and intellectual pursuits, and taught me to examine the ways in which political and historical forces affect the lives of individuals.

Thank you to everyone who encouraged me to struggle with these issues and provided help when I needed it. Special thanks to group participants, whose names have been changed, for sharing their experiences.

shop and unexpectedly was asked to confront and explore my reactions to the Holocaust. The intensity of my responses led me to the realization that the Holocaust has had a profound influence on my life and on my identity as a Jewish woman. I began exploring the impact that the Holocaust has had on other Jewish women, who, like me, were "not directly affected."

Cynthia Ozick (1983) in her article "Notes Toward Finding the Right Question" describes how the unparalleled events of the Holocaust have permanently altered what it means to be a Jewish woman:

> We are not as we were. It is not unnatural that mass loss should generate not only lessons but legacies. An earthquake of immorality and mercilessness, atrocity on such a scale, cannot happen and then pass us by unaltered. The landscapes of our mind have shapes, hollows, illuminations, mounds and shadows different from before. For us who live in the aftermath of the cataclysm, the total fact of the Nazi "selection" appears to affect, to continue to affect, all the regions of our ideas—even if some of those ideas at first glance look to be completely unrelated issues. (p. 135)

Ozick argues that the upsurge of Jewish feminism was caused not by the rise of secular feminism, but by the awareness that arose as a result of our having "lost so much and so many." In our state of vulnerability after the Holocaust, Jewish women became aware of the losses that have resulted from our having been refused the opportunity, century after century, to participate in Jewish practice and scholarship, losses that until recently have gone unnoticed (pp. 135–136). When I discovered this article in early 1993, I was intrigued. Has the Holocaust really affected all the regions of our minds, even those that at first seem as unrelated as the Holocaust and Jewish feminism?

I am a clinical social worker with expertise in the treatment of survivors of trauma. In October 1992, I attended a workshop, "Countertransference and Trauma" led by Yael Danieli, with the goal of learning more about how to manage my reactions to the stories of trauma that I hear from my clients. She began by having us explore our individual relationships to the Holocaust.

When we were asked to recall the first time we had heard about the Holocaust, I had two memories. First, I remembered the execution of Ethel and Julius Rosenberg—the announcement of the execution on television, my mother being upset and leaving the room, my sense of confusion about what was occurring. This memory seemed to be totally unrelated to the question. Next, I remembered thinking: "If I had lived there or the Germans had come here, that would have happened to me! That my father is not Jewish would have made no difference." I felt twelve years old again. I later concluded that my thoughts were most likely a reaction to reading *The Diary of Anne Frank,* first published in English in 1952. The awareness that I could have been in hiding, could have been taken away and killed, whether or not I identified myself as Jewish, permanently altered my sense of safety in the world.

During the remainder of the workshop and for days afterward, I was flooded with thoughts and feelings. I realized how strongly I had reacted to learning about the Holocaust, and how those reactions had shaped, and continued to shape, my life. It cannot be unrelated that I have an interest in the intergenerational transmission of trauma and in the way that political events affect individuals. Nor is it unrelated that I married a Jewish man, and that it has been important to me to instill in my children the Jewish values of pursuing justice and treating the stranger kindly. It also cannot be unrelated that I have been working actively on the problems of Jewish invisibility and an antisemitism. While other factors in my life have certainly played a part in these decisions, I now realize that I was so profoundly touched by the Holocaust that nothing in my life and my view of myself and my world is unrelated.

The following weekend, I attended the First International Conference on Judaism, Feminism, and Psychology: Creating a Shelter in the Wilderness. There I heard one presenter speak about being a child survivor and having been marked for annihilation, and another talk of the Jewish community's having been in mourning since the Expulsion from Spain 500 years before. I wondered about the Jewish women who sat all around me. How had they been affected by the Holocaust? It was likely that some were survivors or children of survivors. Others were, like me, from families that had not been directly affected by the events in Europe fifty years before.

When and what did these women first learn about the Holocaust? What connections, if any, had they made between these horrendous events and their own lives? How will future generations respond to the stories that have been written down, filmed, and videotaped and to visits to Holocaust museums and the death camps? How will we speak of this to our children? What will our children say to their children?

In the weeks that followed, I continued to ask myself these questions. Each time I discussed my interest with a friend or acquaintance, she responded with a story about her own reaction to the Holocaust and was eager to talk. My interest grew. I searched the libraries and bookstores. Among the thousands of books and articles written about the Holocaust, I found only a few that were concerned with the impact on those who had not been directly affected, and even fewer that addressed my interest in the individual emotional impact.

In her article "Survivors Nonetheless: Trauma in Women Not Directly Involved with the Holocaust," Kayla Miriyam Weiner (1995) describes her reaction to seeing newsreels of the concentration camps. "The message was loud and clear, 'This is what can happen to you for no other reason than that you are Jewish'" (p. 223).

Amy Sheldon (1991) in "A Feminist Perspective on Intermarriage," speaks of her strong conviction that her children must be raised as Jews saying "I can't finish what Hitler started" (p. 82). She describes her fear of annihilation:

> I remember sitting in a movie theater in Manhattan when I was about 16 years old in the late 1950s. I was watching Alain Resnais's film "Night and Fog." It was in color, but it moved dramatically into black and white for scenes of the concentration camps. Although I had been hearing and reading about the camps at that time, I hadn't seen the horrors so graphically. It was overwhelming. I sat alone, frozen in the dark, realizing how vulnerable I and my family and friends were just because we were Jews. My Jewish world that I had associated with warmth and security and home was suddenly different. And I was utterly terrified. (p. 86)

In "Split at the Root: An Essay on Jewish Identity," Adrienne Rich (1996) describes seeing films of the liberation of concentration camps. When she told her father, who was Jewish, and her mother, who was not, where she had been, they were not pleased:

> One thing was clear: there was nobody in my world with whom I could discuss those films. Probably at the same time, I was reading accounts of the camps in magazines and newspapers; what I remember were the films and having questions that I could not even phrase, such as *Are those men and women "them" or "us"?* (p. 139)

Years later, she was unable to talk with her sons about the Holocaust because "these things were still too indistinct in my own mind" (p. 148).

Anne Roiphe (1981) shares her reaction to the Holocaust as she talks about the way in which the horrible events are more personal for her as a Jew than for non-Jews:

> There but for the grace is part of it . . . but beyond that there is a bonding, a coupling, a connection with the victims that is as deep as my genes. . . . I believe in 1980 that the Nazis could appear at my children's door; the threat is personal. (pp. 177–178)

Knowledge of the Holocaust can have significant personal impact and lead not only to personal change but to new professional directions. Sociologist Ruth Linden (1993) began her research about Holocaust survivors by interviewing survivors at the American Gathering of Holocaust Survivors in Washington, DC, in 1983. Linden was born after World War II into an "assimilated Jewish-American family apparently unscathed by the destruction" (p. 2). For the first time, she registered a personal connection to the Holocaust when she realized that distant relatives, whose names she would never know, must have died in the ghettos, camps, and gas chambers (p. 69).

Linden describes personal reactions that I had never before seen included in research or clinical reports:

> No boundaries cordon off my research—"the field"—from the rest of my life. Momentary flashes of insight into questions I've pondered for years resound in the deep reaches of my

being. The ineffability of the Holocaust often leaves me mute, trembling with confusion and sadness. (pp. 8–9)

Interviewing survivors had changed my life, radically repositioning me as a Jew and a social scientist. I can think of no single experience up to this point in my life that registered such a decisive impact on my identity. (p. 71)

Judy Chicago, the feminist artist, began her study of the Holocaust when she was asked if she would illustrate a poem about the Holocaust. She had such a powerful reaction to what she learned that she rejected the offer and spent the next seven years creating a body of art designed to convey the human story of the Holocaust. In her book *The Holocaust Project: From Darkness into Light,* Chicago (1993) details the struggles that went into creating the project, including the emotional impact of immersing herself in Holocaust history and images.

My own work on a topic as emotionally laden as the Holocaust was not without its difficulties. My reading put me regularly and repeatedly in touch with stories of horror. At times it was too much, too many horrors, too much sadness. I could not spend so much time thinking about the pain and suffering that victims and survivors endured, about the millions who had been murdered, and of the loss of European Jewish culture. I would turn my attention to other less disturbing pursuits, listening to music, hiking in the hills near my home, spending time with family and friends. As I did so, I would begin to feel guilty. If so many had to endure so much, how could I turn away just because I felt too upset? Eventually, my interest and energy would revive and I would resume my work.

Early on I was concerned about speaking about my reactions to the Holocaust. I worried about how survivors and their children would react. Would I be perceived as trying to eclipse or diminish their pain? I was acutely aware of the difference between being a victim and being a witness, and in no way wanted to detract from the experiences of survivors and their children. As I struggled with this, I gradually became convinced that I could share my reactions. Those of us who are witnesses to the pain and suffering caused by the genocidal policies of the Nazis must not be silent.

In an effort to find out more about women's reactions to the Holocaust, I presented a workshop at the Association for Women in Psychology Conference in March 1994 and facilitated a similar exploration in my *Rosh Chodesh* group. I began by asking the following questions based on those Danieli uses in her workshops:

The Holocaust. What comes to mind when you hear these words? What are you thinking, feeling? Pay attention to your reactions and to your reactions to your reactions.

When was the first time you heard of the Holocaust? How old were you? What did you think? Is there anything about it that you have not been able to let yourself know?

How is your relationship to the Holocaust affected by your age, gender, class, sexual orientation, place of birth, the birthplaces of your parents, your grandparents? How do you think your knowledge of the Holocaust has influenced your sense of yourself as a Jew?

Have you talked with anyone else about how you have been affected? How did they react? Were there things you were not able to say? What kept you from saying them? (Danieli, 1993, pp. 374–378).

Most of the women had difficulty identifying the first time they had heard about the Holocaust. It seemed to them that it was something they had always known about. An exception was Sarah, who recalled her experience in great detail. When she was four, during a children's service at *Rosh Hashanah*, she noticed numbers on the arm of the teacher who was pouring juice. Sarah asked about her tattoo. She recalled the teacher's picking her up, talking to her about how lucky Sarah was, and giving a brief description of what had happened. The teacher encouraged her to ask questions. Sarah went to her parents in the sanctuary and asked them about what the teacher had told her. She still remembers the look of surprise on their faces and a sense that they did not know quite how to respond to her.

Several participants described disturbing images that were triggered by everyday events. While taking a shower, for instance, they would begin to think about those who had been sent to "showers" that were actually gas chambers, or sitting at a railroad crossing they would find themselves thinking about boxcars packed with people going to death camps. Many women tried to imagine how they would have felt or what they would have done if they had been in such overwhelming circumstances.

Tamar said that she felt disturbed by her tendency to identify with victims. As she read about Holocaust survivors, she would try to imagine herself in their situations. She wondered why she would want to do this and would stop herself. She felt a deep sense of discomfort and shame about her imaginings.

The question of safety came up repeatedly. Rebecca said that her concerns for her safety—what she called her paranoia—increased after she had seen *Shindler's List*. She thinks frequently about what she would do if she had to leave the country, with whom she could leave her children, where would she go. She and her husband keep their passports valid at all times. One of her non-Jewish friends could not understand Rebecca's fears even though she too had been to see *Shindler's List*. Leah talked about having only Jewish friends because she did not feel safe enough with non-Jews to allow friendships to develop. Sharon described keeping a pair of shoes by her bed as a child in case she needed to escape. She realized during the workshop that her childhood fears were probably a result of hearing about the Holocaust.

In her article "Antisemitism as Trauma: A Theory of Jewish Communal Trauma Response" Barbara U. Hammer (1995) explains the presence of traumatic responses in Jews who have not been directly affected by the Holocaust. Jewish teachings and traditions emphasize a sense of "oneness" with all Jews. When individuals identify with and internalize the traumatic experiences of members of their community, they experience some of the symptoms of trauma. Their responses become a part of Jewish family and cultural patterns that are passed on to succeeding generations (p. 208).

Rachel talked about being obsessed by the issue of luck. How was it that some families had immigrated to this country and were safe, while others had not? She knew of families in which only one member survived. How could this be? How can we understand forces that can lead to such huge discrepancies in people's fates?

Several women spoke of what they had not been able to let themselves know. Hannah said she had never related really to the Holocaust because "it was something that had happened to others." But, she also had had the feeling that there was something about it that she was keeping from herself. In a setting where others were talking about their reactions to the Holocaust, Hannah realized that "it was there for her, conspicuous in its absence" Dinah's husband and his family had escaped Nazi persecution. In tears she told us that she had never before allowed herself to imagine what might have happened to him. If he had not escaped, she would not have married him and they would not have had their children.

Before I led these discussions I thought of the Holocaust as a traumatic event for all Jews and predicted that participants' responses would reflect feelings of vicarious traumatization. While most of the responses were consistent with this conceptualization, others challenged it. For example, Miriam talked of her first awareness of the Holocaust coming from stories of those who had survived. This left her with an impression of the Jewish People as survivors, able to live through incredible difficulties.

Those of us who have not had direct experience with the Holocaust must keep in mind that survivors have told their stories so that we will be affected—so that we will remember what happened. If we listen and do not react, or keep our reactions to ourselves, we will not remember and will not be able to tell our children. By becoming aware of and speaking up about the ways in which the Holocaust has touched our lives, we who have not been directly affected can contribute to an increasingly complex understanding of the impact that the Holocaust has had on the lives of all Jewish women.

REFERENCES

Chicago, Judy (1993). *Holocaust project: From darkness into light.* London: Penguin Books.

Danieli, Yael (1993). Countertransference, trauma and training. In John. P. Wilson and Jacob D. Lindy (Eds.), *Countertransference in the treatment of PTSD.* (pp. 368 – 388). New York: Guilford Press.

Hammer, Barbara U. (1995). Anti-Semitism as trauma: A theory of Jewish communal trauma response. In Kayla Weiner and Arinna Moon (Eds.), *Jewish women speak out: Expanding the boundaries of psychology* (pp. 221 – 235). Seattle, WA: Canopy Press.

Linden, Ruth (1993). *Making stories, making selves: Feminist reflections on the Holocaust.* Columbus, OH: Ohio State University Press.

Ozick, Cynthia (1983). Notes Toward Finding the Right Question. In Susannah Heschel (Ed.), *On being a Jewish feminist: A reader* (pp. 120 – 151). New York: Schocken Books.

Rich, Adrienne (1996). Split at the root: An essay on Jewish identity. In Wendy
    Martin (Ed.), *The Beacon book of essays by contemporary American women*
    (pp. 134 – 151). Boston, MA: Beacon Press.
Roiphe, Ann (1981). *Generation without memory: A Jewish journey in Christian
    America*. New York: The Linden Press/Simon and Schuster.
Sheldon, Amy (1991). A feminist perspective on intermarriage. In Rachel Josefo-
    witz Siegel and Ellen Cole (Eds.), *Jewish women in therapy: Seen but not
    heard* (pp. 79 – 89). New York: The Harrington Park Press.
Weiner, Kayla Miriyam (1995). Survivors nonetheless: Trauma in women not
    directly involved with the Holocaust. In Kayla Weiner and Arinna Moon
    (Eds.), *Jewish women speak out: Expanding the boundaries of psychology*
    (pp. 221 – 235). Seattle, WA: Canopy Press.

Chapter 28

Violent Legacies—Dialogues and Possibilities

Judith Chalmer

The day before I left for Berlin, I woke in my narrow bed, having left years ago the milk and urine-soaked blankets to which three young sons had crept, tangled in and around a balled-up marriage. Down the hardwood hall, my husband curled into the sigh of the king-sized water bed. I had never smelled the smooth face or the cross seams of the new quilt in which he lay.

The littered room where I slept contained the contraction of my life, its steam and its limitations: Under the bed, a folding ladder to hook over the windowsill for a quick escape. On the far wall, a poster from Amsterdam: "It's only for one night," scrawled in Dutch handwriting over a picture of a young woman on a bike, one of the anonymous ones who risked death during the Nazi occupation in order to find hiding places for Jews such as my then three-year-old cousin and his parents. Chestnuts from last fall's leisurely New England hike. My mother's silver button box, purged and full again after its turn-of-the-century voyage from Russia. A small pile of polished seeds slipped from a necklace I'd been given on a pulsing street corner during the 1960s. Two filing cabinets, my computer, and ninety-some volumes of poetry, upon which I've based a teaching job and my long climb out of fear. Boxes of typed and handwritten correspondence. Brief notes from the Red Cross certifying dates my father was imprisoned in Dachau. Two splashy bedspreads on a shelf in the closet which form the sides of a yearly *succah* in which the boys expect we'll all eat each fall, snow or no snow. My clothes and those outgrown by one or two of the boys. The stitched yellow star my grandmother wore in a Dutch con-

301

centration camp. My parents' death certificates, marriage licenses, birth papers. Natural and invented forms of beauty. Three square feet of bare floor onto which I lowered my feet.

My trip to Berlin had been settled and arranged months before. Three meals a day and a private bath in the marble and mahogany district of Wannsee where Hitler's final solution had been ratified. Five days at a peace center taking part in a dialogue between descendants of Holocaust survivors and descendants of Nazis. The dialogue would be sponsored by a newly incorporated nonprofit, called One-By-One, whose experienced members described themselves as particularly intimate with the trauma of that period in history. At an orientation months earlier, I'd noticed the ease with which dishes were passed and washed by the seasoned members, shoulders hugged, German and English phrases tossed together with the clinking of spoons and the drip of coffee brewing. There were reasons this group held particular promise for me. My suitcase and briefcase were already packed.

The task I woke to that morning, however, was to make a down payment on a duplex three blocks away into which I planned to move when I got back from Germany. I'd taken years to make up my mind. The house I'd found had enough space so the kids could live with me half the time and rental income from the other side almost enough to pay the mortgage. Finally. A way to end the marriage struggle in which a boy and a girl born to rented, peacetime apartments along elm-covered Jewish streets in Buffalo had grown up to enact a violence bequeathed to us as man and woman by a larger culture. Neither one of us, with our postwar expectations . . . the right to move freely across state lines . . . assumptions of equal opportunity . . . the right clothes, the right syntax and skin for job interviews, college degrees . . . had known to lift that violence from the background of which it was made, had dared to see it as a heritage.

Our first summer married we'd taken jobs caretaking a shelter and 10 miles of hiking trail along the spine of Vermont's Green Mountain range. In addition to our garbage picking duties, we'd become accustomed to trading smoke-dried towels for the incoming bikers' permanently wet and muddy ones, hearing confession by glowing coals from people who'd disappear early the next day in the shadows, sending off moldy paperbacks for eventual return by a caretaker at the New Hampshire border. One night we got back late to the cabin, garbage-laden rucksacks pulling heavily at our shoulders, shin-bruised, sweaty, half-scared, and glad for the sound of each other's voices, to find, for the first and only time that summer, no bikers signed in, empty bunks surrounding ours. Privacy. His delight, his hand reaching for mine. Again my terror, sudden cramps, reeling nausea. Frantic search for escape.

The timing of the trip to Germany was bad. I hadn't realized how suddenly decisions would be made about the marriage when I'd first signed up to go to Germany. The day before, resting our mugs on opposite ends of the *milchig* counter, we'd guessed how far we'd have to travel to arrange a *get:* Boston or Montreal, most likely. We'd been married for twenty-five years, a couple from the year we'd turned sixteen years old. We agreed to go through with a get, although it had been perhaps six years since we'd abandoned orthodoxy.

Neither of us had been raised in *frum* households. I don't think we knew we'd be yanking ourselves up by the roots when we decided at the end of that first summer to stay in Vermont. What did we know of northern New England's storm patterns? The feeling of awe that blew over us . . . paused on top of three feet of corn snow in March, amid softwood stands littered with seed husks, wind-blown branches, the dulled edges of small and large tracks, peering into clear space around the boles of sticky pines inside whose rough trunks it seemed something large and warm-blooded must surely have stepped . . . was nothing for which we could find reference in our Jewish upbringings, made up of brass and silver as they were for candle lightings, stainless steel from the kitchen, plastic pearls and blacktop on the road to prayer. The idea of orthodoxy grew on us during the years we lived in the woods, an awkward graft, an exotic experiment.

Our conversion began slowly. When our first son was born I eagerly quit my job as a minor and irritable bureaucrat to take on the traditional role, dreaming my son would become some day the writer I wished to be. The drive to synagogue Friday nights brought a weekly relief. From loneliness. Physical exhaustion. I could sit in the synagogue, meander for an hour uninterrupted in my thoughts, while first one, then another and another babe crowed, crawled, then toddled from lap to mercifully stationary lap. At the *bima*, their father lifted them and leaned into the *bracha*, his voice and his rolling heels a lullaby. The place looked like heaven. Grownups sat still. Babies and kids made all the moves, fingering beards, *tsitsit*, earrings, lips . . . climbing down, away, without anyone losing the tune. After, there was food, people standing and sitting in predictable ways. It was a party, all right.

For our young, newly transplanted Jewish community, gathered after a while not only at synagogue but in dog-haired living rooms and growing sincerity, there were homemade *kippot*, homemade *shofarim*, the sharp edges of newly carved ceremony, *niggun* woven of our many-colored voices on long summer afternoons, sweet wine and *challah* on lilac- and maple-shaded porches. The two of us became our own model couple, a story set down unsteady as the first pot thrown at a novice's wheel, turned and glazed in a day into working receptacles, hosts to a wide-eyed community of rural Jewish renewal. We read the New Age justifications for observing the traditions and repeated those reasons. Being a stay-at-home mother was one of the options, I often said, for an inclusive feminism. Division of labor along traditional lines, as long as it was chosen, I said, was a viable way to claim power. There was so much to do. We organized *seders* and *siyyumim*, rehydrated the local community's long-abandoned *tashlich*. Holiday and *shabbos* meals, not yet kosher at our house, were pot luck in the local covered dish tradition: shit kickers and woolen mittens steamed at the wood stove; broccoli and cheese, with chicken, at the electric. It was the quiet that was hard, uncertainty that seemed so slippery. Later, when friends lugging salad bowls and diaper bags had left, when the kids were lifted from couches and carried back to bed, too much of us was left out of order.

We decided to sell the log cabin and move into town, within walking distance on *yom tov* and *shabbos* from the *shul*. We found an old Victorian with counters and cabinets down both walls of a cavernous kitchen, a front room where we stuffed the kids' toys. We dipped our ladles and *kiddush* cups in the frog pond at the end of the street. I cooked and cooked; our friends' food wasn't *kosher.* The kids railed, then gave up on baseball, chorus, anything that met Friday night or Saturday. We all stayed home. A timer on every light switch, a second sink in the shiny kitchen. Lucky, I bled for seven or eight days each month. There was another week—it was right there in the book—I could wait before plodding back to the *mikveh*. One half of every month I was safe. From the sacred, inviolable right, the one ceremony I dreaded.

It didn't take long. Not more than two or three years before we saw even the certainty of religious tradition wasn't helping. Not long after giving up shabbos restrictions and the promise of family purity, to make the discovery, along with the rest of the culture. There was another explanation. On Parent Education Night at the Worcester Day Care it was me up there on the overhead projector. My life. I'd been sure I was crazy, bad, an oversexed girlchild, a burnt out, unnatural wife. "Childhood Sexual Abuse: Recognizing the Signs." At last husband and wife were taught to say it. I was a victim.

I would not have thought, as little as three months before I'd bought my ticket to Berlin, I'd care particularly about the families, neighbors, fellow parishioners of Nazis. I have never been fond of invoking the word Nazi, or of making blanket comparisons whenever oppression appears, to the specific genocide against European Jews. It's an accident of circumstance that leads me, at the end of the twentieth century, the daughter of Jewish parents, to understand my life and the world in terms of the Holocaust. Now, after having lurched back three times across the ocean—once to beg hidden stories from my aunt, the only member of the first generation in my family still alive; once again to find the families in the Resistance who'd sheltered them; and then again . . . not planning particularly . . . somehow finding something to look up at the eastern border of the Netherlands . . . just in case there was a fast train to Munich . . . if there were some way to feel it, even a single point of barbed wire perhaps, I could take into my body . . . if the concentration camp—*"There is no longer a concentration camp. Do you wish information about the memorial site?"*—would be open . . . to enter Dachau—the understanding I've come finally to respect rather that fear, is the necessity of scars. Going back and back into the Holocaust keeps it ugly, as insistent as the exodus from *mizraim*. Mizraim, as I've begun to see it, is a wound which, praise God, has not been allowed to heal over; liberation understood best in the creases of the body. Forgiveness is not necessarily the goal. Who among the descending generations holds the right to forgive slavery? I'd come to see the task for Jews—the task of continuing to dig and dig for every whiff of the Holocaust—as part of that older, tribal alchemy: turning history into the search for justice. The task for the Germans . . . ?

The room we met in was bare. The only color, the only smell was of our skin, our clothes, our hair. Outside, brightly scarved and mittened skaters circled and crossed freely over the frozen lake to East Berlin. A Jewish American described her vacation in Disneyland. "I was there with my children. The youngest was five. She was too big for a stroller. We decided we would make her walk. The paths were crowded. She was tired. She started to cry. There were balloons and thick legs. She threw herself sideways onto the sidewalk. There was concrete and face paint. I picked her up. My shoulder bag jerked down to my elbow. Everyone was eating. Peanuts and cheese doodles. Slush cones. I told myself if my toes were gone, my fingers, if my parents were gone, sisters, my husband, if there were no place else in the world, if there was only the next step in the dirty snow, if there were holes to fall in, ashen bodies, I wouldn't think about putting her down. I'd have to keep going."

A German woman who grew up in America described her high school education: "I told everyone I was Scandinavian." A Jewish woman crossed her arms over the infant she held in her womb and worried what the child might absorb from the words in the room. A German woman spoke softly of the ministry her father had practiced after the war, having finished with teaching military tactics for the Waffen S.S. A Jewish man described the torture expiring through his survivor-mother's pores, the tips of her fingers, the poisoned liquid of her voice spilling out directly onto him. A German woman wept, "I thought we were a race of monsters."

It was the first time I'd felt like an artifact. The first time I understood my people as a conspicuous absence, rather than as the way I'd always known us in America, a presence. Mourning, sometimes afraid, often loud, our speech full of *tam*. Present. Here.

Good soup simmered slowly downstairs. We broke for lunch. In the dining hall just off the sunporch our shoes mingled under the table. Above my ankles bulged varicose veins. High blood pressure. Gray hairs. Small things, the ones that would have made the difference. I used to study survivors' stories. I knew I'd do anything to survive. Now I'm old, almost forty-five. I'd have been sent to the other line. I take pills for my meager depression. The luxury of it.

After lunch a Jewish woman born in Bergen Belsen after the war, was the first one to shout at the Germans: "You can never apologize to me enough." It was the first rallying point for the two groups. Jews and Germans joined together in defense. "There's no one here who should have to take that blame!" "All the Germans in this room were born after the war." "Are we ever going to move beyond hate?"

As if it were possible to finish with raging at evil. As if moving on were the same as refusing the full bowl of feeling. As if "You can never apologize enough," means, "Try." I remembered my mother's voice the third time I rang her long distance to tell her just what she let happen to me when I was a child. The words she offered before we got ready to hang up could be the most loving thing anyone will ever say to me: "If you want to tell me again, you can."

This year at *seder* I will open my door and say, "Pour out Thy wrath upon the nations." To speak those words is to know the effects of real rage, to keep the promise of solidarity with those who are fueled by it. Not to advocate revenge, but to keep alive that unpretty knowledge of our human capacity. My mother was eighty years old when she invited me to keep saying it. She was willing to hear it, willing to know. Again and again and again.

What appeals to me about the German/Jewish dialogue is its split personality. Support groups are characteristically composed of people who come together to work on a common task. In this group, two distinct tasks are undertaken side by side and together by two different sets of people. Both sets are deeply affected by the same event, but come from opposing sides of the legacy. Who better to understand that a shower is not only a shower but a freak of good luck than those who close down the spigot with thoughts of the dirty roll call they missed by mere decades? Who better to understand that a bed—a real bed to onesel—is a miracle?

*　*　*

"Please. Just get out. Get out of my room."

I hadn't made the deposit on the duplex. Each morning when I picked out socks and turtleneck from a suitcase in Wannsee I tried thinking of the small painted dormitory room as mine. I was mountains away, an ocean away, rivers and train tracks from my family. A Jewish woman trying to make a home in space. I was uncertain what I would do when I got back from my trip. What would it mean to expand out of my room? Where would my husband I then meet? Even we, who crave change, live as man and woman surrounded by currents of violence and fear. People who meet through One-By-One are not asked to pretend the task is the same for Jews as it is for Germans. Yet they have asked, having each learned of the other's task, to meet.

"But I'm not the one who hurt you."

"Leave me alone. Get it?"

Something thick and greasy as smoke was ending my marriage. Something neither one of us had invented. Hadn't we grown up together in the same neighborhood? The cloud of graying hair that flares so beautifully now from my gentle husband's face is tipped with the memory of pine logs peeled and set whole as rafters, of quilts gathered and our huddling between them when the pregnancy miscarried halfway through, of naming in the summer and then sledding down Barf Hill in the winter, of bathing children through fevers, of building on and staining, of our faces searching for creosote in the chimney, one from the bottom, one from the top, of cold coffee and rusty shovels—years and years of sticking it out.

"A lock for your door, for God's sake?"

"Don't stand in here. Get out."

As each of my three sons was born, as each one unfolded his eye, his startled legs, as he curled up under the skirt of his own baggy skin, I suffered the brief disappointment, the searing realization of a possibility lost, a daughter sucked back into the dark of those early hour passages. Then the flood of relief, the good blanket of protection I felt enfolding mother and son. I wouldn't pass it on, the tight walls I knew to be the muscles of a girl, the ugly infusions she'd be bound to absorb from me. It didn't occur to me that my girlhood could be damaging to my boys. Later, they would hide from the fights.

"Nothing has changed here. It's been years, you know. Years. You tell me. How do I know you're working on it?"

"Can't you leave me alone?"

"You won't touch me. You won't look at me. I want to know what you're doing to make this better. I don't believe you want anything to change."

"I'm telling you."

"All I want is a sign. I could put up with it; I could put up with anything if I knew I was ever going to get something for myself out of this. I give in to everything. All you ever say is no."

*   *   *

"I'm telling you, get out of my room.

On the final night of the meetings in Berlin there was a party for members of the dialogue group. It was held at the home of a former soldier in the Waffen S.S. There was food laid out in every room. Here the meat pastries. Here vegetarian. Here the dips. Here the cheeses. Soups. Noodle puddings. Here the fancy cakes. Here the wine. Or bottled water. Cream for your coffee?

The guests at the former soldier's home offered to speak if they could in English. The doctor from "Doctors Without Borders." The minister from the liberal church. The American director from "Children of War." The actor. The artist. People who had decided their own lives. The owner of the house lives there in quiet elegance. His family abandoned him when he began talking publicly about his Nazi past. I entered into that elegance with the chatter in one ear of my mother's Russian immigrant Yiddish scorning the obvious wealth with which my father's German banking family in the other ear calmly prepared to grant severance pay to the Polish servants. Neither side had words for my keeping company with any elegance even formerly associated with the Nazi S.S.

A German woman spoke of her plans to convene groups of Germans who might want to talk among themselves about their inheritance. "What can Germans do? We can bear witness to the history of our country. We can say 'Yes it happened here.' We can listen to each other's pain. There is a difference between guilt and responsibility. I was born after the war. I don't bear guilt for the crimes of my parents' generation. I am a member of my culture. I do bear its responsibilities, including living with its history." The Germans I met through One-By-One are refusing the definition of the Holocaust as a Jewish problem, an event in the victim's history. They don't consider it a finished event for Germany. The Jews who traveled to meet them are refusing to dismiss the German people as monsters.

*   *   *

My husband and I were born in Buffalo, New York. It was 1951. We were both born to Jewish parents. We are blessed, *keineinhorah*, with good health. Among our many forms of wealth, we've also inherited our genders. Our voices have pounded—may they pound no more—with the weight of a built-up, built-in fury, accumulated across generations, oceans, across assorted cultures, from either side of a locked bedroom door. Can we live together with such history? My pig-headed husband, with the sweat of horseradish shining on his earnest brow, his tender tongue made good and full on the shabbos *schmaltz* of his grandmother's kitchen, with the strength of his luscious mind, the goodness of his work, his music, the justice singing deep in his *Yiddishe* soul, and I with my blind groping for voice, for safety, wish together and first for our children's safety and health, the toss of their free heads, wish, both, for easy breaths in a world that welcomes them, that welcomes us fully.

* * *

Among the American guests at the party were an assortment of musicians. Singers, guitarists, a flutist. An impromptu *klezmer* band assembled in the house of the former Nazi soldier. And a Yiddish cabaret. The room was alive with untranslated jokes, teary, wonderful, crooked grins. The doors to all the rooms were open. People in every corner of the house heard the songs.

By the time I'd left home for Berlin the door to my room would no longer stay closed. During the worst of the years it had been pounded so many times the painted wood had split down the center. The hinges at the side creaked open, stiff as a rewired jaw. Inside, against the wall, a bed slat lay where it had fallen on the floor when my bed, with me in it, had been slammed headboard to the wall.

But could traditional roles have been freely chosen when the currencies of power remain traditionally defined? Perhaps a year into shabbos restrictions my Reform upbringing had poked its crabby claw into the *tcholent*. I wanted to wash the windows on shabbos.

"This is supposed to have been a family decision. If you loved me, you wouldn't."

Several years later I had spent tens of thousands of the dollars my husband had earned. Neither one of us would have called it a set-up for extravagant, hot-headed threats.

"I'm not paying for any more of your therapy."

Among the German men at the party that night in Berlin was a smiling man, a Jew whose home is Germany, even after the war, though he'd slept for a while in a small space on a bunk in Auschwitz. Among the German women was a dancer in soft purple and sparkling in every one of her more than eighty years, whose life work remains the site of Ravensbruck, a concentration camp for women, where her mother served time for supporting the German Resistance. Ravensbruck was renowned for medical experiments, particularly on pregnant women. The *klezmer* band struck up a waltz. In the house of the former soldier the old Jew and the old German danced. The old man's voice rang loud above our heads.

My babies. Our sons. What will they make of it? Their mother slamming a metal garbage can through the air, missing their father's head, cutting a scar on the dining room wall? The oldest called out of bed to stop his father's hands yanking his mother by the wrists from the toilet, underwear around her ankles? Their mother's letters in the closet, filled with failed, unfulfilled affairs? The two older boys backed onto couch cushions, their father in the corner, mother weeping cross-legged on the floor with the youngest who willed himself into limpness, who would have produced sleep out of the riot if he could have managed it? What kind of conversation is there to be had at the far end of a legacy when the war is still raging? Though it's been years since we've been physically violent, though my husband confirms the boys' memories of a shattered door, the house, the world, is full of conflicting memories, conflicting definitions. The house, the world. My sons. Our babies.

I was exhausted. I had no heart for the klezmer dance. I sat in a soft leather chair, head back, knees parted. Between them and against the stuffed chairseat leaned a woman with whom I'd become friends in Berlin, with whom I'd felt a deep personal affinity. Her father was chief of gestapo in White Russia, personally responsible for and active in the murder of 40,000 Jews. The two of us rested together. The dancers swayed and sang their way across the dizzy room.

Glossary

Notes:

Hebrew and Yiddish words often have multiple spellings in English transliteration.

Literal translations are in italics.

We indicate h, for Hebrew; and y, for Yiddish terms.

Adonai Elohenu, h: *Lord, Our God.*

Aggadic, h: Nonlegal rabbinic narrative.

Aguna, agunoth (pl), h: A woman who cannot get divorced or remarry because her husband is absent or unwilling to consent to a religious divorce.

Aliyah, aliyot (pl), h: *Ascent.* The honor of being called up during the Torah reading. Also immigration to Israel.

Alte Yiddene, y: *Old Jewess.* Term used with respect and affection or with disdain and ridicule.

Ark: Biblical repository for the stone tablets containing the ten commandments. Modern usage: cabinet containing the Torah scroll(s).

Ashkenazi, h: Jews of Central and Eastern Europe.

B'reshit, h: *In the Beginning.* First words in the Torah.

Balabusta, balebusteh, y: Excellent and praiseworthy homemaker.

Bat/Bar Mitzvah, B'nai Mitzvah (pl), h: *Daughter/son of the commandments.* The religious ceremony marking adult membership in the community at age thirteen. The first girl's Bat Mitzvah was led by Rabbi Mordechai Kaplan for his daughter Judith, in the early 1920s.

Bett Din, h: Court of Jewish law, traditionally composed of three male judges.

Beshert, y: *Fated.* Often refers to the person(s) fated to become a life partner.

Bima(h), h: Podium at which Torah is read.

Bobbe, bubbe, y: Grandmother.

Bobbe meises, y: *Grandmother stories.* Similar to "old wives' tales," can denote respect but more often used dismissively.

Bracha, Barucha, Bruchot (pl), h: *Blessing.* Prayer of praise or thanks.

Brit habat, h: Modern ceremony welcoming a baby girl into the covenant of the people of Israel.

Bris, y: **Brit, Brit milah, Brit mila,** h: *Covenant of circumcision.* Ritual male circumcision eight days after a son's birth.

Britah, h: *Covenant of the daughter.* Modern celebration welcoming an infant daughter.

Bund, y: Jewish Socialist organization.

Camps: Concentration camps.

Challah, Hallah, h: Braided egg-bread traditionally served on Sabbath and Holy Days.

Chasid, h: *Faithful follower.* Member of ultra-religious Chasidic group.

Chaverte, y: *comrade* (female), friend.

Chavurah, h: Study or prayer group functioning with lay leadership.

Chupa, h: Wedding canopy.

D'var Torah, h: *Word of Torah.* A brief talk on a theme or insight from the Torah reading.

Eliyahu Hanovi, h: *Prophet Elijah.* Said to be the forerunner of the Messiah and to appear at the Passover Seder where a full cup of wine is poured for him, and at circumcisions where, among Sephardi Jews, a chair is prepared for him.

Frum, y: Religiously observant.

Ger tzedek, h: *Righteous stranger.* Refers to a convert to Judaism or a person who has done an extrordinary deed such as protecting Jews during the Holocaust.

Get, h: A Jewish religious divorce.

Goy, Goyim (pl), h: Non-Jew(s).

Ha-adam, h: Human being, person.

Haftorah, h: Reading from the Prophets which follows the Torah reading.

Haggadah, h: *Telling* or *Legend.* Most commonly the story of the exodus from Egypt, read at the Passover Seder.

Hai, h: *Life*, also *number 18*. Eighteenth letter of the Hebrew alphabet, also worn as adornment.

Halahha, Halakha, h: Jewish Law.

Halahhic(ly), halakhic, h: In strict accordance with Jewish law.

Hamam, Turkish bath.

Hamsa, h: Hand-shaped amulet, warding off evil spirits, also worn as jewelry.

Hanukah, Chanuka(h), h: Feast of Lights, commemorating the Jewish rebellion and victory over Romans.

Hanukiah: Eight-branched candelabra also called menorah, lit during Hanukah.

Hamantashen, y: *Pockets of Haman*. Three-cornered pastry, filled with poppy seed paste of jam, served on Purim.

Havdalah, h: *Separation*. Ceremony at conclusion of Sabbath and festivals, indicating the separation between holy and mundane, observed with candles, spices, and wine.

Ima, h: Mother.

Indzere, unzere, y: *Ours*. Our own kind, meaning Jews; used during times of persecution when it was not safe to say Jew out loud.

Israel, h: The new name given to the Patriarch Jacob after his night of wrestling with the Divine Angel; also the State of Israel.

Kabbalah/cabala, h: The mystical tradition within Judaism.

Kabbalat Shabbat, h: *Welcoming the Sabbath*. Friday evening religious service.

Kaddish, h: Memorial prayer of sanctification traditionally recited only by male mourners, recently allowed to women mourners.

Kashrut, cashrut: Adhering to kosher practices.

Kavannah, h: Wholehearted intentionality, mindfulness, focused intention.

Keineinhorah, y: *No evil eye*. A phrase used to ward off bad luck.

Kibbutz, h: Collective community in Israel.

Kiddush, h: Blessing over ceremonial wine.

Kippah, kippot (pl), h: Skullcap, yarmulke, head-covering worn by observant Jews.

Klezmer: Jewish music or musicians combining traditional ethnic, folk, and religious melodies.

Kol be-ishah ervah, h: *Woman's voice is indecent*. Talmudic saying quoted to silence women's voices.

Kol Nidre, h: Aramaic, *All Vows*. Most solemn prayer chanted on the eve of Yom Kippur, asking forgiveness of all unfulfilled promises to G-d.

Kosher, h, y: According to Jewish laws, primarily pertaining to preparation and consumption of food.

Kotel, h: *Wall*. Wailing Wall in Jerusalem.

Kotel Ha Ma'aravi, *Eastern Wall*.

Kovnogebernya, y: *County of Kovno (Kaunas)*. Lithuanian Jews from small towns identified their origins by county.

Krystallnacht: German. *Night of Crystal*. The night of November 9-10, 1938, when Nazis broke into Jewish homes, storefronts, and synagogues, breaking crystal and glass as well as burning Torahs and books.

L'Chol Dor Va Dor, h: *From generation to generation*.

Latkes: *Pancakes*: Potato pancakes served during Hanukah.

Leyn, y: Ritual chanting of the Torah portion.

Lilith: Legendary first woman created by God as a companion for Adam. She resisted male control and was succeeded by Eve.

Magen David, h: *Star of David*. Often used decoratively.

Marrano(s) Spanish: *Pig(s)*. Derogatory term applied to Jews who were forced to convert to Catholicism during the Spanish Inquisition.

Matzah, h: Unleavened bread eaten during the week of Passover.

Mazal (mazel) tov, h, y: *Good luck*. Congratulatory greeting.

Mehitzah, h: Curtain separating women from men in Orthodox synagogues.

Mikvah, Mikveh, h, y: Body of running water used for ritual immersion after menstruation or as part of conversion.

Milchig, y: Milk or dairy products or utensils for their use conforming to the laws of kashruth that separate milk and meat.

Mimounah: Judeo-Arabic. Sephardi celebration at the conclusion of Passover, when families hold open house serving non-Passover foods. Mimounah picnics, held on the day after Passover, are often the meeting-ground for potential marriage partners.

Minyan, minyon, h, y: A quorum of ten Jews required for significant parts of religious service, only recently beginning to include women.

Mitzvah, mitzvoth, mitzvot (pl), h: *Commandment of God*. In popular usage a good deed, also the precepts, duties, good acts mandated in Torah.

Mizraim, h. Egypt.

Mohel, h. A person trained in the rituals and procedures of Brit Milah, circumcision.

Moshav, h: *Settlement*. Community of smallholders in Israel with some features of a collective.

Mutti, German: Affectionate diminutive for "mother."

Neshoma, h: Soul, spirit.

Niggun, h: Melody.

Noodge, noodje, y: A caring, constant reminder or person doing the nudging.

Omamma: German. Grandma.

Parasha, h: Weekly portion or Torah reading.

Passover, Pesach, Pessah, h: Holiday celebrating and commemorating the Jewish people's liberation from slavery and exodus from Egypt.

Pilpul, h: Casuastry, intricate mode of discussion originally used by Talmudic sages.

Pirkei Avot, h: Sayings of the Fathers. A section of the Talmud.

Piyut, Piyutim (pl), h: Religious poem or song.

Pogrom(s): Russian. Officially licensed outbursts of mass violence against Jews in Eastern Europe, involving killings, rapes, and looting.

Purim, h: Feast of Esther, commemorating how Queen Esther outwitted the evil Haman and saved the Jewish people from persecution.

Rebbe, y: *Rabbi*. Also charismatic leader and authority figure.

Rebbitzin, y: Wife of a rabbi.

Refusenik(s), Jews in the former Soviet Union who were refused government permission to emigrate, losing their jobs upon applying for exit visas.

Rosh Chodesh, Rosh Hodesh, h: *New moon*. Celebration of beginning the lunar month, has become the focus of women's spiritual groups.

Rosh Hashanah, Rosh Hashono, Rosh Ha Shanah, h, y: *Head of the Year*. Jewish New Year, birthday of the world.

Saba, h: *Grandfather.*

Sabra, h: *Fruit of cactus.* Slang for Israeli-born, prickly outside and soft inside.

Safta, h: *Grandmother.*

Schmaltz, y: Rendered chicken fat; also sentimental, soft-hearted.

Schmini Atzeret, h: *Solemn Convocation.* Eighth and concluding day of the Fall Festival of Succoth.

Seder, h: *Order of service.* Ceremonial feast on the first (2) nights of Passover that includes reading the Haggadah traditionally in Hebrew.

Sephardi(c), Sephardim (pl), h: Jews of Meditteranean area including Spain, Portugal, and Morocco; migrated to Holland, the Americas, and other countries during the expulsion from Spain. Their vernacular is Ladino or Judeo-Arabic.

Shabbas, Shabbot, h: **Shabbos**, y: Jewish Sabbath, beginning at sundown Friday night and ending at sundown Saturday night.

Shabbat Shalom: *Peaceful Sabbath.* Sabbath greeting.

Shalom Bayit, h: *Peace in the home.*

Shanda, Shonde, Shondah, y: *A disgrace or shame.*

Shavuoth: Feast of First Fruits, celebrating the giving of the Ten Commandments; a spring festival traditionally including a reading of The Book of Ruth.

Shehehyanu, h: *Who has kept us alive.* Blessing said on special occasions, thanking G-d for allowing us to reach this season or event.

Sheitel(s), y: *Wig (s)* worn by Orthodox women who shave their hair upon marriage.

Shema, h: *Hear, Israel, our Lord is the One God.* Central prayer of the Jewish People.

Shiva, h: Seven days of mourning.

Shmini Atzeret, h: *Solemn Convocation.* The eighth day of the Fall Festival of Sukkoth.

Shofar, shofarim (pl): *Ram's horn.* Call to repentance on Rosh Hashana and Yom Kippur.

Shtetl, y: The Jewish towns, neighborhoods, and ghettoes of Eastern Europe.

Shul, y: Synagogue or temple, house of prayer.

Siman tov v mazel tov, h: *Good signs and good luck!* Celebratory, congratulatory chant.

Simha, simcha(s), h, y: *Celebration.* Joyous occasion.

Simhat Torah, h: *Celebration of Torah.* Celebrating the completion of the annual reading of the Five Books of Moses followed immediately with reading B'reshit, the first verse of the Bible. This concludes the Holy Day season that began with Rosh Hashanah.

Siyyum(im), h: Celebration(s) when a portion of Jewish learning is completed.

Succah, Sukka, Sukkofh (pl), h: *Shelter.* Harvest hut constructed for the Jewish Holiday of Succoth; observant Jews eat and sleep in the succah during the week of Succoth.

Succoth, Sukkot(h), h: Harvest Festival commemorating the forty years of wandering in the desert.

Tagelach, y: *Bits of dough.* Delicacy made of small balls of dough cooked in honey, combined with candied fruits and nuts. Traditionally served at Rosh Hashanah to sweeten the new year.

Tallis, tallit(ot) (pl), h: Ritual fringed shawl worn by men and lately by women during prayer.

Talmud, h: *Study* or *learning.* Volumes containing the oral law, legend, philosophy, and anecdotes that comprise the central body of Jewish teachings and guidance for Jewish life.

Tam, h, y. *Taste.* Flavorful, tasty.

Tashlich, h: Ceremony symbolically casting sins into a body of water during Rosh Hashanah.

Tcholent, y: A hearty dish kept warm throughout shabbos in order to avoid cooking on the Sabbath.

Teshuvah, h: *Return to Jewish thought and practice.* Also, repentance.

The Temple: Central place of worship in Jerusalem, destroyed by the Babylonians and later by the Romans.

Tikkun Olam, h: *Repair of the world.* Jewish people's responsibility to help repair or heal the world.

Tischlied: German. *Table song.* Usually a poem or song to celebrate an occasion.

Torah, h: Literally the parchment scroll that contains the handwritten Five Books of Moses; in the broadest sense, all of Jewish law and teachings.

Torah portion, Specific portion of Torah read on a particular Sabbath or Holy Day.

Treif, y: Not kosher.

Trop, trope, y: Musical cantillation for chanting Torah or Haftorah.

Tsimmis, y: *Mixture*. Slow cooking dish combining carrots, potatoes or sweet potatoes, sometimes prunes, and/or a piece of meat.

Tsitsit, h: *Fringes*. Knotted fringes on Jewish prayer shawls.

Tu-Be-Shvat, h: Birthday of the Trees, celebrated in early spring with planting of trees in Israel.

Wailing Wall: Remnant of the Jerusalem Temple now used as a special place of worship, also referred to as Western Wall or Kotel, h.

Yahrzeit, y: Anniversary of a person's death using the Jewish calendar.

Yamim Noraim, h: *Solemn days*. Period of self-reflection between Rosh Hashana and Yom Kippur.

Yashir (Yasher) Koah, h: *May your strength be enhanced*. Congratulatory greeting to a person having performed a ritual deed or mitzvah.

Yehus, Yihus, h, y: Family status, usually high status, a family of great learning, wealth, or power.

Yentah, Yenta, y: A meddlesome, gossiping person, usually applied to women.

Yeshiva, yeshivot (pl), h: School of Jewish studies for young men only.

Yiddish(e), y: Yiddish language, also possessing the flavor of the eastern European Jewish culture.

Yiskor, Yitzkor, h: *To remember*. Religious Service of Remembrance.

Yom Kippur, Kippour, h: Day of Atonement, holiest day in Jewish calendar.

Yom tov, h, y: Holy Day.

Zakena, h: Wise old woman.

Zayde, y: Grandfather.

Zohar, h: *Brightness*. Principal book of the kabbalah.

Index

Abraham, as a Jewish father, 250,256
Abuser, dual personality of, 262
Adolescence
  and African American girls,
    234-236
  ethnic impact on, 234-235
  female crisis in, 233
  identity formation, 232-233
  Jewish experience of, 234-236
  and lesbian identity, 234-236
Adonai Elohenu (Lord, Our God),
  225
Aggadic (nonlegal rabbinic
  narratives), 142
Agunot, Aguna (without religious
  divorce), 21,144,268
AIDS, 53
Alcuin Award, 116
Aliyah aliyot (ascent), 153,172,
  182,211,212
 Orthodox and, 6
Allied Jewish Federation, 270
Alpert, Rebecca, 30
Alpert, Richard. *See* Dass, Ram
Alte Yiddene (old Jewess), 205
AMEND, 271
American Dream, 252,257
American Gathering of Holocaust
  Survivors, 295-296
American Jewish community, 179
American Jewish Joint Distribution
  Committee (JOINT), 112
Androcentrism, of Talmud, 142,267
Anne Frank house, 163-164
Anti-Defamation League of B'nai
  B'rith, 219
Antimother, Jewish attitudes, 41
Antisemitic remarks, 159-160,281

Antisemitic society, 26
Antisemitism, 83
  Canadian study, 279,281-282,
    284-285,
  experiences of, 159-160,171,
    189,281-282
  fear of, 131,133,148,149,179,
    203-204
  and feminist agenda, 193
  internalized, 26,32-33
  invisible, 252
  in Prague, 189
  in Tadzhikistan, 107
"Antisemitism as Trauma: A Theory
  of Jewish Communal Trauma
  Response," 298
Antiwoman, Jewish attitudes, 41
Antonelli, Judith, 224-225
Anzaldua, Gloria, 152
Apostasy, 75
Appropriate, 54
Arcana, Judith, on women as child
  bearers, 40-41
Arendt, Hannah, 180
Ark (Torah cabinet), 211
Art therapy, 78
Ashkenazi
  in America, *xxiii*,19,149
  food of, 62
  traditions, 82
"Asocials," in death camps, 30
Association for Women in
  Psychology Conference, 297
  Jewish caucuses, 209
Aunties, 236
Auschwitz, 191,311

Balebusteh (praiseworthy homemaker), 231
Baptism, 72
Bar Mitzvah (son of the commandments), 5,49,169-170
Baruchas (blessings), 220,226
Bat Mitzvah (daughter of the commandments), 5,24,98,99, 153,211,223,224,227
Battered woman syndrome, 263,265, 275-276
Battered Woman's Research Center, 268-269
Battered women
  in the Jewish community, 261
  in Metro Denver, 268-275
Batterers, reason given for, 265
Beck Torton, Evelyn, 32,152
Bedouin woman, giving birth, 89
Beer Sheba, 172-173
Beit Yakov School, 208
Bereavement, issues of, 263
Bergen Belsen, 307
Berlin, 160-163,205,301,302
  Holocaust memorial, 162
Beshert (fated life partner), 29
Beth Jacob synagogue, 213,214
Bett, Beth Din (Court of law), 126
Bezalel Art School, 112
Bimah (Podium), 47,153,212,304
Birth family, of converts, 127,133
Bisexual, 30
B'nai B'rith Youth Organization, 19
B'nai Mitzvah (daughters/sons of the commandment), 5,11
Bobbe (grandmother), 120
Bobbe meises (grandmother stories), *xxi,xxiv*
Body, Jewish, 285-287
Bonaparte, Napoleon, 81
Bonds for Israel Corporation, 169
Bosnia, genocide in, 185
Boulder Action for Soviet Jewry (BASJ), 100,108

Brandeis University, 231
Braun, Eli, 266,267
Breaking-point, battered women, 265
Breast cancer epidemic, 53
Bremen, Germany, 58
Bridges, 209,224
Bris, Brit, Brit Milah (circumcision), 9,11,12,84,127
  feelings about, 14
  Sephardic tradition, 90-91
Brit habat (naming ceremony), 15-16, 127
"Broken Column, The," 195
"Bronze Horseman, The," 97
Brown, Laura, 173
Brown, Lyn Mikel, 242
Brown v. Board of Education, 177
Bukharan Jews, 101,109
Bund (Jewish Socialist organization), 64
Burial, guidance, 121

"Camps, The," 49,61. *See also* Concentration camps; Death camps; Extermination camps
Canada
  make up of antisemitism/sexism study, 279-280
  Montreal, Jewish community in, 19
  Toronto, 81
  Winnipeg, 119
Castrating mother, 251
Castration anxiety, 14
Catholic church, 76
Catholic priest, 72
Catholic school, study at, 96
Catholic shame, 174
Catholicism, 73,74,75,79,254
Challah (bread), *xxi,*64,222
Chanukah (Festival of Lights), 50,88,237,238
Chasid (faithful follower), 216
Chaverte (comrade) Novak, 190

Chavurah (study or prayer group),
205,228,284
Chesler, Phyllis, 233
Chicago, Judy, 175,296
"Childhood Sexual Abuse:
Recognizing the Signs," 305
Child-rearing theories, feminist, 34
"Children of War," 309
"Choosing My Religion," 182
"Christ-killers," antisemitic remark,
281
Christmas
celebration of, 50,70,149,237-238
issues of celebration of, 21,22,23,
24,27,239-240
Chupa (wedding canopy), 19
Circumcision. *See also Bris*
issues of, 9-11
and Jewish identity, 84
mother's experience, 93
Civil rights, queer, 32
Civil Rights Movement, 252
Cocreators, 227
Cohen, 83
Colon, Christobal, 256
Colorado, 269,270,271
Colorado Jewish Family Services,
270,274,275
Columbus, Christopher, 254
"Come home," 228
Coming In Prayer, A, 257-258
Coming out, 33,34,150-151,228
"Coming-to-oneself," 190,193
Commentary, 192
"Communion," playing at, 96
Community
and Jewish identification, 11
longing for Jewish, 194
Comparative religions, teacher
of, 224,227
Comsomol, 107
Concentration camps, 302,305. *See
also* Camps; Death camps;
Extermination camps
Concubines, 41

Conservative practice, 6,147
Conservative synagogue, 3,6,19,179
Conservative tradition, 82,135
Consistoire de Paris, 81,82
Construction workers, story of, 249
Contraceptive information, 256
Conversion
and authenticity, 132-133
ceremony, 126
to Judaism, 98,99
rise in, 135
Converts
acceptance of, 136
and Jewish observance,
130,132-133
job description, 134
and their birth families, 127
Cooper, Howard, 17
Coparenting, 35
Cossacks, 49
"Countertransference and Trauma,"
292
Country Club, 46
Couscous, 87
Cremation, and Jewish law, 23
Cycle of violence, 265
Czar, 49
Czechoslovakia, Prague, 69

Dachau, 301,305
Dalai Lama, 223
Danieli, Yael, 292
Dass, Ram, 175
Daughter, rabbi's, 3-4,8
Day schools, 3,24
Death camps, 97,162. *See also*
Camps; Concentration camps;
Extermination camps
Denver Jewish community,
267,268,270-275
Denver University School of Law,
109
Depression, 77
DeWoskin, Shelia, 226-227

Diamant, Anita, 13,17
Diaries (Kafka's), 188
Diary of Anne Frank, The, 293
Diaspora, 254
"Dinner Party, The," 175
Dinnerstein, Dorothy, 233
"Dirty Jew," antisemitic remark, 281
Divorce, and battered women, 266,269
"Doctors Without Borders," 309
Domestic violence, no training about, 272
Domestic Violence Institute, The, 269
Domination, 180
Down by the Riverside, 232
Dubner, Stephen, 182-183
D'var Torah (Word of the Torah), 43,226

Easter, celebration of, 70
Easter eggs, decorated, 50
Ecumenica discussionl, exclusion of women, 203
El Al, 171
Eliyahu Hanovi (Prophet Elijah), 222
Eliyahu's chair, 91
Emerson College, 164-165
Engendered Lives, 248,250
Epistemological foundations, 247,248
Ethical culturalists, 183
Ethical tradition, Jewish, 173
Evangelical Christians, 179
Exclusivity, feelings of, 178,179,180
Expulsion, from Spain, 254,293
Extermination camps, 75. *See also* Camps; Concentration camps; Death camps
Eye-for-eye, self-defense, 264,266

Families, African-American, 248
Family
   Christian definition of, 248
   matriarchal, 248
   meaning of, 31
   violence in, 261-262
"Family of choice," 35
Feminist "click," 193
"Feminist Perspective on Intermarriage," 294
Feminist Seders, 56
Feminist theories, and child rearing, 34
Feminist Therapy Institute, 173,175
Festivals, observance of, 127
Fiddler on the Roof, 19
Fifth Commandment, 39,44
Fiorenza, Elisabeth Schussler, 216
First International Conference of Judaism, Feminism, and Psychology, 201,247,293
First International Jewish Feminist Conference, 140
Florida, Boca Raton, seniors community in, 185
Focus groups
   Canadian, 279-280
   main themes of, 280
Food
   backward, 48-49
   religious tradition, 62
Fourteenth International Conference of Gay and Lesbian Jews, 30
France, Jewish community of, 81
Franco, Francisco, 72
Freud, Sigmund, 250
Freudian premise, no accidents, 191
Friedan, Betty, 233
"A Friend of Kafka," 191
Friendship
   with non-Jews, 7-8
   with other Jews, 7
Frum (religiously observant), 130,303

Gay and lesbian rights, 157,181
Gender, as containment, 45
German Resistance, 311
German/Jewish dialog, 307
Germany, post Nazi, 160-163
Ger tzedek (righteous stranger), 127
Get (religious divorce), 21,25,
    268,303
Gilligan, Carol, 233,242
Girl Scout Camp, 226
God
  belief in, 154
  doubts about, 5-6
  women and ritual, 16-17
Goddesses, ancient, 117,175
Goldman, Emma, 151
Good girls, 233
Gordonia, 112
Gottlieb, Lynn, 175
Goy, Goyim (non-Jews), 179
Grandmother
  Ashkenazi, 61-62
  Sephardi, 60-61
Grandparent-grandchild bond, 59
Grandparents, difficulties of role,
    63-64
Greenberg, Blu, 141,224
Greenhorns, 46
Grinch, The, 22

Hagaddah. See Haggadah
Hagar, 214,251
Haggadah (Passover story), 131,185
  lesbian-feminist, 151
Halakhic (Jewish religious)
    conversion, 98,99
Halakhic Judaism, restrictive nature
    of, 144
Half the Kingdom, 139
Hallah. See Challah
Hamam (Turkish bath), 84
Hamentashen (pastry), 98
Hammer, Barbara U., 298
Hanukah. See Chanukah

Hanukiah (Menorah), 88
Harvard Graduate School, 232
Havdalah (separation), 220,222
Healthy courage, 236
Hebrew, language of, 19,61,116,
    214,253
Hebrew, studying the language
    of, 99,266
"Hebrew people," 30
Hebrew University, in Jerusalem,
    112
"Hebrews," 30
Hegel, on community, 143
Heilman, Samuel, 215
"Helper" program, battered women,
    274
Helpline, 274
Heschel, Susannah, 212
Heterosexism, 31
  internalized, 31-32,33
Heterosexist stereotypes, 35
High Holy Days
  observance of, 127
  services, 47,77
  sermon on domestic violence, 273
Hillel, 169
Hillel's dictum, 219
Historian of Religion, 125,128
History, Jewish idea of, 129,174
Hoffman, Howard, 267
Holiday creation, role of, 22
Holland, 163
Holocaust
  impact of, *xxiii*,23,26,32,149,
    239,240,254,291-299
  loss of spiritual leaders, 228
  memorial, 185
  refusal to believe, 169
  survivors of, 61,188,253-254,293
  to understand the, 98
Holocaust Project, The: From
    Darkness into Light, 296
Homoerotic tensions, in Kafka's
    work, 194-195
Homosexuals, in death camps, 30

Honi, story of, 142
Honor, meaning of, 39-40
hooks, bell, 184
House Un-American Activities
    Committee (HUAC), 96
Human Development and
    Psychology, 232
Hyrrcanus, R. Eliezer ben, *xxi*

"I don't know," 237-238
Identity formation
    conversion narrative and, 129
    and ritual observance,
        132,136,212,320
"Ima's Not on the Bima," 206
In Search of Eden, 118
Independence, woman's right to, 269
"Indians," 254
"Individualization," 64
Industrial Workers of the World, 167
Inquisition, 73,188,254
Interdating, as taboo, 7,8
Interfaith marriage, 19
    issues of, 20
Intermarriage
    attitude toward, 83,130
    experience of, 19-27
    impact on children, 26
    Jewish male practice, 288
International Committee for
    the Women of the Wall, 144
International Conference
    on Feminism and Orthodoxy,
        143
International Sex Roles Conference,
        171
Intourist Hotel, 103,105
"Invisible minority," 136
Iraq, 60
Isolation, 70
    from Judaism, 20-21,22
    spiritual, 22

Israel
    battered women
        shelters fundraisers, 270
        training, 276
    emigration to, 112
    issues about, 227
    and Jewish identity, 11,79,113,
        114,171-173,231
    right of return, 135
Israel-Arab war (1965), 169
"Israelites," 30
Ithaca (NY), 3,205

Jacasta, 250,251
Jerusalem, 81,99,150
    Arab quarter, 150
    cemetery in, 120
    Mea Shearim, 116
Jesus, 72
Jew
    right kind of, 50
    with feminist analysis, 36
"Jew bag," antisemitic remarks, 159
Jew in the Lotus, The, 223
"Jew-Bu," 224
"Jewing down," antisemitic remark,
        281
Jewish activists, 51
Jewish adolescence, experience
    of, 234-236
Jewish American Princess, 240-241,
        285,286
    jokes about, 248
Jewish Baby Book, The, 13
Jewish community
    ambivalence toward, 178-179
    patriarchal hegemony, 142
Jewish education, 3,11,134,143
    women and, 202-203
Jewish families, queer, 35-36
Jewish Family Service agency,
        Denver, 270
Jewish guilt, 174
Jewish history, learning of, 11

Jewish identity
  forming of, 11-12,167,213
  in Israel, 11,150
  in United States, 11-12,23
Jewish Lesbian Torah study group,
  152
Jewish males, internalized
  antisemitism, 287-288
Jewish meditation techniques, 223
Jewish mother, 240-241
  jokes about, 248
"Jewish princess," antisemitic
  remark, 281
"Jewish question," 188,248
Jewish renewal, 228
Jewish Renewal, 181,185
Jewish Response to Family Violence,
  271
Jewish retirement home, 171
Jewish Woman in America, The, 41
Jewishness, authentic, 190,191,
  210,223
Jews
  and African Americans,
    151-152,160
  Latin American, 253,254
"Jews Against Apartheid," 151
Jezebels, orthodox feminists as, 141
Joe Hill, 232
Johnson, Barbara, 152
Josef, K., 187
Joys of Yiddish, The, 128
Judaism
  antiwomen attitudes, 203-204,
    205,207
  class on, 77
  and feminism, 24-25,127,134-135,
    224,251-252,262,282
  Halakhic, 144,267

Kabbalah (mystical tradition), 220
Kaddish (memorial prayer), 263
Kafka, critique of his work, 194-195

*Kafka and the Yiddish Theater: Its
  Impact on His Works,* 187
Kahlo, Frida, 195,196
Kansas, Topeka, 170
Kaplan, Aryeh, 223
Kaplan, Mordecai, 156
Kashrut (kosher practices), 62
Kavannah (intention), 29,220
Kaye/Kantrowitz, Melanie, 152
Keineinhorah (no evil eye), 310
Kibbutz (collective community),
  150,173
Kiddush (blessing of wine), 133,304
"Kike," antisemitic remarks, 159
King Mihai of Romania, 112
Kippot (skullcaps), 6,103,133,304
Klepfisz, Irma, 152
Klezmer (Jewish ethnic music) band,
  310,311
Kol Nidre (All Vows)
  contents of, 78
  service, 47,53
Kosher (food ritual), 98,149,
  167-168,304
Kotel, 144,268. *See also* Wailing
  Wall
Kovnogebernya (Lithuanian county),
  xxii
Krystallnacht (Night of Crystals), 58
Kwanza, 238

Labor Zionist, 231
Ladies Home Journal, 46
Latkes (pancakes), 88,232
Learned helplessness, 202
Learned ignorance, 148,155,201-202,
  204,219
Lentl, 152-153
Lerner, Michael, 181
Lesbian identity, 193
Lesbian rabbi, 148
Lester, Julius, 222
Letter bomb, 26
Letters (Kafka's), 188
Levi, Jacques, 191

Levi, Yitzhok, 191
Leyn (ritual chanting of Torah
        passage), 211,214,216
    in English, 216-217
Liberal pluralism, 177
Life, 46
LILITH, 119,185,209,224
Linden, Ruth, 295
Lithuanian, 61,81,205
Living a Jewish Life, 17
Lorde, Audre, 152
Los Angeles, Jewish neighborhood
        in, 170
Los Angeles Times, The, 171
Lovesong: Becoming a Jew, 222
Lox, 232
Luebeck, Poland, 57
Lutheran minister, 72
Lutheran religion, 70,74
Luxembourg, Rosa, 151
Lux Radio Theater, 46
Lycee Francais, 83
Lycee Francais de Barcelone, 72
Lying, about religious faith,
        70,71,72,82
L'chol Dor Va Dor (from generation
        to generation), 64

"Magical thinking," 71
Mairie (city hall), 82
Male violence, problem of, 269
Manhattanville College of the Sacred
        Heart, 74
Mapam, 150
"Marital therapy," and domestic
        violence, 272
Marranos, 73,78,79,254
Marriage
    meaning of, 31
    as solution, 75
Marriage, Family, and Child
        Counselor, 78
Marycliff Academy, 74
Marynoll missionary nun, 74

Masada, 172
Masochism, Jewish mother's, 43
"Matriarchs, The" 40
Mea Shearim, Jerusalem, 116
Mehitzah (curtain), 267
Mental health professions,
        mother-blaming, 41,42
Michigan State University, 170
Middle child syndrome, 4
Mikvah, Mikveh (ritual immersion),
        84,99,126,135,267
Milchig (dairy) counter, 303
Miller, Jean Baker, 42,233
Mimounah (Sephardic celebration),
        89
Minyan, Minyon (quorum), 182,
        212,263
    exclusion from, 135
"Missing commandment, The," 211
Missouri, Springfield, 39
Mitzvoth
    (commandments), Orthodox and, 6
    (good deeds), 95
Mizraim (Egypt), 305
Modern Language Association,
        192-193
Modern Screen, 46
Mohel (performs circumcision),
        10,12-13,91
Montreal, participants in
        antisemitism/sexism study,
        279-280
Morality, and religion, 6-7
Morocco, Sephardic experience, 60
Moshav (settlement), 150
Moslem lands, Jews of, 87
Mother, honoring of, 39-40
Mother-blaming, by mental health
        professionals, 41,42
Mothers
    African-American, 248
    unappreciated, 42
Mother's Day, 42
Mount of Olives, 120
Ms. magazine, 193

Multicultural discussion, exclusion
  of women, 203
Mutti (mother), 58,59

Name, change of, *xxiv*,83
Narration, conversion, 128,
  129-130,136
National Women's Studies
  Association, 193
  Jewish caucuses, 209
Nawal, 242
Neshoma (Soul), 99
New Yorker, The, 192
*Nice Jewish Girls: A Lesbian
  Anthology*, 32,193
Niggun (melody), 304
"Night and Fog," 294
Nobel prize for literature, 192
Noodje (nudge), 221
Normandie, France, 69,76
"Nose job," *xxiv*,241,287
Not knowing enough. *See* Learned
  ignorance
"Notes Toward Finding the Right
  Question," 292

"O Hevruta, O Metuta!" 142
Observance, Jewish, 127,220
Oedipal complex, 250,256
Oedipus, 250,256
Okin, Susan Moller, 184
Old Testament, access to, 116
Omamma (grandmother), 57
One-by-One, 302,308,309
Orthodox congregation, Berkeley,
  182
Orthodox practice, 6
Orthodox Quarter, Mea Shearim, 116
Orthodox synagogue, 6,19
Orthodox tradition, 82,135,136,203,
  208,231,267
  view of women's education, 201
  women, view of, 284

Orthodoxy, refusal to speak, 140
Outreach congregation, 77
"Oven rider," antisemitic remark,
  160
"Oy Luck Club, The," 221
Ozick, Cynthia, 211,292
  on Jewish feminism, 292

Palestine, 75
Paley, Grace, 242-243
Pappenheim, Bertha, rescue
  activities, 58
Parasha (weekly Torah reading), 152
Paris, France, 69
Passah. See Pesach
"Passing," 235-236
Patriarchal religion, 25,224
Pearl Harbor, 172
"Perpetual care," 120
Pesach (Passover holiday), 22,39,88
Phi Beta Kappa, 96
Photoplay, 46
Pilpul, 264
Pirkei Avot (Sayings of the Fathers),
  217
Piyut, Piyutim (religious song/
  poem), 90
Plaskow, Judith, 40,182,212,216
Pogroms (official antisemitic
  violence), 111,254
Poland, 57,61
  Warsaw, 191
Political resisters, 233
"Politics of Difference, The," 178
Prague, 188,189
Prayer
  group, women's, 267
  Orthodox women and, use of, 154
Pre-Oedipal phase, 251,256
Primordial Goddess plate, 175
"Problems of Intermarriage," 23
Progoff, Ira, 175
Project Safeguard, 271
Protestant prohibitions, 174
"Providers," 41

Psychology of Adolescence, 232
Puah, 157
Purim (feast of Esther), 98
    Sephardic tradition of, 88
Purity laws, 135,181

Queer
    meaning of, 29-30
    parenting, 30
Queer Jews, 29
Queer parents, as a gift, 34

Rabbi
    as midwife, 157
    role of, 155
    women's, ordination of, 147
Rabbinical Council, 272,273
Rabin's assassination, 175-176
"Raised as a resister," 236
Ravensbruck, 311
Reasonable woman standard,
    275-276
Rebbitzin (Rabbi's wife), 57
Reconstructionist
    identify as, 30
    practice, 6,147,156,284
Reconstructionist Rabbinical
    College, 147
Reform family, 82
Reform practice, 6,147
Reform synagogue, 6,98
Reform tradition, 82,284
Refugees, women and children, 256
Religion
    changing denominations, 183
    vs. love, 21
Religious fundamentalism, 179
Religious observance, 6,11,62,232
Religious values, imparting, 64
Response-ability, 227
"Revenge of Ignorance, The," 187
Rich, Adrienne, 294
Ridwas, 201

Ritual space, as male territory, 212
Robert, Marthe, on Kafka, 189
Robinson, Tracy, 235
Rogers, Annie, 232,234,237
    on the Holocaust, 295
Role model, grandmother as, 59,62
Romania, 111
Rose Hospital, 270
Rose Hospital Foundation, training
    program, 273
Rosenbergs, execution of the, 293
Rosh Chodesh (New Moon), 209,
    284,297
Rosh Hashanah (New Year),
    22,39,81
    Sephardic tradition of, 91
Rosh Hashono. *See Rosh Hashanah*
Rumanian, 69,81
Russian culture, study of, 95
Russian language, 95
Russian Revolution, 97

Saba (grandfather), 16,63
Sabbath candles, 26,149
"Sabbath-mindspace," 225
Sabras (Native born Israeli), 112
Sacred space, 212
Safe feeling, as Jew, 282
Safety
    of Jewish people, 26-27
    in post holocaust world, 293,298
Safta (grandmother), 16,63
Samplers, *xxvii*
Sara, 251
    as codependent, 250-251
Schacter-Shalomi, Zalman, 216,223
Schindler's List, 225,298
Schmaltz (sentimentality), 310
Second World War, 61,69,73,160
Secular Jews, 111,213,219
Seder, 88,98,251
    attending a, 97,185,256
    feminist, 56,152
    leading a, 206

Self-defense
   battered women and, 264,265
   legal burden of, 264
Self-identity, Orthodox, Jewish
      feminist, 141
"Self-induced television epilepsy,"
      42
Sephardic culture, 60-61,62,175
Sephardic Jews, differ from
      Ashkenazi, *xiii*
Sephardic traditions, 82
Sexism
   Canadian study, 279,283-284,
      284-285
   at home, 283
   in Jewish community, 284
   in Judaism, 43,225,277
   in the workplace, 283-284
Shabbat (Jewish sabbath), 8,11,77,
      85,126,127,130,220,222,226,
      304
Shabbat Shalom (peaceful sabbath),
      133
Shalom Aleichem Folkshule, 190
Shalom bayit (peace in the home),
      xxiii,62,261,269,270,271,272
Shanda, Shonde, Shondah (disgrace),
      50,179,261,262,269
Shavuot (Feast of First Fruits), 89
Shehehyanu (blessing), 210
*Sheila Levine Is Dead and Living
   in New York*, 181
Sheitels (wigs), 140
Sheldon, Amy, 294
Shema (prayer), 99,220
Shifra, 157
Shiva (mourning period), 54,263
Shmini Atzeret (Solemn
      Convocation), 92
Shofarim (ram's horns), 304
"Showers," 297
Shrine of the Book, The, 99
Shtetls (ghettos), 46,178,179
Shul (synagogue), 6,47,304.
      See also Synagogue; Temple

Siegel, Rachel Josefowitz, 42
Siman tov and Mazel tov (good signs
      and good luck), 212
Simchas (celebrations), 21,22
Simhat Torah (Celebration of Torah),
      92
Simpson, O. J., testimony
      about, 268,276
Singer, Isaac Bashevis, 125,191
   translator of, 192
Single-sex public schools, 177
Siyyumim (celebrations), 304
Smith, Beverly Jean, 236
Social community, need of, 142
Socialists, 183
Southern Review, 192
Soviet Criminal Law system, 109
Soviet Union, Jews in, 100
Spain, 72,78
"Split at the Root: An Essay on
      Jewish Identity," 294-295
Standing Again at Sinai, 216
Storytelling, enjoyment of, 215
Success stories, survival strategies,
      180
Succoth, Sukka (harvest festival), 92
Sukkah (shelter), 249
Surrey, Janet, 42
"Survivors Nonetheless: Trauma
      in Women Not Directly
      Involved with the
      Holocaust," 294
"Suspicion and remembrance," 216
Switzerland, 205
Synagogue
   attending, 76
   class aspect of, 47
   gay and lesbian, 32
   Lausanne, Switzerland, 206
   Montpelier, Vermont, 213
   in Moscow, 101
   non-Jewish partner in, 22
   role of, 12

Tadzhikistan, Dushanbe, 100, 102-105
Tagelach (dough cookies), *xxi*
Tallis, Tallot, Tallit (prayer shawl), 6,144,170
Talmud, 142
  mixed gender study group, 266,268
  Steinsaltz translation, 266
  women's study group, 182
Talmudic dialectic, 227
Talmud Torah (school), 114,115
Tam (taste), 306
Tao, 225
R. Tarfon, 217
Tashlich (cast water), 304
Tcholent (hearty dish), 310
Tel Aviv, 150
Temple, call aspect of, 47
Ten Commandments, 39
Terrifying Love: Why Battered Women Kill and How Society Responds, 266
Teshuvah (return), 223
Therapy, 77
Theresiensadt, 69
Third World women, 253
Tikkun, 185
Tikkun Olam (repair of the world), *xxix*,35,227,255,262
Tischlied (table song), 57
"Tivona," 226
Torah (five books of Moses), 40
  binders, *xxvii*
  covers, *xxvii*
  literacy, 215
  reading lessons, 182
  scroll, as sacred object, 212
  studying, 220
Torah portion (Scriptural reading), 40,211
Toronto, participants
    in antisemitism/sexism study, 279
Transgendered, 30

Tree planting, 47
Trial, The, 187,188,194
Trials of Eve, The, 116,117,118
Trief (not kosher), 150
Trop, trope (musical scheme), 214,220
"True I," 237
Tsimmis (stew), *xxi*
Tsitsit (fringes), 304
Tu-Be-Shvat (tree birthday celebration), 88
Tunisia, 82,86
Turkey, Sephardic experience, 60-61

Ultra-Orthodox tradition, 82,208
UNICEF calendar, 115
Unitarian congregation, 170
United States, Jewish identity in, 11-12
United Synagogue Youth (USY), 213
University of Chicago, 125
University of Judaism, 175

Vancouver, 205
Vegetarianism, 150
Vermont, 205,211,232
  Green Mountain range, 302
Vessels, women as, 41
"Vicarious traumatization," 261
Vienna, 188
Violence
  against women, and Judaism, 262-263
  sexual, 256
Virgin Mary, 41,242
Visibility, as a Jew, 26
Vows, under duress, 78

Waffen, S. S., 306,309
Wailing Wall, 172,208,268
Wake, 23
War of Independence, Israel's, 150

Ward, Janie, 235
WASP, 85
Weiner, Kayla Miriyam, on the
    Holocaust, 294
Wolf, Christa, 190
Wolf, Yosef, 208
Woman Question, 248
Women
    affiliation within Judaism, 6,179
    and illiteracy, 256
    Jewish, showpieces, 41
    and Judaism, 134-135,136,
        181-182
    as killers, 275
    ritual observance, 143
    and Torah, 144,206
Women's Liberation Movement, 253
Women's role, unappreciated, 42-43
Woolf, Virginia, on art and life, 196
Wounds of Gender, 195-196

Yad Vashem, 172
Yahrzeit (death anniversary), 263
Yamim Noraim (solemn days), 81
"Yasher Koah," 154

Yehus (family status), 58
Yellow star, 301
Yenta (meddlesome gossip), 134
Yentl, 152
Yeshiva, Yeshivot (religious schools),
        3,82
Yiddish
    language, 19,192-193
    plays, 188
    studying, 188,191
    theater, 190
    women writer's in, 193
Yiskor (remembrance service), 263
Yitzkor (Remembrance) service, 53
Yom Kippur (Day of Atonement),
        53,150
    observance of, 81,91-92,207
    sermon, 179
Yom tov (holy days), 304
Young, Iris Marion, 178

Zakena (wise old woman), 63
Zayde (grandfather), 119
Zionism, 169

Order Your Own Copy of
This Important Book for Your Personal Library!

CELEBRATING THE LIVES OF JEWISH WOMEN
Patterns in a Feminist Sampler

_____ in hardbound at $49.95 (ISBN: 0-7890-0086-5)

_____ in softbound at $19.95 (ISBN:1-56023-913-1)

COST OF BOOKS_____

OUTSIDE USA/CANADA/
MEXICO: ADD 20%_____

POSTAGE & HANDLING_____
(US: $3.00 for first book & $1.25
for each additional book)
Outside US: $4.75 for first book
& $1.75 for each additional book)

SUBTOTAL_____

IN CANADA: ADD 7% GST_____

STATE TAX_____
(NY, OH & MN residents, please
add appropriate local sales tax)

FINAL TOTAL_____
(If paying in Canadian funds,
convert using the current
exchange rate. UNESCO
coupons welcome.)

☐ **BILL ME LATER:** ($5 service charge will be added)
(Bill-me option is good on US/Canada/Mexico orders only;
not good to jobbers, wholesalers, or subscription agencies.)

☐ Check here if billing address is different from
shipping address and attach purchase order and
billing address information.

Signature_____

☐ **PAYMENT ENCLOSED: $**_____

☐ **PLEASE CHARGE TO MY CREDIT CARD.**

☐ Visa   ☐ MasterCard   ☐ AmEx   ☐ Discover
☐ Diners Club
Account # _____

Exp. Date _____

Signature _____

Prices in US dollars and subject to change without notice.

NAME _____

INSTITUTION _____

ADDRESS _____

CITY _____

STATE/ZIP _____

COUNTRY _____ COUNTY (NY residents only) _____

TEL _____ FAX _____

E-MAIL_____
May we use your e-mail address for confirmations and other types of information? ☐ Yes   ☐ No

Order From Your Local Bookstore or Directly From
The Haworth Press, Inc.
10 Alice Street, Binghamton, New York 13904-1580 • USA
TELEPHONE: 1-800-HAWORTH (1-800-429-6784) / Outside US/Canada: (607) 722-5857
FAX: 1-800-895-0582 / Outside US/Canada: (607) 772-6362
E-mail: getinfo@haworth.com
PLEASE PHOTOCOPY THIS FORM FOR YOUR PERSONAL USE.

BOF96

OVERSEAS DISTRIBUTORS OF HAWORTH PUBLICATIONS

AUSTRALIA
Edumedia
Level 1, 575 Pacific Highway
St. Leonards, Australia 2065
(mail only) PO Box 1201
Crows Nest, Australia 2065
Tel: (61) 2 9901–4217 / Fax: (61) 2 9906-8465

CANADA
Haworth/Canada
450 Tapscott Road, Unit 1
Scarborough, Ontario M1B 5W1
Canada
(Mail correspondence and orders only. No returns or
telephone inquiries. Canadian currency accepted.)

**DENMARK, FINLAND, ICELAND, NORWAY
& SWEDEN**
Knud Pilegaard
Knud Pilegaard Marketing
Mindevej 45
DK-2860 Soborg, Denmark
Tel: (45) 396 92100

ENGLAND & UNITED KINGDOM
Alan Goodworth
Roundhouse Publishing Group
62 Victoria Road
Oxford OX2 7QD, U.K.
Tel: 44–1865–521682 / Fax: 44–1865-559594
E-mail: 100637.3571@CompuServe.com

GERMANY, AUSTRIA & SWITZERLAND
Bernd Feldmann
Heinrich Roller Strasse 21
D–10405 Berlin, Germany
Tel: (49) 304–434–1621 / Fax: (49) 304–434–1623
E-mail: BFeldmann@t-online.de

JAPAN
Mrs. Masako Kitamura
MK International, Ltd.
1–50–7–203 Itabashi
Itabashi–ku
Tokyo 173, Japan

KOREA
Se–Yung Jun
Information & Culture Korea
Suite 1016, Life Combi Bldg.
61–4 Yoido–dong
Seoul, 150–010, Korea

MEXICO, CENTRAL AMERICA & THE CARIBBEAN
Mr. L.D. Clepper, Jr.
PMRA: Publishers Marketing & Research Association
P.O. Box 720489
Jackson Heights, NY 11372 USA
Tel/Fax: (718) 803–3465
E-mail: clepper@usa.pipeline.com

NEW ZEALAND
Brick Row Publishing Company, Ltd.
Attn: Ozwald Kraus
P.O. Box 100–057
Auckland 10, New Zealand
Tel/Fax: (64) 09–410–6993

PAKISTAN
Tahir M. Lodhi
Al-Rehman Bldg., 2nd Fl.
P.O. Box 2458
65–The Mall
Lahore 54000, Pakistan
Tel/Fax: (92) 42–724–5007

PEOPLE'S REPUBLIC OF CHINA & HONG KONG
Mr. Thomas V. Cassidy
Cassidy and Associates
470 West 24th Street
New York, NY 10011 USA
Tel: (212) 727–8943 / Fax: (212) 727–8539

**PHILIPPINES, GUAM & PACIFIC TRUST
TERRITORIES**
I.J. Sagun Enterprises, Inc.
Tony P. Sagun
2 Topaz Rd. Greenheights Village
Ortigas Ave. Extension Tatay, Rizal
Republic of the Philippines
P.O. Box 4322 (Mailing Address)
CPO Manila 1099
Tel/Fax: (63) 2–658–8466

SOUTH AMERICA
Mr. Julio Emöd
PMRA: Publishers Marketing & Research Assoc.
Rua Joaulm Tavora 629
São Paulo, SP 04015001 Brazil
Tel: (55) 11 571–1122 / Fax: (55) 11 575-6876

**SOUTHEAST ASIA & THE SOUTH PACIFIC,
SOUTH ASIA, AFRICA & THE MIDDLE EAST**
The Haworth Press, Inc.
Margaret Tatich, Sales Manager
10 Alice Street
Binghamton, NY 13904–1580 USA
Tel: (607) 722–5857 ext. 321 / Fax: (607) 722–3487
E-mail: getinfo@haworth.com

RUSSIA & EASTERN EUROPE
International Publishing Associates
Michael Gladishev
International Publishing Associates
c/o Mazhdunarodnaya Kniga
Bolshaya Yakimanka 39
Moscow 117049 Russia
Fax: (095) 251–3338
E-mail: russbook@online. ru

LATVIA, LITHUANIA & ESTONIA
Andrea Hedgecock
c/o Iki Tareikalavimo
Kaunas 2042
Lithuania
Tel/Fax: (370) 777-0241 / E-mail: andrea@soften.ktu.lt

**SINGAPORE, TAIWAN, INDONESIA, THAILAND
& MALAYSIA**
Steven Goh
APAC Publishers
35 Tannery Rd.
#10–06, Tannery Block
Singapore, 1334
Tel: (65) 747–8662 / Fax: (65) 747–8916
E-mail: sgohapac@signet.com.sg